HE 243 TUR

Turning the Corner?

Blackwell
Publishing

Turning the Corner?
A Reader in Contemporary Transport Policy

Edited by

Francis Terry

Blackwell Publishing

BLACKWELL PUBLISHING
350 Main Street, Malden, MA 02148-5020, USA
9600 Garsington Road, Oxford OX4 1JF, UK
550 Swanston Street, Carlton, Victoria 3053, Australia

The right of Francis Terry to be identified as the Editor of this Work has been
asserted in accordance with the UK Copyright, Designs, and Patents Act 1988.

First published 2004 by Blackwell Publishing Ltd.

Library of Congress Cataloging-in-Publication Data has been applied for

ISBN 1-4051-1915-2

A catalogue record for this title is available from the British Library.

Set in 10.5/12pt Palatino
by Graphicraft Limited, Hong Kong
Printed and bound in the United Kingdom by Page Bros (Norwich) Ltd

The publisher's policy is to use permanent paper from mills that operate a
sustainable forestry policy, and which has been manufactured from pulp processed
using acid-free and elementary chlorine-free practices. Furthermore, the publisher
ensures that the text paper and cover board used have met acceptable
environmental accreditation standards.

For further information on
Blackwell Publishing, visit our website:
www.blackwellpublishing.com

CONTENTS

1. Introduction: Transport Policy in Uncertain Times

FRANCIS TERRY

In a summary of some key strands in British transport policy over the past few years, the author argues for greater clarity of thinking about the place of market forces in transport and more coherence in government strategy. Significant progress is being made by transport professionals in working towards the objectives set out in the 1998 White Paper, but the results so far are fragmented geographically and poorly related to other aspects of public policy. There are encouraging signs in the infrastructure of training, investment and planning for transport, but too many resources are wasted through inefficiencies in the structure of transport industries which remain pseudo-competitive or quasi-monopolistic.

This volume is based on a collection of articles on transport written for the quarterly journal *Public Money & Management* since the Labour administration took office in 1997. The collection is supplemented by a number of other papers written specially for this work, or drawn from other sources and worthy of wider dissemination. Many of the contributions strike a hopeful – even optimistic – note about British transport policy. Over the period since the Conservative Government's Green Paper *Transport: The Way Forward* (DoT, 1996), a developing consensus has emerged among professionals about both the sources of current problems and the range of remedies that can be applied. The problem is how to apply those remedies, and even more importantly, how to carry public opinion with them.

In the White Paper *A New Deal for Transport: Better for Everyone* (DETR, 1998), Labour proposed a plethora of measures that were expected to achieve the main principles advocated in its predecessor's Green Paper (though without, of course, acknowledging any direct connection between the two pronouncements). Those principles included a reduced dependence on private cars for mobility, devolution of transport decisions to the lowest practical level, a closer link between prices and the wider costs of transport, and a much improved framework for transport planning. In that sense, it looked as though a corner had been well and truly turned.

FRANCIS TERRY is an Adviser on transport policy and funding and Visiting Fellow in the Interdisciplinary Institute of Management at the London School of Economics.

The challenge of market forces

With the benefit of hindsight, it now seems that while the Conservative diagnosis remains largely correct, and the Labour prescription was both enlightened and enthusiastic, some critical success factors were missing. First, the Green Paper had included among its key principles a statement that the 'efficiency of markets needs to be strengthened' (DoT, 1996). Some regarded this as a ritual item of lip service to earlier policies that had led to the deregulation of long-distance coach and local bus services and the privatisation of the railway network. It was hoped, and expected, that Labour would drop it. However, it is a principle that seems to survive implicitly in much that the present government does, undermining much else that is done to achieve better integration and stronger coordination of transport services. It is a principle whose practical worth needs urgently to be re-evaluated.

Competitive markets are undoubtedly a powerful stimulus to driving out inefficiency in transport operations, as elsewhere. The trouble has been that marketisation is a very blunt instrument, with unpredictable effects in a policy area where predictability is all. Among management, the quest for greater efficiency is liable to be confused with more short-term measures of economy, often taken in an effort to satisfy private shareholders. Thus the bus industry in the later 1980s shed large numbers of staff, cut back investment in new vehicles and sold off garage sites for development. Yet in 2003, the bus industry was striving to recruit 32,500 drivers and retain them through better standards of training and career development (CPT, 2003). The backlog of under-investment has caught up with the industry to the point where it now needs to spend £500 million per year on new buses for at least the next five years. In London, garages are being re-acquired at enormous cost in an area of inflated land prices.

Similarly, in the rail industry any hopes that the application of market forces could bring benefits to passengers through greater efficiency were speedily and resoundingly dashed. Competition *in* the market was a lost cause from the start, because rail travel is already subject to powerful competition on many routes from air and road – a discipline that had already sharpened up British Rail's operations over many years. Competition *for* the market, through the process of franchising groups of train services to train operating companies (TOCs), has had generally unsatisfactory results for passengers and is unpopular with the industry. It involves much wasted expenditure in the preparation of bids that may turn out to be unsuccessful, while the costs of subsidies from government are probably much higher, if only because private operators need a margin of profit. Most of the hoped-for benefits of private investment and management are lost through inefficiencies like these, along with huge transaction costs in a fragmented system.

The problem for the present government, if it really wishes to rely on market disciplines, is to find ways that they can be effectively applied in transport while securing the level of service that voters want. At the moment, it has the worst of both worlds: ostensibly committed to using private sector operators, but unable to grant them greater freedom on account of the deleterious effects of market failure.

Coach, bus and rail

An interesting case example is the National Express Group's long-distance coach operations. When National Express, originally part of the National Bus Company (NBC), was privatised, it rapidly wiped out the competition and for many years has had an effective monopoly on many routes. To maintain dividends, it has usually chosen to withdraw from unprofitable routes or make other economies, rather than stimulate new business (apart from a few airport feeder services). It has, however, generally benefited from rising demand, a reflection of overall economic conditions. Some observers would say it has become complacent: content with an adequate return on the business that it has, unwilling to risk much in new development. Yet if Government really intends to reduce road congestion 'below current levels' by 2010 – as it declared in the *10-year Plan* (DETR, 2000) – it has to find ways of remedying the inadequacies of the coaching market.

In local bus services, a parallel dilemma exists. Since the component parts of the NBC, which operated stage-carriage services, were sold off, massive consolidation of the industry has taken place. Now, just three or four major groups effectively 'control' local bus services across large areas of Britain. Competition nominally exists, but passengers see no real benefit from it; indeed it is arguable that they seldom did even in the period immediately after deregulation. The Office of Fair Trading for long imposed norms of anti-competitive behaviour that obstructed much of the government's professed commitment to better integration and coordination of public transport. Again, it is high time to sort out this confusion of purpose.

The inconsistency in transport policy is perhaps most marked in relation to the railways. The privatisation of other major state-owned industries, in the course of the 1980s and early 1990s, was popular and produced significant gains in efficiency and investment. It may have seemed a logical step to sell the railways off as well. Unhappily, the analogy was false. Unlike gas or electricity, which are also network industries, railways do not provide a service that everybody needs. Rail is obliged therefore to charge people as and when they use the service. In the absence of uniform, buoyant demand, attempts to move the railways to full-cost pricing – covering both infrastructure and train operations – is self-defeating (Terry, 2001). Or, to put the point rather differently, the broad economic benefits from having a good communications network can seldom be fully reflected in charges at the point of use. In the case of the road system, practically nobody thinks it even worth trying. Yet the government remains wedded to the form of a privatised rail system long after the hope of any benefits to passengers, the economy or the Exchequer have evaporated.

3

Investment

It seems unlikely that current transport policy will win much favour with the populace until Government confronts these fundamental issues over the appropriate place for market forces. Instead, it has preferred to trumpet the scale of investment that it hopes to see coming into transport services, including the road network. This is unfortunately a weak compromise. Level of investment is an input measure, not a measure of output; still less is it a measure of socially desirable outcomes. As such, it is very little help to us in knowing whether the targets erected for transport policy are ever likely to be met. The fact is (as the contributions by Shaoul in this volume demonstrate) a great deal of investment in the privatised world of British transport is ineffective, if not actually wasted. It is wasted through being directed into channels like the London Underground Public–Private Partnership (PPP) that are not only inherently inefficient, but also lack adequate control.

So, in simple terms, it seems that large-scale public spending on transport is making up for lack of political courage, at least for the time being. Yet this situation cannot last, as the Director of the Strategic Rail Authority, Richard Bowker, has realised (Bowker, 2003). While Britain's railways absorb more public money than at almost any time in their existence, passenger and freight traffic levels remain largely static and performance continues at a lamentably low level, with just under 80 per cent of passenger trains arriving 'on time' (in many cases this means arriving within ten minutes of the correct time). Soon, the railways will be under pressure to do more with less, within a framework that is vastly more complex, inefficient and, in many people's eyes, less safe.

Professional development

One area where professional initiative, taking heart from the fine words of the White Paper, has begun to make progress is in transport planning. After a long period in which local authorities and other agencies severely pruned their transport staffs, it has become clear that the realisation of Government's goals cannot be achieved without more and better-qualified planners. A transport planning skills initiative has been launched jointly by various professional bodies and supported by the government. The Transport Planning Society, formed in October 1997, has become a valuable stimulus to good practice. The requirement for highway authorities and passenger transport executives (PTEs) to produce local transport plans (LTPs) has been an overdue and salutary reform. Sadly, and with an infirmity of purpose which many recognise as a hallmark of present policy, the government has recently relaxed its requirement by allowing authorities classed as 'excellent' in their overall performance to give up producing an LTP if they wish.

It is clear however that, despite the vagaries of national policy, many local authorities and all of the PTEs are making effective use of their responsibilities in transport planning – and it is at the local level that reduced congestion, better integrated transport and easier access to destinations will be experienced by ordinary people. The spirit of the White Paper, with its many examples of innovation and good practice, is slowly being translated into practice. It is a pity that the pattern remains so fragmented, with improvements in some places counterbalanced by a 'do minimum' or 'just build more roads' philosophy in other places. Perhaps the most striking example of what can be done by local initiative is the successful introduction of congestion charging in central London, an initiative of the Mayor from which Government did its best to distance itself for fear of a public opinion backlash.

At the regional level, planning for transport remains problematic, especially in the southeast of England (as the contributions by Harman, and Harman and Bolden, in this volume explain). Here, it is acutely evident that policies on transport must be closely interrelated with policy aspirations across a wide diversity of other fields: housing, employment, industry and the economy generally. Government recognises the importance of many of these interrelationships, but seems to lack either the technical capacity or the political will to make truly strategic choices. Transport is too often left to fit in behind one or other big initiative in other fields. A recent example is John Prescott's (2003) announcement of a 'step change in housing supply' in the southeast, to be delivered through a plan for sustainable communities, which shows a cavalier disregard for the transport implications. Another example of the reluctance to think through the transport implications is the policy towards airport expansion.

An encouraging development, alongside the renewed interest in transport planning, is the concern to raise standards of management in the transport industries. Management training was a serious casualty of the privatisation era, as bus and rail companies sought to trim their overheads. The British Transport Staff College closed, the various training establishments operated by British Rail were sold off, and graduate recruitment schemes were mostly dropped. Now, it has become apparent that simply poaching good managers with the offer of higher pay is a short-term ploy that does not really address the problem. Through the Confederation of Passenger Transport, helped by wider initiatives from publicly supported bodies like the learning and skills councils, training at all levels in the bus industry is being strongly promoted. The rail industry likewise, has at last recognised that a coordinated effort is needed to rectify the desperate shortage of technical training and management development. Among other initiatives, a Centre for Rail Skills has been formed.

Thus it appears that on the local scene and at the operational level, transport is indeed 'turning the corner'. Professional skill, working sometimes (but not always) in partnership with local political will, is genuinely helping to contain traffic growth, improve access for all and open up journey opportunities. Often the environment is benefiting also, but the trend away from motor vehicle usage is very weak, while the prospects of ever catering adequately for all the desired movement by car are hopelessly remote (see the contribution by Goodwin in this volume). International comparisons can be deceptive, but in transport they have much to tell us. The enormous resources of the United States, with its vastly more spacious land area and ready willingness to spend public money, has given up trying to solve urban congestion through road construction. The small, densely populated countries like the Netherlands and Singapore have, at the other end of the scale, demonstrated convincingly how people can live, work and move about efficiently and cheaply without necessarily having to depend on cars.

Conclusion

While the United Kingdom can undoubtedly learn from such comparisons, the focus of this volume is on providing some insights into how British solutions to the many self-inflicted British problems could emerge. It is not an attempt to give a comprehensive or even a particularly rounded picture (air and maritime transport are largely excluded); but it does try to set out some constructive criticism and suggest how we might learn from past mistakes.

References

Bowker, R. (2003). A speech to the Rail Passengers' Council. Reported in *Modern Railways* 60(652) (January).

Confederation of Passenger Transport (CPT) (2003). Private communication with the author.

Department of the Environment, Transport and the Regions (DETR) (1998). *A New Deal for Transport: Better for Everyone* (Cmnd. 3950). London: HMSO.

Department of the Environment, Transport and the Regions (DETR) (2000). *Transport 2010: The 10-year Plan*. London: DETR.

Department of Transport (DoT) (1996). *Transport: The Way Forward: The Government's Response to the Transport Debate* (Cmnd. 3234). London: HMSO.

Prescott, J. (2003). *Sustainable Communities: Building for the Future*. London: Office of the Deputy Prime Minister.

Terry, F.R. (2001). 'The nemesis of privatization: Railway policy in retrospect', *Public Money & Management* 21(1).

2. Solving Congestion[1]

PHIL GOODWIN

This chapter, originally presented as the inaugural lecture for the Professorship in Transport Policy at University College, London in 1997, comments on the rapid evolution of transport policy in Britain as road building was increasingly seen as an inadequate solution to traffic congestion, eventually giving way to the official adoption of demand management as a strategic approach. The process was started by the Conservative administrations during the 1990s, and led to the Labour transport White Paper in 1998. The change was underpinned by considerations of fundamental traffic theory, research findings on induced traffic, environmental and economic impacts, and emerging policy experience of the effects of re-allocating road space. It is suggested that ways of measuring congestion, and methods of forecasting traffic, both need to change.

My starting point is a paper by Smeed and Wardrop (1964), which is surely one of the great classic papers of transport studies. It demonstrated convincingly, if somewhat counter-intuitively, that if everybody travelled by the slow method of transport (namely, bus), they might all travel faster than if they all travelled by the fast method (namely, cars). The reason why this is true is the fundamental defining relationship of traffic science – the speed-flow curve. This shows that the more traffic uses a road, the slower it goes, the effect becoming more and more severe as the traffic flow approaches the maximum capacity of the network, until finally overload is so extreme that all vehicles are unable to move. We may define 'congestion', therefore, as the impedance that vehicles impose on each other due to their interaction. This helps us to understand that the underlying cause of congestion is not road-works or taxis or accidents: it is trying to operate with traffic flows too close to the capacity of the network, when any of these transient incidents will have a disproportionate impact.

Armed with this powerful insight, Smeed and Wardrop calculated that since the number of cars required to move a given number of people is much greater than the number of buses, then a transfer from car to bus would enable the traffic to go faster and, in certain circumstances, this is enough to

---

PHIL GOODWIN is Professor of Transport Policy at University College, London.

offset the extra time spent waiting for the bus, walking to one's destination and so on. But there is a catch. Whatever anybody else does, for each individual, it is nearly always faster to travel by car, and there is normally little or no incentive to do otherwise. It is one of those cases where Adam Smith's individuals pursuing their own best interests do not add up to Jeremy Bentham's greatest good for the greatest number.

Road pricing

The benefit can only be delivered by intervention, either in the allocation of road space – through bus lanes and so on – or by pricing. Through his chairmanship of the Committee on Road Pricing in the Ministry of Transport in 1964, Smeed made another important contribution to our understanding of transport policy when he demonstrated the practical validity of the proposition that economic welfare would be increased if road use, perceived as a 'free' good, were charged for. The reason is that each driver, in using roads in congested conditions, imposes delays on everybody else, and these delays have a cost not taken into account in his or her personal choices. Therefore some journeys are undertaken for which the benefits to each driver are less than the costs they cause to everybody else, and the overall use of resources – *waste of resources* – is greater than it should be.

Sadly, the practical history of road pricing so far has been marked by flirtations, studies, cold feet, and pricing *interruptus*. The reason for this, in my view, is that for a quarter of a century nobody took seriously the implications of a couple of lines of calculus in an appendix to the Smeed Report, which revealed – but obscurely, as through a glass, darkly – that although pricing certainly reduces congestion, the larger part of actual benefit from road pricing does *not* consist of this congestion relief. The benefit sits, 'locked-up', in the revenue collected, and it is only released when the revenue is used.

More subtle recent analyses show that if road pricing were implemented in a way that also had environmental benefits, and was geared to providing economic advantages to freight vehicles and buses, then the direct benefits could be magnified. The core point remains: the calculated benefits to a considerable extent are crystallised in the revenue streams. This is why discussion of road pricing without explicit attention to the use of revenue streams is *inherently* unlikely to be able to command a consensus in its support. I would advocate this as an axiom of contemporary transport policy.[2]

Thus there are two important policy propositions about how to solve congestion that have now been with us for a generation. Congestion could be less if people travelled by slower methods of transport; and if they paid for what they now think of as free. I would be among the first to acknowledge that as policy statements, these two statements somehow lack that magnetic allure that could bring them into the manifestos of politicians. The banner 'slow and expensive' fails to inspire. However, let me suggest another axiom. If there is a policy that genuinely increases efficiency, then there must be *some* way of implementing it that can win support: there are benefits to be had and there are more people who stand to gain than lose.

'Predict and provide'

So why do the basic propositions sound so unattractive? Where is the flaw in the argument? Where *was* the flaw in the argument thirty years ago? One flaw was that the tools we had for understanding how individuals make their travel choices were misleading and tendentious. Another was that economic orthodoxy, quite wrongly, classified the revenues produced by charging for congestion costs as a 'tax' – thereby ensuring that discussion of their application would be rejected as the heresy of hypothecation. Yet the real barrier to implementation was that the spirit of the time was heading in an entirely different direction. There was on offer an easier, more comfortable, painless, modern, more exciting way of solving congestion. We could simply build our way out. If traffic levels get too close for comfort to capacity, increase the capacity.

From the late 1950s onwards the transport planning orthodoxy was 'predict and provide'. The approach was: *first we forecast how much traffic there will be, and then we build enough road space to accommodate it.* This resulted in a rapid, huge expansion of road capacity, and produced the national network of motorways. Nowadays, we cannot imagine life in a modern economy without them. Yet this was also the approach that resulted in some things that we now, mostly, have come to realise were a grievous mistake, like the destruction of the heart of some of our city centres to make room for urban motorways. Here, our imagination of life without them is easier and, in many places, town centre road capacity is indeed now being reduced or closed and the space returned to more productive use, though alas many historic structures have gone forever.

Good or bad, the high point of 'predict and provide' was, by one of the ironies of history, its final hour: the programme of road building announced in the 1989 White Paper *Roads to Prosperity* (DoT, 1989), based on the National Road Traffic Forecasts of the day. This was the last time any government transport policy tried – even partially, and with caveats and exceptions – to devise a roads programme intended to 'meet the demand'. It was launched with the greatest of fanfares but, even by the time of the launch, the process that would lead to its abandonment was under way, and was largely completed by about 1995 under the last Conservative Government. This is not a party-political difference. The flaw was that even such a programme would not keep pace with traffic growth.

Let us suppose road capacity is expanded at a rate less than traffic growth. What follows? The consequence is a matter of arithmetic, not politics. On that trend, the ratio of vehicles to mile of road can only increase, and therefore logically congestion is likely to get worse, not better (although this does not, of itself, mean 'traffic will grind to a halt', since congestion can get worse in intensity, duration, geographical spread or some combination of these). Supply of road space will not (because it cannot) be increased to match demand; therefore, demand will have to be reduced to match supply. In practice, 'predict and provide' actually meant, inevitably, 'predict and *under*-provide', and a strategy with road building at its heart would not deliver improvements in travel conditions. This simple insight was at the core of what became known as 'New Realism', in a project initiated by the Rees Jeffreys Road Fund in the late 1980s (Goodwin *et al.*, 1991).

In the mid-1990s, the same idea started to be extended to inter-urban roads, especially after 1994 when the government's Standing Advisory Committee on Trunk Roads Assessment (SACTRA, 1994) reported that road construction in conditions of congestion normally results in an increase in the total volume of traffic. This reduces the period of relief from congestion, and consigned to history the untenable assumption that the total volume of traffic is unaffected by travelling conditions. SACTRA's report opened the way to recognising that the volume of traffic is – in part – the *result* of policy, and is therefore subject to some degree of choice.

This stage of my argument can be summarised in two propositions:

- we cannot match the supply of road capacity to the unrestricted forecast demand for it; and
- demand is not inexorable, external or given: it is subject to influence.

Taken together, these propositions marked the change from self-fulfilling forecasts to self-defeating forecasts. As Owens (1995) argued: 'predict and provide' became 'predict and prevent'. This was the reason – not just a change in fashion or shortage of funds – why during the 1990s demand management has become part of the transport policy of every political party. Transport policy *in principle* everywhere started developing certain common themes. The previously fringe idea started to become mainstream: the growth of traffic will have to be slowed down, and in some locations the actual traffic level will have to be reduced, or even removed.

In part that implies reversing the long-term decline in public transport. We are probably talking about an overall market for public transport that should expand at around 3 to 5 per cent a year, sustained for thirty years; and in some locations, the logic of policy suggests much more dramatic levels of growth – say, 25 per cent in two years, 100 per cent in five – achieved by changing relative prices, or the re-allocation of road space, or both, and investing in new systems where the old ones cannot be sufficiently improved. In all cases, a strong contractual commitment is required between public agencies and commercial operators; favourable treatment, but only in exchange for better services.

The 'new realism'

This fundamental change in provision is only part of the answer to problems of congestion. We now recognise the need to reinvent safe, attractive streets in which it is normal for children to walk or cycle to school; to reinvent the old custom of home delivery of shopping; to rediscover the role of land-use planning to reduce journey distances; to look for ways of participating in social activities that generate less traffic.

The new policy toolbox includes pedestrianisation, traffic calming, and traffic management aimed at maintaining a quality margin of reliability by reducing flows to significantly less than capacity. Once again, pricing is everywhere discussed, as the only tool of traffic restraint which has the 'double whammy' of ensuring that resource costs are covered in the choices people make, and also providing the funds to pay for improvements. These tools were part of the national debate on transport called for by Brian Mawhinney in December 1994, as much as they were in the manifestos[3] for the general election in 1997.

There is an important point about this list of policies. While the *overall impact* is intended to reduce the total amount of traffic, it does so by a combination of measures, some of which are restrictive (and which, on their own, could hardly expect enthusiastic public support) with others that provide improvements in the quality and attractiveness of travel conditions (and which, on their own, would certainly be popular but do not result in a reduction in traffic). Within this policy context, decisions about road capacity are quite logically at the end of the list, not the beginning – not because we shall never again see any new road capacity, which would be absurd, but because it is not possible to design a new road until it is decided what traffic load to design it for. That now implies a policy choice, not a forecast. It can only be assessed *after* taking account of the combined effect of the whole policy package. The National Road Traffic Forecasts issued in October 1997 at last recognised this explicitly: 'different policies will result in different forecasts' – seven words that unpacked seventeen years of practice. These words must, I believe, displace the 1980 House of Lords ruling that the National Road Traffic Forecasts could not be a subject of discussion or challenge at local road enquiries. And not before time.

While many of us now agree on such principles, converting them into practice has been painfully slow, unconvincing and inconsistent. I want now to shift the focus of this essay to some research carried out with my colleagues Sally Cairns, Joyce Dargay, Graham Parkhurst and Petros Vythoukas that bears on the practicality of some of these policies. If road capacity will be inadequate to meet all the demands on it, are there ways of using it more effectively? This issue does not only, or even mainly, relate to pushing more vehicles along a road by clever traffic signals or one-way systems. It relates to reallocating space away from 'general traffic' to more selective uses: bus or cycle lanes, disabled travellers, emergency services, lorry lanes, or

11

pedestrianisation. In each case, we deliberately change the use of space as a tool to achieve more efficient use of the network, environmental advantage, enhanced street attractiveness or improved safety. The problem, however, is that all of these *improve* conditions of movement for the favoured users, but tend to *reduce* capacity for other classes of traffic.

Stability or dynamism?

Now, the technical assessment of such measures has most often been calculated on the assumption that all traffic displaced from one street will simply divert to another. If this is true, the predicted effect is at best displaced congestion, at worst total traffic chaos. For this reason, time and again such measures have been considered, assessed, but rejected; or they have been implemented in the most reduced, watered down, and ultimately ineffective, form.

The interesting point is that many other cities, often led by politicians who arrogantly disbelieve such technical advice, have introduced such measures and succeeded. Often there has been a short period of disruption lasting a few days, but no gridlock and no prolonged traffic chaos at levels worse than those that already prevailed. Sometimes there has not even been a short-term problem. The ubiquitous comment has been: 'the traffic has disappeared and we don't know where it has gone'. You may remember the tone of utter bewilderment with which the London *Evening Standard* (3 February 1997) reported that when Hammersmith Bridge was closed for repairs, the anticipated total breakdown of traffic flow simply did not happen.

We need to understand exactly what is going on in such cases. Can it be that traffic really does disappear? Researchers at the University College London Centre for Transport Studies are currently[4] studying some hundreds of these experiences, but it is already public knowledge in a dozen countries that there are many occasions where capacity has been reallocated or reduced, without causing damaging disruption and chaos.

Of course, this is encouraging, but how can it be? Consider what people actually do when travelling conditions change – they can change their driving styles to bunch up more, they can alter their route, the time of day they travel, the frequency of trips, the destinations they choose, the location of their home and workplace, the method of transport, the arrangements they come to with family or neighbours, the sequence of activities on a round trip, the substitution of trips for other forms of communication, and many others. All of these responses are influenced by the real world, but also by the complex and not always accurate perceptions people have of the real world. This complexity is sometimes difficult for transport professionals to accept because conventional transport assessments are largely built around a view of travel as stable and repetitive: the commuter who makes the same journey every day, the shopper doing the same journey every week. Without question, such repetitive patterns exist, and they dominate our perceptions of our own lives, as well as our interpretation of other people's. Such a view is reinforced when we see roughly the same traffic conditions at roughly the same time, day after day.

This apparent stability is composed, we now know, of volatile, unstable, changing undercurrents – what the pollsters call 'churn'. It is surprising (although Peter Bonsall *et al.* (1983) and Steve Atkins (1985) both noticed this years before its significance was realised), but actual individuals in the traffic queue even at the same time on two successive mornings are not, in most part, the same individuals. Every year anything up to one-third of people change their jobs, up to one in seven move house. They receive a pay increase or they are sacked. People leave home, get married, have babies. Their children change school. Some get divorced. They retire. A member of their family dies. If car ownership grows by a steady 2 per cent in a year, what that really means is that 12 per cent of households increase their cars, and 10 per cent reduce them. At each of these life events there may be a reason to reconsider travel patterns and choices.

So the response to changes in travelling conditions is composed of at least two quite different processes: first, there are responses by specific individuals, limited by habit, the desire to experiment (or not to), ignorance, preferences, and by binding – but not permanent – domestic and economic constraints. For these, minor adjustments may be quite swift, but bigger changes proceed at the pace of change in their own lives and the pace of evolution of their attitudes and tastes. Second, each day or year some individuals simply leave the system and are replaced by different people making a new set of trips. These, being new, can react to whatever prevailing conditions they find, sometimes bringing a more open mind to the new situation. As a result, broadly speaking, the process of adaptation to a new policy starts on day one, but takes between five and ten years before it is near enough to completion to get lost in other, even longer term processes. Such responses are difficult to predict precisely, but they are vitally important because they are give us space and time to manage the effects of policies on traffic.

Effects of congestion

What about the effects on the economy? The evidence on that is still uncertain,[5] but we can start to address this question. First, I have to say I cannot endorse statements of the form 'congestion costs the economy £15 billion a year', updated from time to time by inflation, and implying an annual dividend of £1,000 waiting to be distributed to each family. This is a convenient, consensual fiction. It is calculated by comparing the time spent in traffic now, with the reduced time that would apply if the same volume of traffic was all travelling at free-flow speed, and then giving all these notional time savings the same cash value that we currently apply to the odd minutes saved by transport improvements. This is a pure, internally inconsistent, notion that can never exist in the real world: if all traffic travelled at free-flow speed, we can be quite certain that there would be more of it, since at least part of the time saved would be spent on further travel, and further changes would be triggered whose value is an unexplored quantity. It is a precise answer to a phantom equation.[6]

While the number is suspect, I do not at all challenge the wide agreement that time, energy and money spent in traffic jams is a waste, and that continuing current trends in traffic growth will have unacceptable effects on economic efficiency. This is primarily due to increased congestion resulting in slower, and more variable, journey speeds and is real, not fictional. Then the *prima facie* expectation about policies aimed at reducing traffic in congested conditions should be that they will have *positive* effects on the economy. Now it is surely axiomatic that this could only be true if the policies themselves are well-judged. The case is clearest in relation to road pricing, which is itself based on an economic argument: policy instruments to reduce traffic, which make firms and individuals pay the full marginal economic costs of their journeys, must increase economic efficiency and therefore create (or allow) greater economic welfare.

What then about the effects of policy instruments using regulation, restrictions, rationing or traffic management? My view is that this must depend on the form of discrimination used. Primarily, it means that instruments tending to favour economically productive or efficient travel by reducing economically unproductive or inefficient travel could improve economic efficiency. (So freight movements may sometimes need to be given precedence over passenger movements; high utilisation passenger vehicles given priority over low utilisation vehicles, and so on.)

My argument here is that if we are in conditions where congestion is itself wasting economic resources, then traffic restraint – clever traffic restraint – is good for the economy, not bad for it. This is primarily a theoretical argument, but we do have one set of crucial empirical evidence. It is now established that reducing traffic levels in town centres can improve the level of turnover and competitive position of those towns, provided this is done with style and ambition, and with favourable related policies including high-quality public transport access. Much of that evidence has come from Carmen Hass-Klau (1993) and others from other European countries that are some twenty years ahead of the United Kingdom in this area of policy; but we are now starting to grow our own experience that tells much the same story (SACTRA, 1999). In any case, we can be certain that the economic functioning of places like central London depends on being able to have access to a labour force who simply could not get to work under the traffic conditions that would obtain if they all travelled by private car.

Such an argument should not be used to justify careless restrictions in traffic, unaccompanied by appropriate other measures. Yet it is reasonable to argue that policy measures designed to slow the rate of growth in road traffic, or where necessary to reduce its absolute level, can protect economic efficiency from the greater threat of congestion, and should therefore be welcomed, not feared. The case for this is clearer when the measures are 'in tune' with economic principles, especially in relating prices to full marginal costs, though they may also apply when using other measures.

At this stage, let me summarise my conclusions so far. Solving congestion does not depend on building new roads; indeed, liberating our minds from this assumption has been an important step in allowing us to consider wider and more effective methods. I maintain that, broadly, we can do this, if we want, without increasing spending – or at least, without increasing taxation and public sector spending – because the cash flows already spent inefficiently on travel can be recycled in a way that reduces traffic and simultaneously improves the quality of streets, public transport and access to activities. Even if we decide not to use the price solution, reallocation of road space offers net benefits without high cost. I maintain that the policies that do this most effectively have converged with those that contribute best to environmental improvement, enabling a 'green-gold coalition' of environmental and economic advantage. Done properly, this enhances economic efficiency rather than diminishes it, and therefore provides the possibility of better material standards of living in a way that does not diminish the moral and spiritual quality of life.

The need for conceptual advance

Yet serious concerns remain. Our ability to treat the new policies analytically, to understand their effects, and to assess their costs and benefits is seriously hindered by our inheritance of an analytical toolkit that is bright, impressive, of unchallengeable intellectual achievement, and wrong. It was Wardrop, nearly half a century ago, who provided the theoretical core of modern transport modelling practice by suggesting that drivers choose among alternative routes for the same journey by picking that route that gives the minimum journey time. If too many chose the most direct route, it becomes congested and less attractive. There is then an incentive for drivers to use an initially rejected longer route. Adjustments continue until equilibrium is reached when no individual can make a further improvement as a result of any individual choice. When this obtains, all routes used between any origin and destination have the same journey time, any other possible route being slower, and not used.

Wardrop's rules were originally worked out assuming that the only choice open to the driver is which route to take. This was initially only a simplifying assumption, but as often happens, it became entrenched in practice for many years – the Department of Transport made such an assumption for most new motorways between 1970 and 1994. Most small-scale schemes in towns still make this assumption, though this practice, not before time, is declining. Increasingly it is accepted that other responses must be allowed for, but what has not been recognised is the implications of allowing for them on the concept of 'equilibrium'.

Suppose we accept that long-term transport demand responses are different, and usually bigger, than short-term responses, because behavioural responses are time-dependent and include adjustments that take years to be completed. This observation is so in tune with what we know informally about the human condition as to seem commonplace, even trivial, and I do not expect it to be challenged. Thus we can say, for example, that the effects of pedestrianisation are that there is an immediate impact on traffic, often a short-term negative effect on trade that lasts a year or two, then a growth in the number of pedestrians and retail turnover. The effect of bus fare changes seems to be that passenger response after the first year may be doubled (or thereabouts) after five years. Motoring cost changes have a small immediate effect, but are still working their way through car ownership and use ten years later. The effect of changes in transport infrastructure on land use patterns start very swiftly (sometimes even before the infrastructure is opened) but may not be completed for a generation or more.

Such observations are absolutely crucial to political strategy. We need to know how long it takes for these effects to build up in order to know which policies must be implemented first, and which may be left until later. There is hardly a more important political question. Regrettably, the most-widely used analytical tools have *nothing* to say about sequence and timescale, because they treat end-states: notional equilibrium conditions that may never apply at all, but even if they will apply, we cannot say when. Not only that, but even their description of the end-state may be biased. In technical terms, the necessary condition for the sorts of models we use (mostly based on cross-section analyses, or on time-series analyses which, quite unnecessarily, fail to take account of the delays in responses) to deliver correctly estimated equilibrium relationships is that the variables of interest should not have changed systematically in the period before the observation, for a time long enough to have allowed the effects to settle down.

If the adaptation period is in the order of years, this condition is rarely, if ever, likely to apply in conditions observable in modern economies in the real world. Therefore, the parameters estimated from cross-section observed data will not, in general, be successful in describing equilibrium relationships from observation of uncompleted processes. This suggests that improved understanding will depend on treating travel behaviour as a *process*, not a state. In this way, we will be better able to comprehend the process by which travel habits are formed, or broken, the process by which cultural values and patterns of travel behaviour are transmitted from person to person, between producer and consumer, or from generation to generation, and how the constraints acting as barriers to change themselves get stronger, or relax, in the course of individual, household and social growth.

Of course, it may be that in understanding these processes, a mental construct of conditions under which things would be stable could be helpful in defining the rules of motion under which they actually operate. Martin Mogridge *et al.* (1987) have pursued an approach like this which gives useful insight into how a decline in public transport can lead to lower speeds of car travel. However, our current assessment techniques have a flavour of predicting the result of the match from a photograph taken in the middle of it. We cannot sustain the assumption that we observe equilibrium in travel surveys, or the assumption that a future forecast describes the equilibrium on any specific, known, date.

However, abandoning these substantially weakens the scope of cross-section analysis, and the credibility of current methods of long-term project evaluation that discount a 'known' time profile of future costs and benefits to a net present value. On the other hand, a move from ideas of equilibrium to ideas of process strengthens our ability to assess issues of great importance for policy – how long it takes for policies to have an impact, the consequences of a different order of implementation, and the special problems involved in seeking to reverse well-established trends. And it may actually lead to the adoption of simpler, more transparent, and more tractable models, rather than adding another layer of complexity to an already incomprehensible set of black boxes. This should be simplest of all for the national forecasts, for which there is no great technical obstacle to using such an approach already: a bit of a lost opportunity, I think, which I hope will be corrected soon. Until then, there are reasons for being very alert to the possibility of bias when using the new procedures to assess the effects of new policies.

Conclusion

From an academic perspective, I see the transport agenda as requiring three changes. A change in policy, for which the time feels ripe. More difficult, a change in methodology, which until now has seemed less welcome. And third, which at the moment I feel least confident to define, perhaps we need to rewrite the textbooks as well, and reconsider the skills we want our students to learn. That's for a later time. A final observation – the province of the politicians – is to ask 'what about votes?' If there is a policy that makes peoples' lives easier, more comfortable, less stressed, that improves the quality of the air they breathe, makes the economy more efficient, and improves their own health and that of their children, and which offers some chance of making things better rather than just slowing down the pace at which they get worse, then I like to think they will vote for it.

If that seems unrealistic, the evidence of opinion surveys, focus groups and so forth does lend some support for a change in public mood. I believe we are engaged in one of those historic transitions that looks quite different when you are in the middle of it to what it looks like in retrospect. Consider the great liberal reforms of the nineteenth century – abolition of slavery and child labour; the introduction of free, compulsory education; the concept of public health; the construction of a system of drains; clean running water; the right to vote. All of these, at the time, seemed revolutionary, threatening or infringements of the liberty of the citizen, or too expensive, and there were

17

long arguments about them. In retrospect, they seem logical, fair, efficient and absolutely good value for money. Subsequent generations even wonder why it took so long, and why there was so much fuss about it.

I see the current situation in transport in similar terms. Mass car ownership offered us a control over time and space that no previous generation has ever had, and we took it up willingly and enthusiastically, but it has got out of hand. It has now started to defeat its own advantages. There is much talk of a 'level playing field', but playing fields are never level, which is why we change ends at half time. It is now half time – literally: we are probably about halfway to the levels of traffic that would eventually apply if trends continue unchecked, and that just will not do. So we need to find a better way or ways. It may all seem very complicated just at the moment, but we do our children no favours if we confine them to a car-dependent mobility. And I think our grandchildren will wonder what took us so long.

Notes

1 The Inaugural Lecture was given at University College London on 23 February 1997, under the title 'Solving Congestion (when we must not build roads, increase spending, lose votes, damage the economy or harm the environment, and will never find equilibrium)', during a period when the author was chairing a panel of advisers helping to write what became the 1998 White Paper *A New Deal for Transport* (Cmnd. 3950). Subsequent developments were noted in a series of public lectures sponsored by the Transport Planning Society, and a number of published papers: notably Goodwin (1999, 2003). The footnotes and some references have been added later, but the text itself has not been amended to take account of later developments, which have been mixed.

2 The legislation under which London launched its congestion charging scheme in February 2003 provided for the revenue to be kept by the local transport authority and applied to transport improvements.

3 The Labour Party Manifesto was one of the source documents for John Prescott's White Paper *A New Deal for Transport: Better for Everyone* (DETR, 1998).

4 Subsequently published as Cairns *et al.* (1998).

5 Subsequently collated in SACTRA (1999).

6 This approach, against the advice of the author, later underpinned the government's forecasts of the effects of its policies (DETR, 2000; DoT, 2002), and was criticised by the House of Commons Transport Committee (2002) for doing so.

References

Atkins, S. (1985). 'Experience from a Repeated Travel Survey'. Extract from doctoral thesis, University of Southampton.

Bonsall, P., Jones, C. & Montgomery, F. (1983). 'Who Goes There? A Disaggregate Look at the Stability of Traffic Flows'. Working paper, Institute for Transport Studies, University of Leeds.

Cairns, S., Hass-Klau, C. & Goodwin, P. (1998). *Traffic Impact of Highway Capacity Reductions: Assessment of the Evidence*. London: Landor.

Department of Transport (DoT) (1989). *Roads to Prosperity*. London: HMSO.

Department of Transport (DoT) (2002). *Delivering Better Transport: Progress Report*. London: HMSO.

Department of the Environment, Transport and the Regions (DETR) (1998). *A New Deal for Transport: Better for Everyone*. London: TSO.

Department of the Environment, Transport and the Regions (DETR) (2000). *Transport 2010: The 10-year Plan*. London: DETR.

Goodwin, P.B. (1999). 'Transformation of transport policy in Great Britain', *Transportation Research* (A) 33: 655–699.

Goodwin, P.B. (2003). 'Towards a genuinely sustainable transport agenda for the UK'. In I. Docherty & J. Shaw (eds), *A New Deal for Transport*. Oxford: Blackwell Publishing (in press).

Goodwin, P.B., Hallett, S., Kenny, F. & Stokes, G. (1991). *Transport: The New Realism*. Report No. 624, Transport Studies Unit, University of Oxford.

Hass-Klau, C. (1993). 'Impact of pedestrianisation and retailing: A review of the evidence from Germany and the UK', *Transport Policy* 1(1).

House of Commons Transport, Local Government and Regions Committee (2002). *10-year Plan for Transport* (Eighth Report of Session 2001–2002). London: TSO.

Mogridge, M.J.H., Holden, D.J., Bird, J. & Terzis, G.C. (1987). 'The Downs/Thomson Paradox and the transportation planning process', *International Journal of Transport Economics* XIV(3).

Owens, S. (1995). 'From "predict and provide" to "predict and prevent"? Pricing and planning in transport policy', *Transport Policy* 2(1): 43–49.

Smeed, R. & Wardrop, A. (1964). 'An exploratory comparison of the relative advantage of cars and buses in urban areas', *Institute of Transport Journal* 30(9): 301–305.

Standing Advisory Committee on Trunk Road Assessment (SACTRA) (1994). *Trunk Roads and the Generation of Traffic*. London: HMSO.

Standing Advisory Committee on Trunk Road Assessment (SACTRA) (1999). *Transport and the Economy*. London: TSO.

3. Greater London: Growing or Shrinking? – A Discussion[1]

TERENCE BENDIXSON

A key strategic issue in planning for the southeast of England is the need to provide for huge numbers of new homes. The author describes a series of studies that have reviewed the principles – economic, architectural, social and environmental – to be observed in achieving this growth. Perhaps most problematic is the provision of transport infra- structure to underpin the projected development, and the inability of government to focus adequately on the long-term planning and investment this requires. Much depends on the ability of the London Mayor, in the absence of coherent action by central government, to address this need. Early indications are encouraging, although the Mayor lacks many of the powers and resources to tackle the tasks that lie ahead.

London and its economy are shaped by a complex mix of forces. Global influences, such as the state of financial markets, determine employment and investment in the City of London, the expensive parts of the housing market and immigration by foreign professionals. The capacity of the roads and railways radiating from the capital, and the availability of houses along their routes, help to decide how many households move out to the Home Counties and beyond. The availability of homes and the quality of what is on the market within London help to determine how many households opt for city living. The quality of schools, perceptions of street crime, travelling conditions on the London Underground and the railways are other factors that play some part in deciding whether the population of Greater London grows or falls. The important point about this is not that the workings of the economy of a world city may be too complex to describe, though probably they are, but that the economy and demography of a city such as London are under the influence of a wide range of constantly varying forces.

From new towns to an 'urban renaissance'

Post-1945, London saw a long period of population decline. Traditional employers such as the Port of London shed labour and moved outwards. At

TERENCE BENDIXSON is a Visiting Fellow in the Department of Civil and Environmental Engineering at the University of Southampton and Secretary of the Independent Transport Commission.

the same time, local authorities demolished street after street of dense Victorian terrace houses and replaced them with more spacious estates modelled, to some extent, on the visionary planning of Le Corbusier. Meanwhile, modern industries were expanding in towns such as Hatfield and Reading, and new towns were under construction in most of the Home Counties. An exodus of Londoners was inevitable, although this did not justify the town planners calling it 'overspill'.

This picture remained roughly accurate until 1979 when the Conservatives under Margaret Thatcher wound up the new towns programme, reduced the scope of local authorities to build houses and removed obstacles to the building of suburban drive-in shopping centres and business parks. Yet the Tories, notwithstanding their power base in the shire counties, found they could not ignore the cities. Riots in Notting Hill Gate, Bristol and elsewhere drew attention to one kind of urban problem – high levels of unemployment. Michael Heseltine threw himself into the issue with characteristic energy and inaugurated a new set of planning instruments all aimed at promoting private, as well as public, investment in inner cities. These tools included urban development corporations, enterprise zones and garden festivals.

Nowhere in Britain was the effect of Michael Heseltine's energy more evident than in London. One by one, the pieces of what is almost a new city fell into place in the former Docklands. The office skyscrapers of Canary Wharf, the Docklands Light Railway, London City Airport, the Jubilee Line extension, the Channel Tunnel Railway station at Stratford and even the dreadful Millennium Dome were all decided upon and got under way. Even a rail link to Heathrow, Europe's leading airport, was put on the agenda. There was no grand design. There was no master plan. It was all done as the City of London does things, by taking one step at a time and relying on brilliant 'fixers'.

The swing of the pendulum from its position in the 1960s was by then complete. Whereas new towns set in regional plans were the flagship urban developments of postwar governments, by the 1990s, top priority was going to reviving existing cities by bringing back into use sites that were disused, underused or abused. Someone coined the term 'urban renaissance'. In London, the revival of Docklands was extended downstream and renamed the 'Thames Gateway'.

New Labour – New thinking

This was roughly the position when in 1996 Tony Blair's 'New Labour' Government ousted the long-ruling Conservatives. The new brooms arrested further out-of-town retailing, set up an Urban Task Force and promised a White Paper on cities. They gave Londoners, whom Mrs Thatcher had emasculated, a Greater London Authority and, as it turned out, Ken Livingstone as Mayor. Labour went on to publish its unprecedented 10-year plan for

21

transport and promised a White Paper on airport development. The Mayor published a London plan, and had the guts to introduce road user charging.

What are the implications of all this for London? Within the context of the global economy and its effect on the City, the government had fixed the main forces that would shape the capital over the next two or three decades. They are:

- The strength of London's urban renaissance – Thames Gateway.
- The goals of the London Plan.
- The capacity of radiating motorways and railways.
- The expansion of road user charging.
- Airport expansion.
- Social deprivation and inner city crime.

London's 'urban renaissance'

London, like Britain's other big cities, faces a problem set out by the Urban Task Force in 1999: 'How can we improve the quality of both our towns and countryside while at the same time providing for almost 4 million additional households in England over a 25 year period?' (DETR, 1999). Key phrases in the report are:

- Compact urban development
- Excellence in urban design
- Priority for pedestrians, cyclists and public transport passengers
- Developing on 'brown field' land and recycling existing buildings must become more attractive than building on green field land
- Partnership with local people

'Protecting the countryside' is currently understood to mean building fewer houses in rural areas and more in existing towns and cities. The target, as set out in John Prescott's urban White Paper (DERT, 2000a), the first on urban affairs for 20 years, is to build, by 2008, 60 per cent of new houses on brown field land or in converted buildings. Apropos the capital, the White Paper said:

London stands apart as a city competing in a global context especially in financial and cultural activities. . . . It is the second most densely populated region in Europe. Despite having the highest GDP per head of any English city, it also has one of the lowest rates of overall employment and contains one of the largest concentrations of deprived areas. (DETR, 2000a: Paragraph 1.11)

London also featured in research on *The State of English Cities* (DETR, 2000b), published concurrently with the White Paper. In this report, Professor Brian Robson and his colleagues drew attention to Greater London's population increase of 232,400 between 1991 and 1997, and to forecasts of a growth in population of 9.4 per cent (21.4 per cent in households) for the period 1996 to 2021. Robson *et al.* also observed one of London's peculiarities. Whereas rates of net out-migration from most British conurbations are highest for the better

Table 1. Satisfaction with local area by type of area, 1998/1999 (percentage)

Area	Very satisfied	Fairly satisfied
Urban	35	40
Suburban/urban	42	40
Suburban	55	34
Suburban/rural	64	28
Rural	77	19

Source: *Living in Urban England: Attitudes and Aspirations* (DETR 2000a, Table 3).

off and best qualified residents, 'London experiences high rates of loss of skilled manual and managerial workers, but holds onto professional workers better than other conurbations' (DETR, 2000b: 16). Gentrification is a London speciality.

Housing density and suburban living featured prominently in the urban White Paper. The government noted that only 9 per cent of the English population live in the centres of towns and cities at a density of around 85 people per hectare. Most live in places they think of as suburbs (DETR, 2000a: Paragraph 1.14). However, the government went on to commit itself to pushing the density of new housing upward towards the 35 to 40 dwellings per acre characteristic of many nineteenth-century districts. Elsewhere the White Paper points out that the satisfaction of households for the places in which they live is lowest in cities, middling in suburbs and highest in villages. While rising satisfaction may be determined by declining settlement size, the behaviour of neighbours and other factors, it is notable that it also correlates with declining density (see Table 1).

This underlines the popular attitudes that face the promoters of an urban renaissance, although given the findings of Professor Brian Robson set out above, it may be that there is more satisfaction with living in 'urban' conditions in London than elsewhere in the country. Inner London undoubtedly has some very desirable neighbourhoods.

The London plan

A draft of the Mayor's *Spatial Development Strategy* was published in 2002 (GLA, 2002). In it, Mayor Ken Livingstone analyzed the state of the capital and set out his vision for its future:

- London is today experiencing phenomenal growth. This growth is without parallel in any other UK city. This rapid expansion, of population and jobs, stems from London's exceptional dynamism, attractiveness and advantages in the new era of economic globalisation.
- To sustain and improve London's environment, this increase must be absorbed without expansion into the existing Green Belt or encroaching on

London's internal green spaces . . . (and) without destroying the historic heritage of the city. (GLA, 2002: xi)

- Expansion of London into its surrounding region, the path chosen during much of the 19th and 20th centuries, would be environmentally unacceptable, particularly for the surrounding regions, and is ruled out by current government policy. (GLA, 2002: xii)

Later on, the plan suggests that any attempt to hold back a forecast net growth of 700,000 people and 636,000 jobs by 2016 would 'degrade the economic efficiency of the city, decrease the quality of life of Londoners and damage its environment' (GLA, 2002: Paragraph 1A4/5). London's population growth is forecast to come from natural increase, plus international immigration minus out-migration mostly to southeast England. The most significant increases are foreseen amongst 'rejuvenating' cohorts aged 15–29 and 45–59. Job growth is expected in financial and business services, but also in hotels and catering, retailing, and health and education.

This vision of a higher density 'compact city' follows the reasoning of Lord Rogers in *Towards an Urban Renaissance* (DETR, 1999). However, it has not gone unnoticed that, at a time when high density cities such as Barcelona are being held up as models for London, residents of such places, like Londoners in the past, are moving to the suburbs.

The capacity of radiating railways and motorways

Trains currently carry 466,000 workers in and out of London every day. The new Channel Tunnel link into King's Cross Station and Stratford in east London, and CrossRail I connecting places in the eastern and western Home Counties via Heathrow and Canary Wharf (but not yet funded) will provide increased capacity. The Independent Transport Commission (ITC) asked Professor Sir Peter Hall and Dr Stephen Marshall to consider the effect on land use in England of these and all the other transport proposals in the government's 10-year plan for transport (DETR, 2000c). Hall and Marshall (ITC, 2002) assumed that the rail projects planned for London would be delivered, that long-distance commuting from counties at and beyond the fringes of Southeast England would increase, and that within Greater London congestion charging would make London 'more attractive to high-income groups . . . particularly small, childless households' (ITC, 2002: Paragraph 2.7.3). The ITC, in its assessment of Sir Peter's work, judged that the Department for Transport had given too little cognisance to the 'tension' between urban regeneration and investment in radial transport infrastructure and urged the government to fill the gap when it updated its 10-year plan (ITC, 2002: xv).

With railway finance now devoted more to maintenance than new works, only the Channel Tunnel Rail Link is under construction but, in addition to services to the Continent, it will provide paths for new, high-speed commuter services from now remote parts of east Kent. If, eventually, CrossRail I is built and the capacity of other lines is expanded, it is hard to believe that they will not give rise, as Professor Hall suggests, to additional long-distance commuting. Could anything stand in the way of this effect? One possibility is an ending of the subsidy for season tickets, currently running at about 50 per cent of the full fare. With the Treasury interested in all transport becoming self-financing, it may not be so far-fetched as it seems.

House prices in London are higher than elsewhere in England. In 1995–1997, only one-third as many houses were sold for less than £20,000 in Greater London as in remote rural districts (DETR, 2000b: Table 11). This contrast between London and remote country prices, even though it throws no light on the cost of houses bought by managers, hints at one of the attractions of long-distance commuting.

Road user charging

Given that London's roads are already crowded, even though 40 per cent of London households do not own cars (but ownership is slowly rising), increasing the population by raising densities could make driving even more difficult. Might it even help to push some people out of London? The Mayor's solution is to reduce driving and promote greater use of walking, public transport and cycling. The £5 a day charge for entering central London introduced in February 2003 was a significant step in that direction. Cutting road traffic by about 17 per cent creates opportunities not just for improving bus services but, for instance, taking out obsolete one-way schemes and creating streets for people. Furthermore, the revenue from charging, though less than forecast, will help pay for these and other transport improvements. Two possible extensions of road user charging have already been mooted. One is to expand the existing zone into Hackney in the east, and Kensington and Chelsea in the west. The other – the front runner – is to create a new zone around Heathrow Airport to deter driving to and from the new Terminal 5 and help finance public transport improvements.

Airport expansion

Heathrow Airport in west London employs, directly and indirectly, 102,000 people and, with its worldwide connections, is a major attractor of investment. At the end of 2000, Heathrow was handling 64 million passengers per annum (mppa) and London's five major airports (including Heathrow) were handling 116 million. Forecasts by the Department for Transport of unconstrained demand show London's total rising to 300 mppa by 2030 (DfT, 2002). If Heathrow, with Terminal 5 now under construction, gets a new runway, its capacity could rise to 116 mppa. Given the airport's location inside London, this would add to noise nuisance, but keep some of the additional 12,000 airport jobs within the capital and so contribute to the goals of the 10-year plan (DfT, 2002: Table 7.5).

Expansion at Stansted in North Essex would lift employment from 8,000 to as much as 72,000, transform the airport's predominantly rural surroundings (DfT, 2002: Paragraphs 9.33–9.35), and fit nicely into the 'potential' London–Stansted–Cambridge growth corridor set out by the government in its Regional Planning Guidance for the South East (RPG 9).

When the government proposed a completely new four-runway airport on the Thames estuary marshes at Cliffe in Kent, it took everyone by surprise. Cliffe would generate from 41,000 to 61,000 jobs in a labour market where residents grossly outnumber jobs (DfT, 2002: Table 11.4). It could be linked to the Channel Tunnel railway and 'have positive effects in terms of regeneration [for] the Thames Gateway', the centrepiece of Greater London's urban renaissance. However, like the expansion of Gatwick, it always seemed an improbable choice and has now been dropped.

The White Paper on airport expansion (Secretary of State for Transport, 2003) has now been published, setting out the government's decisions. Stansted in Essex, although opposed, has far fewer environmental problems than other sites and is adjacent to the M11 urban growth corridor. This, and its railway access to London and the Midlands, makes it the first choice for short- to medium-term expansion expansion. Heathrow, because of its advantageous position within Greater London and the scope for railway connections to the West Midlands and the Southwest, is the choice for longer-term expansion provided environmental issues can be resolved. Congested road access is a problem, but could be addressed by a road user charging zone. This leaves the problem of Heathrow's extensive noise footprint and the powerful opposition it creates to expansion. Whether such environmental opposition is worth more votes than those of the very large numbers of people whose jobs depend on the airport is something that the Secretary of State will no doubt be examining carefully.

Social deprivation and inner city crime

The three districts with the highest proportions of deprived residents in England are in London. They are the boroughs of Hackney, Tower Hamlets and Newham – all in east London (DETR, 2000b: Table 8). Unemployment, low income, poor housing, expensive housing, low achievement at school, poor health and high levels of street crime are all characteristic of such places. Yet wealthy parts of London such as Kensington and Chelsea also contain wards that are in the poorest quintile in the country (Kensington and Chelsea Partnership, 2002).

Districts subject to such deprivation create two distinct kinds of movement: those living in them who can move out do so; and the social conditions within them deter all but those with no choice from moving in. In the context of the Mayor's vision for Greater London, such neighbourhoods contribute to a high-density city where much travel is on foot or by bus, but their reputations generate a sense of fear and anxiety that spreads beyond their boundaries.

Discussion

Forecasting is a dangerous trade. In London's case, the high growth in jobs in financial services characteristic of the 1990s has already turned downwards. However, assuming that, in due course, the financial markets revive and that when they do global trade will again increase, hiring will presumably replace firing. Meanwhile, Britain's relatively buoyant economy, and perhaps the attraction of the English language, are helping to keep the inflow of economic migrants at a high rate. The Mayor's growth forecasts depend on both.

Other factors that support the Mayor's plan include the reluctance of the Home Counties to permit house builders all the plots they want, and Mr Livingstone's undertaking to minimise 'the need for London's employment to be supported by increased commuting' (GLA, 2002: Paragraph 1B.17). If the Mayor can do all that he promises – and it is a big if – he may indeed slow the rate of London's long-standing diaspora.

Higher commercial and residential densities will be essential to delivering such a future and, with the ubiquitous Lord Rogers as his Chief Advisor on Architecture and Urbanism, the Mayor puts much emphasis on high-quality design as a painless path to liveable dense development. The plan links higher residential densities to convenient public transport, and proposes 240 to 435 dwellings per hectare in the central area, 55 to 110 dwellings in inner boroughs and 30 to 65 dwellings in suburban town centres.

Conclusions

London has been growing in population and extent for hundreds of years. After 1945, the population within the capital began to decline as those seeking suburban lifestyles moved beyond the metropolitan green belt. Since the 1980s, however, this pattern has changed, and in 2002 Greater London was estimated to be both gaining and exporting about 51,000 people a year (GLA, 2002: Paragraph 1A 15). The Mayor has seized on these conditions and seeks, with his vision of a more populous, higher density, design-led metropolis, to reinforce London's position as one of three global financial centres. His success in this will depend on both a continuing inflow of refugees and professionals in business services, and on the interaction of an array of push-pull factors. Some of them have been examined here.

Sceptics take the view that the current strength of 'pull' factors (which attract people to London) is a flash in the pan. They grant that growing numbers of young resident professionals and other small households are gentrifying the inner boroughs, occupying warehouse conversions and buying tens of thousands of new riverside apartments. Moreover, they argue that the larger numbers of refugees from the Middle East and elsewhere, like earlier migrants before them, will, as they prosper, move from cramped lodgings in the inner city to more spacious homes in the suburbs and the Home Counties. In this scenario, London will revert, before long, to being a net exporter of people.

27

Another scenario is that the attractions of long-distance commuting and suburban lifestyles are losing some of their traditional power. Professor Andrew Daly, for instance, in a review of factors underlying travel, noted the emergence internationally of a distinct new, non-car-owning, inner city lifestyle (Rand Europe, 2003). Perhaps the suburban dream is becoming a car-dependent suburban nightmare. Given the frustrations of commuting to and within very large European cities, given the growth of sophisticated business services, and given too the excitements and stimulants of living in a vibrant, 24-hour 'continental' city, perhaps the emergence of a new thirst for city living should not be a surprise.

Uncertainty must remain, however, about the outcome for London of the contest between push and pull factors. Putting aside external economic and demographic forces, can Mayor Livingstone deliver sufficient affordable homes to maintain the quality of essential public services? Can he combine higher commercial and residential densities with less travel by car and less nuisance from road traffic? A key factor here is the £5 a day charge to drive into central London. It is a mechanism for reducing car use and financing alternatives, and already the Royal Borough of Kensington & Chelsea, which is just outside the pay zone, is lobbying to be included. Might other boroughs follow suit?

Another straw in the wind is the action of St James Homes, a leading London house builder that is building flats with good public transport access. Instead of offering purchasers parking slots that require space, it offers membership of a car-hire club (St James Homes, 2003). In Paris, too, Mayor Betrand Delanoe is intent on a cautious revolution. He plans to ban cars from the city centre, replace riverside roads with walks and parks, and reintroduce trams (see 'It wasn't all bad', *The Week*, 1 February 2003). If Mayor Livingstone is to put 'pull' factors on top and deliver a higher density London, he must improve the quality of life. In doing so, he probably has no option but to reduce the space devoted to driving and parking cars.

Note

1 This paper has not been reviewed by Members of the Independent Transport Commission. It was written by the Secretary of that body in a personal capacity.

References

Department for Transport (DfT) (2002). *The Future Development of Air Transport in the United Kingdom: South East*. London: HMSO.

Department of the Environment, Transport and the Regions (DETR) (1999). *Towards an Urban Renaissance*. London: HMSO.

Department of the Environment, Transport and the Regions (DETR) (2000a). *Our Towns and Cities: The Future, Delivering the Urban Renaissance* (The Urban White Paper). London: HMSO.

Department of the Environment, Transport and the Regions (DETR) (2000b). *The State of English Cities*. London: HMSO.

Department of the Environment, Transport and the Regions (DETR) (2000c). *Transport 2010: The 10-year Plan*. London: HMSO.

Greater London Authority (GLA) (2002). *The Draft London Plan: Draft Spatial Development Strategy for Greater London*. London: Greater London Authority.

Independent Transport Commission (ITC) (2002). *The Land Use Effects of 'The 10-year Plan'*. Report by Sir Peter Hall and Stephen Marshall. Available online at: www.trg.soton.ac.uk/itc.

Kensington and Chelsea Partnership (2002). *Renewing Our Neighbourhoods*. London: Royal Borough of Kensington & Chelsea.

Rand Europe (2003). *Proceedings of Colloquium on 'Issues for Transport Policy Research*, Churchill College, Cambridge, 30 January (forthcoming).

Secretary of State for Transport (2003). *The Future of Air Transport*. London: HMSO.

St James Homes (2003). www.stjameshomes.co.uk. Click on 'developments', then 'North Woolwich'.

4. Climate Change and a Sustainable Transport Policy[1]

MAYER HILLMAN

The author argues that the concern of governments worldwide to ingratiate themselves with their electorates militates against a radical reform of transport policy in the direction of restraining and discouraging the seemingly insatiable demand for mobility. The effect of the resultant carbon emissions on climate change is potentially catastrophic. The need for reform is not merely a matter of reducing car use and substituting a proportion of journeys by public transport – although worthwhile in terms of reducing congestion, this has an insignificant impact in relation to the massive reduction in air pollution that is required to obviate climate change.

Public policy decisions taken over the past few decades give a strong impression that politicians, perhaps understandably, have been loath to adopt measures that run counter to what they believe people want. That is so even where this preference can be seen to be largely or totally inspired by the public's limited appreciation of the longer term consequences of the decisions. This is particularly evident in the transport sector where the social, environmental and ecological damage can be considerable. This essay attempts to highlight a disturbing instance of this where the incompatibility of policies catering for growth transport and those intended to deliver a sufficiently adequate response to the prospect of climate change from excessive use of fossil fuels is obvious.

During the past decade alone, the National Travel Surveys in Britain show that average journeys have increased in length by 12 per cent, those for work by 17 per cent and those for shopping by 27 per cent. Over the last 20 years, average mileage by car and rail has risen by 58 and 34 per cent, respectively, and average speeds by 19 and 13 per cent, respectively. The number of visits abroad by residents of the United Kingdom travelling by air has increased more than four-fold. The British government now forecasts a 40 per cent increase in road traffic over an equivalent period in the future. Rail travel is planned to grow by 40 per cent in the next 10 years, and air travel by 5 per cent *each year*.

MAYER HILLMAN is Senior Fellow Emeritus at the Policy Studies Institute, London.

Against this background, it seems logical to judge that the government should do what it can to cater for this public wish to travel further and faster by greater investment in the necessary infrastructure and service provision. At the same time, it is clear that the journeys should be made with more comfort, security and convenience – as budgets allow. Moreover, it is preferable if, within reason, the cost of travel can be partly offset by some form of subsidy.

Current strategy and its limitations

As evidence of the pressures that have been brought to bear on delivering such a strategy – more spending on transport, but at a lower cost to users than if they were required to pay all the associated costs of provision – it is only necessary to recall a few recent events. Demonstrations in the United Kingdom in 2000 in support of lower petrol prices can be cited, as can the cross-party consensus and widespread public, political and media support for substantial investment in the railways without any indication that the costs should be met out of the fare-box. Indeed, the absence of demonstrations about the escalating costs of upgrading the West Coast rail line from the originally quoted price of £2 billion to the current estimate of £9 billion could also be mentioned in this context.

Accordingly, central and local government politicians, advised by their transport and planning experts, have been working, and largely continue to work, towards the delivery of a better quality travel environment, increasingly free of congestion, delay and other time losses, risk and inconvenience, and at a concessionary price. The government's 10-year transport plan (DETR, 2000) and its decision on Terminal 5 at Heathrow Airport illustrate the extent to which the unwritten goal of public policy has been to meet as much as possible the rising demand for road, rail and air travel.

Only three significant limitations requiring any substantial deviation from this strategy appear to stand in the way. First, there has been the insufficiency of public money from the Treasury – an everlasting difficulty in the absence of determining any end-state, particularly in terms of accessibility and speed. Second, there have been some legislative changes reflecting environmental concerns, notably those regarding noise and air pollution, and local opposition to new developments on these grounds. However, the growth in all forms of motorised mileage suggests that, in general, these have not had a dramatic impact on the pursuit of the 'further, faster' goal of policy. One of the few exceptions is the ban on so-called 'night-time flying', though even here it could be observed that 'daytime' flying starts at 6am when the great majority of the affected population living near airports are very likely to still be in bed. And third, there has been the continuing problem associated with the insufficiency of road space in urban areas and difficulties in acquiring land and property there.

An allied and complementary inspiration for aiming to achieve as much growth as possible in the transport sector can be noted. For the past few

31

decades, a future of 'universal car ownership' has been anticipated in which the geographical limitations of walking are removed through the medium of technological advances enabling travel without physical effort over longer and longer distances and at higher speeds. For those unable to benefit from the availability of a car, an enhanced public transport system would be available. The outcome of this wider availability of cars can be easily identified in the rising use of motorways. It has been assumed that their provision would extend access to a vastly increased catchment of opportunities leading to enrichment of the quality of life of those who can use them. Eventually, it was thought, nearly everyone would enjoy the benefits. However, while in the short term this network of high-speed roads has enabled people and freight to be moved around more efficiently and economically, in the longer term, its success has carried the seeds of its own destruction. Owing to the impossibility of meeting the growth in demand that the motorways have generated by extending the geographical area in which their users can operate, congestion and delay, especially in and near the urban areas served, are an all-too-common feature of the reality of daily travel on them.

Unsustainable growth

Pursuit of this policy of seeking to enable people and goods to travel further and faster is reflected in the decisions of successive governments and in the increase in mileage noted earlier. In turn, each one has given its strong support, with one government revealing somewhat more predilection for road building followed by one perceiving somewhat more that public transport is a public service and therefore deserving of a bigger share of the transport 'cake'. Nevertheless, the growing demand for personal travel by car and freight movement by lorry has been the background against which, with all-party support, a substantial and continuing road building programme has been maintained. This has sought to increase both the vehicle capacity of the road network and bypass construction to relieve communities of the exigencies of through traffic in small towns and villages.

The proposed huge investment in public transport services – particularly rail – over the next decade again indicates government determination to cater for the growth in travel demand, particularly over long distances and at high speed. And it also continues to be government policy to ensure that the infrastructure necessary to minimise the need for limits on growth in travel is in place. Indeed, this was a key argument that the Inspector for the Terminal 5 Inquiry deployed in recommending that the Secretary of State grant approval for its construction.

Until fairly recently, no need was seen for even considering the sustainability of this process in the context of the growing demand for road, rail or air travel. Nor was any attention paid to the possibility that policies on restricting demand may need to be contemplated in light of reports of the Intergovernmental Panel on Climate Change (see Houghton *et al.*, 1997), the Royal

Commission on Environment and Pollution (RCEP, 2000) and government responses to these reports. The continuing availability of resources (materials, land, and private and public finance), combined with technological advances and human ingenuity, has allowed for the rising demand for travel by car and long-distance rail and air journeys to be met to a lesser degree than proponents of the free market would have wished, but nevertheless far exceeding former expectations. That demand appears to be never-ending and no government appears to anticipate any need to cap it in the foreseeable future.

The implications of climate change

Now, however, we are at a defining moment in history at which we have to come to terms with newly acquired and unpalatable evidence. The signal that the world is now receiving is akin to one stemming from divine intervention. The problem arises from manmade activities exaggerating the Earth's natural greenhouse characteristics that have so far enabled it to support life. Climate scientists have established that the planet has a finite capacity. This is totally insufficient to act as a reservoir to absorb the greenhouse gases that are the by-product of our present and projected lifestyles without its climate being seriously destabilised. If we are to act as responsible 'stewards' for present and future generations, the ecological imperative of protecting the planet for the future must represent an *essential* background against which decisions are made. This requires extreme thriftiness in our consumption of finite resources.

Nearly all the hottest years since records began have occurred since the mid-1980s. The tundra in north Canada, Alaska and Siberia is slowly melting, releasing methane gases that in turn are a significant contributor to the world's climate. Already changes have been observed in the character of the Gulf Stream, which in the opinion of the government's former chief scientist, Sir Robert May, are 'awesome'. Given the powerful links between growth, not least in the transport sector, and fossil fuel use that appear to be associated with these catastrophic changes, the otherwise attractive adjective 'sustainable' has lost its meaning in any debate on policy aimed at accommodating growth.

A special issue of *Town and Country Planning* edited by the author included articles (Hillman, 1998a, 1998b) setting out the dramatic extent to which fossil fuel-dependent transport activities must be curtailed rather than subjected to policies of containing their growth. It showed that, within the time-scale available to offset serious worldwide social, economic and environmental damage from climate change, technology cannot conceivably provide a realistic way out. It argued that severe limits will have to be imposed on the use of fossil fuels by international agreement. The Rio, Kyoto and Berlin conferences on climate change are part of this process – along with the 'Rio + 10' conference in Johannesburg in 2002.

The Intergovernmental Panel on Climate Change has called for a reduction of carbon dioxide emissions of at least 60 per cent. This target has been accepted and recommended to the British government by the Royal Commission on Environmental Pollution (RCEP, 2000). Obviously, as has been argued for many years by the Global Commons Institute, the reduction will have to be achieved according to an agreed framework which it has called 'contraction and convergence' (see Meyer, 2000). This proposition stems from the obvious fact that the populations of the Third World cannot be expected to reduce their emissions by making the same contribution as populations of countries in the West. In these affluent countries, this means that average *per capita* carbon emissions must be reduced from their present level by *over 90 per cent* – that is, a reduction of 10 per cent each year for 25 years. It does not require any stretch of the imagination to conclude that there are neither moral grounds for proposing, nor political prospect of obtaining, international agreement on any other than an equity basis. If that highly challenging target is not met, the disturbing consequences of climate change that we are beginning to witness will very likely intensify, and the costs of coping with them will very likely rise sharply.

All aspects of our fossil fuel-dependent economic activity and personal lifestyles must come under scrutiny. No one can expect to be excused from contributing towards meeting the target. Indeed, the case for transport being obliged to set a higher target could be justified. Reference can be made to the fact that much mileage is inessential – certainly less essential than maintaining comfort conditions in the home and at work. The need for travel is also more amenable to change through the medium of reducing locational decisions such as those for commuting or leisure. Air travel too will have to be involved in the negotiations on how this target is to be met because the release of greenhouse gas emissions in the upper atmosphere is a particularly damaging practice. In light of this, the absence within the foreseeable future of renewable energy sources for aircraft propulsion cannot be cited to justify the current scale of air travel, let alone its expansion (Hillman, 1998c).

What does a reduction of over 90 per cent in carbon dioxide emissions mean for the typical household in the United Kingdom when related to its current annual average of over 25 tonnes? To illustrate the significance of this figure for lifestyles, it is important to appreciate the contribution of each component of our energy-consuming activities. At present, each household's share for the operation of power stations and refineries is the cause of about 11 tonnes of these emissions; for industry, 5.5 tonnes; for domestic uses, mainly heating, 3.5 tonnes; and for transport, 4.5 tonnes. Within that transport component, the car is the primary source of emissions. It accounts for over four times the annual tonnage that an equitable ration for each person represents for *all* their fossil-fuel consuming purposes. And the emissions on one person's round trip by air from London to Florida, based on the aviation fuel used and typical aircraft seat occupancy on such flights, accounts for 1.8 tonnes, that is nearly double that annual tonnage. It is very apparent that the *household* 'ration' of 2.5 tonnes, that is one-tenth of the current level, will stretch only to the most essential of energy-intensive activities.

The role of transport policy

Clearly, the scale of change is so considerable that it will necessitate much less choice and a substantial re-ordering of priorities unless there is some phenomenal breakthrough in technology to eliminate the human-sourced causes of climate change. Within reason, use of motorised transport will have to be heavily curtailed. A primary solution obviously lies in promoting *local* patterns of travel – ones that can be met on foot, cycle or bus. However, a brief examination of the policies and practices of the past few decades that have influenced current patterns, and that at present look likely to be continued with only minor modifications, suggests an unwitting discrimination against such a direction of policy. This is most evident in the allocation of transport investment, the great majority of which has been earmarked to improve that part of the transport infrastructure enabling faster and more extensive travel by air and rail, high-quality tramway systems and increasing the capacity of the existing road network.

How has this come about, given the growing understanding among relevant professions – though not in the population at large – of the issue of climate change and its implications for future transport policy? Some of the explanation can be seen to lie in a number of fallacious assumptions that are frequently reflected in discussion of the changes needed. First, it is thought that the most effective way of minimising energy-wasteful patterns of travel – especially conserving finite fossil fuels – is by bringing about a significant transfer of journeys currently made by car to public transport (Hillman, 1996). However, in the United Kingdom, at current occupancy levels, fuel use per passenger kilometre by public transport is only about 20 per cent lower than by car. Moreover, that percentage difference is reducing as technology is applied to getting more kilometres out of the litre of fuel put into a car's tank.

Second, and allied to this assumption, is the belief that a major contribution to lowering greenhouse gas emissions can be made by making more efficient use of fuel in motor vehicles. However, by lowering the unit cost, this all too often leads to the generation of *more* energy demand. In turn, that has encouraged the public to buy vehicles with more engine capacity and higher levels of performance without incurring additional running costs.

Third, it is thought that speed is not a sufficiently significant factor in the pursuit of policies on reducing fuel use and thereby carbon emissions, whereas it represents a highly significant element. Higher speeds by road, rail and air require not only more intensive use of fuel, but also promote longer distance journeys. Given the need to *minimise* fuel use, this latter outcome has even more undesirable effects than the former.

The 'buck' cannot continue to be passed from the responsibility of individuals to that of government, for its decisions are too heavily influenced by electoral rather than public interest objectives. The necessary targets for greenhouse gas emission reductions will only be achieved if there is due recognition of the link with individual lifestyles and working practices. If the delivery of sustainable patterns of activity is to be more than expressions of intent, then there must be far more personal, as well as political, commitment. Dramatic change is necessary to reflect a growing understanding that, in aggregate, fossil fuel-using activities are having deleterious effects on the health of the planet, particularly as the carbon emissions from them remain in the atmosphere for up to 100 years.

Conclusions

At the heart of the matter in this key domain of transport policy lies the difficulty for decision-makers of considering radical alternatives to the strategies they have been pursuing. So far, their actions appear to reflect a desire to enable people to travel further, faster and more cheaply, if not by car, then by public transport. Successive governments have pandered to the public's apparently insatiable appetite for this component of their lives. They have continued to rely on the illusory belief that growth in travel, including by air, need have no limits imposed on it and that, where serious problems are identified, they can be unquestionably resolved by a combination of technology and ingenuity. For this reason, no significant policy initiatives are even being considered for assessing the consequences of growth in this domain of public policy.

However, there is now sufficient objective evidence of the unsustainability of this process, not least that stemming from the implications of climate change. The strategies necessary to advance this require the adoption of targets set to *substantially* reduce both the volume and speed of road, rail and air traffic over a predetermined number of years. Not only will this deliver what must be the key objective of transport policy – that of preventing serious damage to the health of the planet – but it is also likely to make important contributions to achieving a wide range of other social, health and local environmental objectives.

Climate change and urgent action on its implications, not least in the sphere of transport, must be placed at the top of the political agenda (see also Hillman, 2000). The harsh reality that must be faced is that if our individual lifestyle results in the production of more than its fair share of greenhouse gas emissions, then there are only two possible outcomes: either others will have to be denied their fair share or, more likely, the planet's climate will be destabilised, with all the awesome consequences that are already being witnessed. This predicament is the consequence of past failures in acting collectively on our responsibilities, both directly as individuals and indirectly as electors who, in a democratic society, can influence political decision-making. In all conscience, we cannot continue to bury our heads in the sand on this issue.

Note

1 This article was previously published in *Proceedings of the Institution of Civil Engineers: Municipal Engineer* 151(1) (2002): 91–94, and is reproduced here by kind permission of the Institution of Civil Engineers.

References

Department of the Environment, Transport and the Regions (DETR) (2000). *Transport 2010 – The 10-year Plan*. London: HMSO.

Hillman, M. (1996). 'The future of public transport: The dangers of viewing policy through rose-tinted spectacles', *World Transport Policy and Practice* 2(3).

Hillman, M. (1998a). 'Why climate change must top the agenda'. In M. Hillman (ed), *Town and Country Planning* (special issue on climate change), October.

Hillman, M. (1998b). 'Carbon budget watchers'. In M. Hillman (ed), *Town and Country Planning* (special issue on climate change), October.

Hillman, M. (1998c). 'The Implications of Climate Change for the Future of Air Travel'. Written Statement for the Terminal 5 Inquiry, Government of London.

Hillman, M. (2000). 'Coming to terms with 21st century reality', *Town and Country Planning* (special issue on 2050 visions), January.

Houghton, J.T. *et al.* (1997). *Global Warming: The Complete Briefing*, 2nd edn. Cambridge: Cambridge University Press.

Meyer, A. (2000). *Contraction and Convergence: The Global Solution to Climate Change*. London: Green Books.

Royal Commission on Environmental Pollution (RCEP) (2000). *Energy: The Changing Climate* (22nd report). London: HMSO.

5. Bringing Buses up to Standard

STEPHEN JOSEPH

This chapter, based on a report published by Transport 2000 in December 2002, analyzes current failings of public bus services in Britain and sets out an agenda for change. It explains why bus services are important, describes the main obstacles to efficient and effective operation, and proposes a range of specific measures and more general policies that are designed to achieve a radical transformation. Reforms of the regulatory environment, funding structure and local authority powers are advocated, leading to an anticipated growth in passenger appeal. The conclusion is that present policy suffers from a confusion of objectives, lack of strategic vision and a misallocation of resources.

Buses are in many ways the forgotten wing of public transport and despite the aspirations of the present government's White Paper on transport (Prescott *et al.*, 1998), in many places services are inadequate or unreliable. The present situation was analyzed in depth by the author in a report (Joseph, 2002) that forms the basis of this essay. Although buses may lack the glamour of rail transport, they are the only form of public transport available for most people without cars, and are often the only way of reaching shops, employment, education, friends and family. They are nothing less than a social lifeline.

Buses services are important for three principal reasons:

- *Environmental* – Government has a long-term policy commitment to reduce car use, yet it seems reluctant to take stronger initiatives in promoting buses as an alternative, along with walking, cycling and more extensive use of the railways. High-quality local bus services are one element in a set of alternatives to car use, but to be accepted as a realistic alternative, they need to offer speed and comfort and near-absolute reliability and punctuality. They also have to be reasonably available, which means high frequencies at almost all hours.
- *Social inclusion* – High-quality, affordable bus services help people without access to a car to reach other people, goods and services. Vehicles have to be accessible and bus stops have to be sited so that they are reachable.

STEPHEN JOSEPH is Executive Director of Transport 2000.

- *Economic* – Buses can help to tackle congestion by reducing peak-time car use and enabling people without a car to reach jobs and training, thus giving employers a larger recruitment pool. Buses can also enable access to tourist and leisure areas while reducing car use and parking.

The reality of bus services today

In practice, it is only too evident that bus services in Britain do not measure up to the kinds of objectives outlined above. Among the major obstacles to improvement is, first and most obviously, congestion. This does not just apply to urban services, but to rural routes as well, once they enter the towns and cities. Congestion makes buses unreliable and unattractive to those who have a choice. Why get out of your car only to sit on a bus in the same traffic jam? Congestion adds to the operator's costs, sometimes markedly, and also discourages drivers from joining the industry because of the frustration it causes on the job.

The causes of congestion are complex and variable, depending on local circumstances. It is often aggravated by violations of traffic law such as illegal parking, but enforcement is a very low priority for the police and the Home Office. Bus priority measures have only a limited effect on this: bus stops and bus lanes are subject to problems of illegal parking too, as well as the general lack of enforcement. Often, priority is not given in the places where it is most needed, either for fear of offending motorists or because it is deemed impractical in engineering terms (though this is usually based on pro-car views of road use and design).

Availability of bus services is also patchy. Most large urban areas have a reasonable service level on many main routes during normal work and shopping hours. In fact, frequencies and service quality on such routes and times is improving in many places, as the larger bus companies promote high frequency 'metro' services, following the example set originally by Brighton and Hove buses. For small and medium-sized towns and suburban areas, and for evening and weekend services, the picture across Britain is much more mixed. In this respect, there is a clear contrast with London, where buses operate on most central area routes until the late evening and an extensive network of night buses is also provided.

It can also be argued that bus services, whether deregulated and supposedly market-led, or regulated as in London and Northern Ireland, have been slow to respond to new developments and travel patterns. Work by Transport 2000, in conjunction with travel 'generators' such as employers, hospitals and tourist attractions, has shown great frustration towards unresponsive operators (as well as some good practice); yet those we have worked with are the very institutions responsible for bringing business to the bus industry.

The best practice in terms of identifying potential new markets and developing service and fare offers to meet social and economic needs seems to come from some of the Passenger Transport Executives (PTEs) – for example,

South Yorkshire's Travel Options Planning Service – and from some of the smaller operators. The performance of the major bus groups is variable: some parts are imaginative and responsive, while other subsidiaries are poor. Even London Buses has proved slow to alter often very long-standing service patterns to meet new needs or to cater for large new developments.

Rural bus services are particularly variable, as the work by Transport 2000 on Rural Bus Grant has revealed (Woracker, 1999), with service levels and networks ranging from good to non-existent across comparable areas. Inter-urban bus services (not coaches) are also highly variable across comparable areas. Allied to this, on the 85 per cent of services operated commercially outside London, there is no regulatory control on frequency or starting and finishing times. Services can be changed or withdrawn at 42 days' notice. Therefore, it is impossible for an employer or a developer (or any other travel generator) to plan with certainty as to the level, or even the existence, of a bus service on any particular route unless it is run under contract to them or the local authority.

Service quality – in all its aspects – is also hugely variable. There has been significant investment in new buses in most areas and the use of popular low-floor buses is now widespread. Rural Bus Grant and various Challenge Funds have stimulated new services and ideas. On the other hand, from the user's perspective, aspects of the bus industry are prehistoric compared with other service sectors. For example, information in all its aspects ranges from good to non-existent, ticketing systems and fares structures can be difficult to use or understand, and 'customer care' is often very poor indeed. 'Exact fare only' systems can also slow up buses significantly, especially when combined with a lack of pre-boarding tickets.

Networks, again, are extremely variable. Connections and interchanges between buses, or between buses and trains, range from good to poor and, by European standards, even the best in Britain is barely adequate for most people. Buses carrying bikes or the provision of cycle parking at bus stops and stations, normal in some countries (even in parts of the United States), are still very rare. Inter-available or area-wide tickets are still unobtainable in many places. Here there is a specific obstacle in the form of competition policy which, given the penalties, deters operators from entering into any agreement with other operators that might be seen as acting as a cartel. It is clear that the consumer's interests are not being met here and we will return to this later.

Fares are a further problem. Real trends in fares have seen increases above inflation and also above motoring costs since bus deregulation in the mid-1980s; but even before that, fares outside the metropolitan areas were rising above inflation. The end of fare subsidies at deregulation accelerated the trend for a time. While concessionary fares have softened the impact of fare rises on some groups, the increases have had a big impact on poorer households and people. They have also made buses less attractive for car users, especially where perceived costs (mainly parking charges) are low. Subsidies by employers for bus services and bus fares have been treated as a taxable perk (unlike workplace car parking), though some exemptions have recently been made and more may follow.

Public funding for bus services is below that in many European countries and much of it is either national and not specific to an area (e.g., fuel duty rebate) or ring-fenced for certain groups (e.g., concessionary fares) or types of service (e.g., rural services and school travel). While Local Transport Plans (LTPs) give five-year capital funding for bus priority measures or bus infrastructure improvements, revenue funding for subsidising services has not increased. Bus revenue funding is also not ring-fenced in the allocations of revenue support grant from central government to local authorities, unlike highway maintenance, and has to fight for priority with other non-statutory services. Revenue funding is also decided annually: there is no long-term revenue funding framework.

Industry trends

Current trends in the bus industry do not offer much hope that market-led approaches by themselves will sustain any moves towards constructive change. Industry costs are increasing for a number of reasons. Although the government provides a significant rebate on fuel duty, it seldom takes account of the full cost of fuel price rises. Wage costs have risen and companies are having to pay more to recruit and retain staff, after years in which wages and conditions of employment have been generally reduced. Recruitment and retention are also affected by rising numbers of attacks on staff while on duty. Congestion increases operating costs because more buses are needed to run the same service, although fewer people are available to run them. These increases can no longer be absorbed by cost-cutting: if anything, there are now too few staff rather than too many and there is no 'fat' to cut. In many situations, fare increases are the only remedy. On top of this, the Traffic Commissioners have been fining operators for cancellations and unpunctuality, to which operators have responded either by re-scheduling services to cater for the worst congestion or withdrawing those they know they cannot run reliably.

The result of these trends is that local councils are being expected to subsidise services without extra funds; yet their ability to do this is hampered by the increases in tender prices that operators demand for subsidised services (up by 21 per cent in 2002 according to the Association of Transport Coordinating Officers). Even where councils, or in some cases a major employer or other traffic generators, do embark on policies that can be considered favourable to buses, the response from operators is not always positive.

The framework of regulation

Folowing the deregulation of the bus industry in 1985, services outside London remain subject to four main sorts of regulation:

- The Traffic Commissioners, who register services, have recently been getting tough on badly performing bus operators, but their scope and powers are limited. They do not take account of traffic congestion and have no jurisdiction over local authorities; so, for example, operators are blamed for highway authority failures to give buses priority, or even for delays when roads are closed for maintenance. The Commissioners have a limited range of penalties: they can deregister or fine operators or sometimes stop them running services. In many cases, this means that passengers lose out.
- The Office of Fair Trading (OFT), which applies the Competition Acts to the bus industry, interprets its remit narrowly, looking at competition *within* the bus industry rather than competition *between* buses and other modes of transport. As already noted, it has stopped operators from making agreements to accept each other's tickets or run regular interval joint services because it believes that this means anti-competitive cartels. A recent directive giving block exemption from the Competition Acts for joint ticketing schemes is still very narrowly drawn and operators' legal advisers are still wary of any scheme that might fall foul of the OFT.
- Local authorities have highway powers, with Traffic Regulation Orders and conditions used to regulate bus priority, bus stops, etc. They also have a direct public transport role, with duties under the Transport Act 2000 to draw up bus strategies and to promote public transport information. They have powers to subsidise non-commercial bus services and to develop quality bus partnerships. If they can show that other provisions will not work, authorities can apply for powers to impose Quality Contracts – that is, area-wide franchising of bus services. District councils have a duty to provide at least half-price concessionary fares schemes for pensioners.
- The Vehicle Inspectorate regulates operators as to vehicle standards and maintenance, and the industry is also subject to more general oversight by the Health and Safety Executive.

Note that (unlike all other regulated utilities or privatised services) there is no statutory user representation or input into any of these regulatory frameworks (apart from a requirement in the Transport Act 2000 for local councils to consult users when compiling bus strategies). Bus users in England and Wales have only a non-statutory appeals body run by the National Federation of Bus Users and the Confederation of Passenger Transport. In Scotland, a Bus Users' Complaints Tribunal has been established with powers to hear complaints and award compensation to users, but it is not related to other regulatory bodies.

Pro-bus policies

Much of the argument about bus policy has tended to focus on regulatory issues. The remainder of this chapter sets out what a more comprehensive agenda for improving bus services could look like. At the local level, it would mean, first, a clear framework of objectives, targets and measures to reduce traffic and social exclusion and to promote a modal shift to public transport, walking and cycling. Such a framework could not credibly exist without complementary planning policies that require travel plans to be drawn up for new developments, preferably based on reducing parking standards, promoting higher density development and locating development where it can easily be served by public transport, including buses (as well as on foot and bicycle). There has to be long-term commitment to reversing the trend of recent decades in which new developments have been approved often with totally inadequate planning for the transport implications.

Second, traffic management policies are needed that both manage and price car use properly, and give priority to buses (as well as to trams, cyclists, pedestrians and taxis). This means realistic on- and off-street parking charges and controls, speed management, car-free or bus-only areas, priority networks and lanes, and junctions to allow buses (and other key groups) to take precedence over other traffic. Again, such measures are fruitless unless backed up by traffic law enforcement so as to reduce illegal parking, especially in bus stops and on bus lanes, and other traffic offences (speeding, jumping red lights, etc.) that impede buses.

These general policies have a number of implications: bus policy and planning cannot be considered in isolation. A town that does not have charges for car parking or has developments with very large car parks attached cannot expect to have very attractive or commercial bus services, and can generally expect significant and growing congestion in which buses will be caught up. Local authority bus strategies cannot therefore be judged on their own. They will have to be looked at within the context of LTPs and development plans.

Local authority powers

All this sets the context for thinking about local authority powers over bus services. As already noted, at present councils cannot, except through taking on quality contract powers, influence timetables or fares of commercial services, and amendments that would have enabled quality partnership agreements to extend to cover these were rejected during the passage of the Transport Act 2000. The bus industry is strongly opposed to local authority powers to intervene on timetables, routes and fares. The current situation thus seems to offer 'all or nothing' controls to local authorities: either no say on commercial services, or complete powers to specify every detail of all services, on the London franchising model.

There are two big problems with this position. First, in many areas, especially rural areas, operators do not in practice use their commercial freedom very much. In some areas, such as Dumfries and Galloway, almost all services are tendered and in these places a move to quality contracts would lose operators very little freedom and might even help them by allowing for longer term planning. Second, there can and should be options between

London-style full specification of services and fares, and no involvement at all. There are examples of tendering arrangements in other European countries where costs and subsidy have been reduced, services have increased and patronage has remained stable. For example, in Helsingborg, Sweden, the operator can lose the contract if patronage falls by more than 3 per cent, or if customer ratings of quality fall below certain standards (see Preston, 2001).

The problem remains, however, that local councils vary enormously in terms of vision, capacity and competence, and in their attitude to buses. Giving greater powers to local authorites could mean that some areas would get worse rather than better. There is also the risk that councils will divert funds from savings on profitable routes to pay for schools and social services rather than better public transport. That might be a good thing overall, but would not meet transport objectives. An increase in powers would not of itself answer the problem of where the much-needed additional funding is to come from.

Central goverment

The answer lies partly in the role that central government plays, and in particular the need for a *national pro-bus policy*. This should include:

- The application of competition law to the bus industry should be reformed, with a new 'public interest' test that would allow a wide range of agreements between operators, provided these did not actively exclude or work against other operators. This on its own would tend to reduce real bus fares in many areas.
- Reforming the Traffic Commissioners, giving them a brief to consider the full range of problems affecting operators, including traffic congestion, and to raise entry standards into the industry so that operators have to meet certain quality criteria before being allowed to run services. They and the Vehicle Inspectorate should have increased resources to fulfil their role effectively.
- Enabling proper enforcement of traffic law, including enforcement of bus priority and bus stops, within the context of decriminalised parking regimes.
- Giving users a proper voice, through proper funding for the bus user forums pioneered by the National Federation of Bus Users and through trials of other methods of user involvement, such as panels or hearings arranged by the Traffic Commissioners.
- Tax relief for employers' support for bus services and fares, possibly through a travel vouchers scheme, as suggested by the Open University and others (Open University *et al.*, 2000). Removing fiscal and regulatory barriers to flexible services (e.g., VAT on small vehicles).

These are specific measures, but they need to be set within a framework that promotes pro-bus policies from local authorities with a focus on ensuring that councils use their current powers properly. This framework should include:

- Guidance to councils on buses, including indicative targets for bus services and for minimum bus access to key facilities and services. The guidance could also cover developer contributions to bus services to ensure that new developments are served by good bus services from the start. Guidance and briefing should also be given specifically to councillors on the powers they have and on good practice in bus services.
- Government scrutiny and comment on bus strategies, rewarding good ones with praise and high settlements, and criticising and giving low settlements to authorities with poor strategies until they improve.
- An audit of local authority delivery of their part of current quality partnerships – in particular, high-quality bus infrastructure and bus priority.
- Pressure on local authorities to deliver high-quality information and ensure delivery of Transport Direct (the national public transport information service).
- National initiatives to promote the image of the bus – for example, a competition for high-quality design in bus infrastructure and a 'superbus' designation for services meeting agreed standards of quality and frequency.

More generally, we need to think of buses as part of a public transport network, and linked to other modes. Community transport and taxis need to be integrated into public transport networks, with interchange, connections and through ticketing, so as to have far more flexible public transport. Demand-responsive door-to-door services feeding from main bus and rail routes should be commonplace and a key part of public transport networks. This will have the effect of bringing public transport nearer to people's doors and overcoming one of the fundamental difficulties of access for those without a car.

There can little doubt that improved bus services will require extra public funding, but funding can be made more effective if the current system is also reformed. First and foremost, the cost of public transport needs to be affordable. Bus fares have increased substantially in real terms, while motoring costs have stayed constant, and this trend has to be reversed. The way local authorities are funded for bus services should be undertaken as part of the current review of local government finance and should involve five-year revenue funding arrangements for bus support linked to bus strategies (with appropriate checks to ensure that councils deliver the services promised). This would give greater certainty to councils and operators alike in planning services, and would supplement the five-year capital funding arrangements through LTPs. This funding could incorporate all or most bus support, including school transport, rural transport and concessionary fares, so making council bus funding subject to a single agreement with central government.

A number of experimental services have been set up through the rural bus challenge scheme and now the urban bus challenge scheme. The government needs to evaluate these properly, to reach firm conclusions on approaches that appear to work well in meeting its objectives, and then ensure that these enter the mainstream through the five-year funding arrangements and the guidance to local authorities suggested above. Experiments with other new types of services are needed, such as express and limited stop services in urban areas.

The operators

A package of measures on these lines offers significant benefits to operators and they should be expected to respond accordingly. This could be done through a national partnership agreement, where operators agree to meet government targets and objectives with specified commitments – for example, on information, accessibility and driver training. There are precedents for this: operators have agreed to quality and investment targets at recent 'Bus Summits', and coach operators have promised to introduce concessionary fares in return for rebates in fuel duty.

Conclusion

This strategy has the merit of giving enhanced powers to the local authorities that will make the best use of them and show what is possible. In the longer term, council powers and coverage might be made more general by giving a duty to plan, promote and coordinate public transport networks. Where appropriate, this could involve the creation of new PTEs covering a number of authorities, thus allowing high-quality networks backed by pro-bus policies to spread across the country.

The lack of a strategic approach is at the root of many of the current problems with bus services: at the local level, the focus of bus management and councils alike is too often on day-to-day problems or on detailed issues about existing services. There has been an assumption by many operators and local uathorities alike – engendered partly by the Transport Act 1985 – that they are providing a 'safety net' service for those without cars. Yet there are signs of change. Pressure from investors for organic growth in the bus industry have pushed operators to try to change the established culture, and the Transport White Paper and Transport Act 2000 have pushed local authorities towards a more strategic approach. Park-and-ride services have shown that it is, in principle, possible to design a local bus service that people with cars will use. The more radical measures canvassed here aim to build on the prospects for change.

References

Joseph, S. (2002). *Bringing Buses up to Standard*. London: Transport 2000.
Open University *et al.* (2000). *The Potential for Further Changes to the Personal Taxation Regime to Encourage Modal Shift*. London: Department of the Environment, Transport and the Regions.

Prescott, J. *et al.* (1998). *A New Deal for Transport: Better for Everyone* (Cmnd. 3950), London: Department of the Environment, Transport and the Regions.

Preston, J. (2001). In A. Grayling (ed), *Any More Fares?* London: Institute for Public Policy Research.

Woracker, D. (1999). *The Rural Thoroughbred: Buses in the Countryside*. London: Council for the Protection of Rural England/Transport 2000.

6. The Impact of Evidence on Transport Policy-making: The Case of Road Construction[1]

FRANCIS TERRY

For many years, lack of consensus about the goals of transport policy resulted in evidence being used selectively to justify particular policies, rather than to establish whether (when judged against suitable criteria) the policies were actually working. Forecasts of traffic growth were taken as evidence of the need for road construction programmes; now, the phenomenon of 'induced traffic' has led to a re-think, and a more evidence-based approach to transport policy.

Unlike some other public services where the fundamental aims of policy seem relatively stable for generations, transport policy objectives are almost perpetually in contention. In health, there is at least broad agreement about the basic aims of promoting good health, treating illness and providing medical care. In the operation of the criminal justice system, most people would subscribe to the aims of deterring crime, as well as punishing and rehabilitating offenders. In these services, the focus of debate among professionals and politicians is about the *means* to achieve recognised aims, and the contribution of research is to establish 'what works' from an intellectually coherent reading of the evidence. Passenger transport is different, and it is perhaps significant that, until the publication of the White Paper entitled *A New Deal for Transport: Better for Everyone* (DETR, 1998), government had shied away from a declaration of overall transport policy since 1976, preferring instead to pursue a diversity of *ad hoc* and sometimes inconsistent measures.

The debate over policy aims usually comes down to a contrasting pair of arguments:

- Concern to reduce the negative impacts of transport and travel on the environment and society, and even to reduce the volume of transport *per se*.
- Demands, especially from business and motoring organisations, to improve transport flows in the interests of economic development and competitiveness.

FRANCIS TERRY is an Adviser on transport policy and funding and Visiting Fellow in the Interdisciplinary Institute of Management at the London School of Economics.

Characteristic of this debate has been the use of evidence to support policy preconceptions on either side of the argument, rather than to resolve it. This is not just a peculiarity of the United Kingdom: the same is true in other European Union countries (ICCR, 1997). The reasons, perhaps, are not hard to find. For most of us, passenger transport (by car, bus, train, bicycle, etc.) is a much more integral part of normal daily life than, say, healthcare or the operation of the criminal justice system. All of us have regular direct experience of the transport system and have views about it, conditioned by an enormous range of locational, economic, social, environmental and even emotional factors (Steg & Tertoolen, 1999); it is not an exclusive domain of the experts.

The tension between individual preferences and collective impacts is a key characteristic – perhaps the defining dilemma – of transport policy. 'Freedom of movement' – at least within national borders and, increasingly, across them – is generally regarded as a basic human right. By extension, the means by which individuals nowadays exercise the greatest range and flexibility of movement is through motor vehicles; yet the unlimited exercise of freedom of movement by car has detrimental effects that responsible government, sooner or later, has to address. Research in connection with the preparation of the second Dutch National Environmental Policy Plan (NEPP, 1993) is instructive in this context. It showed that while public consciousness of environmental issues (in general) was high, this was not accompanied by any wish to restrain one of the principal causes of pollution and damage to the environment – namely, car use.

Ambivalence in official policy-making can be seen therefore as no more than a reflection of inconsistencies in attitudes and behaviour at the individual level. Government limitations on car use could easily be represented as infringing the rights of individuals and, in such circumstances, democratic governments would be wise to tread with caution. It is tempting for them to think instead of providing attractive alternatives to cars, particularly for urban and inter-city journeys, in the hope that motorists will make enlightened choices. Yet the experience of cities in continental Europe suggests that this is a 'false trail'. Cheap and efficient public transport has little appeal for the habituated car-driver and more often encourages people who do not have access to a car to make journeys that were previously awkward or impossible. We are back to the thorny issue of restricting freedom of movement.

Against this background, a consideration of 'what works' in transport policy is at least partly determined by one's philosophical starting point, and the key questions are easier to answer at the tactical level than in terms of total strategy. Nevertheless, the British government appears more interested in addressing the strategic question now than for a long time in the past, even though it is clearly in no hurry to reach any decisive conclusions. Since debates over policy are often sharply focused in relation to the growth of road transport, evidence in this area is the principal theme of this article; parallel issues and arguments do, however, arise over the provision of public transport facilities by rail, air and, to more modest degree, by bus.

Growth of road traffic

In the decade after 1952, the number of passenger-kilometres travelled by car in the United Kingdom doubled; after 1958, cars accounted for more journeys than any other single mode; within another five years, car journeys accounted for more than twice the passenger-kilometres travelled by all other surface transport modes combined (DoT, 1996a). The trend moved inexorably upwards until 1989, when it seemed to falter, before continuing upwards at a reduced rate. The trend in passenger-kilometres has been accompanied by huge growth in the numbers of vehicles using the road system and the numbers of people holding licences to drive.

The government response to this pattern of demand has been characterised as 'predict and provide' (Goodwin, 1993). Throughout the 1960s, 1970s and 1980s, spending on new road construction averaged over £2 billion annually (in today's prices). The determination to respond to soaring demand reached a climax in the 1989 White Paper entitled *Roads to Prosperity* (DoT, 1989a), in which the government set out proposals for expenditure on road schemes of around £18 billion (1997 prices) over the following ten years.

These grandiose plans were progressively modified as the recession of the early 1990s took hold, making it essential to cut public spending. The government hoped, however, that the private sector would replace at least part of the cuts through the development of the Private Finance Initiative (PFI) and that motorway tolling would raise new income for road schemes (see DoT, 1989b, 1993). Use of the PFI in a road construction context was strongly promoted, although only a very few major schemes have gone ahead since the use of 'shadow tolls' rather than motorway tolls has been shown to represent questionable value for money (Buchan, 1996; National Audit Office, 1998) and it seems unlikely that further such schemes will now be built. A summary published by the Department of Transport (1996b) showed that, despite the ambitions of the 1989 White Paper (DoT, 1989a), real-terms expenditure on national road construction and improvement in England fell from £5.165 billion in 1990–1993 to a projected £3.823 billion for the period 1996–1999. Support to local authorities, chiefly for maintenance of the existing system, was set to fall from £2.691 billion in 1990–1993 to £2.305 billion in 1996–1999.

Official recognition that the declared policy was becoming unsustainable appeared with the Green Paper entitled *Transport: The Way Forward* (DoT, 1996), which canvassed a range of diverse and more environmentally friendly objectives for transport policy. The present government announced a major review of trunk road and motorway spending shortly after it came to office in May 1997, leading to an announcement in August 1998 that out of 156 proposed new schemes, roughly one-third would go ahead with public funding, 13 with private funding and the rest would be either cancelled or referred to other bodies (chiefly regional or local authorities) for decision. The transport

White Paper (DETR, 1998), published earlier the same month, made it clear that the thrust of transport policy would in future be towards promoting alternatives to car use, with a very much lower level of public spending available for new road schemes.

The remainder of this article examines the nature of the evidence that underpinned the very substantial investment in road building over the previous thirty years, the way it was interpreted and used, and the rise of alternative interpretations lying behind the shift of policy signalled in the White Paper.

Nature of the evidence

The evidence used to support major road construction in the past relied heavily on statistics and forecasts of traffic growth. Collection of statistics about car ownership and numbers of qualified drivers is administratively simple (through the licensing system), and few people would seriously doubt that the task was performed other than to the highest professional standards: in that sense, road transport statistics constituted 'hard evidence'. Apart from the statistics, it should be also recorded that the Department of the Environment, Transport and the Regions (DETR), and previously the DoT, allocated about £30 million annually to research into transport problems of all kinds, including some £9 million on road safety. Although the findings from such research also constitutes evidence, its impact on policy towards road construction has typically been at the technical level of implementation. The research agenda has been strongly conditioned by its relevance to current policy – meaning that it focused on better ways of achieving the goal of building roads rather than suggesting alternatives thereto.

Forecasts

The former DoT's practice was periodically to produce National Road Traffic Forecasts (NTRF) for a period of up to thirty years ahead. Although their relationship to public expenditure planning has never been precisely defined, they were used as part of the general case to Treasury in annual public expenditure negotiations. The forecasts made in 1989 (DoT, 1989c) are especially interesting because they acted as the touchstone of policy for most of the Conservatives' remaining period in office up to 1997. The published forecasts consisted of two variants: a high forecast of 142 per cent increase in traffic between 1988 and 2025, and a low forecast of an 83 per cent increase. The growth projections were closely linked to forecasts of economic growth, such that over the period 1988 to 2000, the increase in traffic was expected to be virtually the same as assumed growth of GDP, although traffic was assumed to grow more slowly thereafter.

51

Separate forecasts were made for each major class of vehicle, as follows:

- *Cars* – It was assumed that the observed relationship between increase in income and increase in car ownership would continue until 90 per cent of the population of driving age (i.e., 17–74) own a car. The distance travelled by each car was assumed to increase one-fifth as fast as GDP per head, and to be reduced by 1.5 per cent for every 10 per cent increase in the price of fuel in real terms.
- *Light goods vehicles* – Vehicle-kilometres were assumed to increase in direct proportion to GDP.
- *Heavy goods vehicles* – Again, growth was assumed to be directly related to GDP, though other factors were incorporated, such as an assumption that the roads' share of freight would continue to increase and that most of the additional freight would be carried by the heaviest vehicles.
- *Buses and coaches* – Vehicle-kilometres were expected to remain static at 1989 levels.
- *Others* – Remarkably, no forecasts at all were made for travel on foot or by bicycle, moped or motorcycle.

Aside from the forecasts, detailed statistics have also been kept of road accidents for more than seventy years. These too, are relatively simple to collect from police records, though the way the data are recorded does not always make it easy to analyze the causes of accidents. Nevertheless, they constitute an important ancillary source of evidence on which policy has been based over many decades.

Using the evidence

For much of the postwar period, road traffic forecasts were the driving force behind British transport policy and a principal criterion for deciding on public investment in transport infrastructure. Priorities for investment were, to some extent, influenced by accident statistics ('black spots' being targeted for improvement), but a number of other, more politically important, reasons – not examined in detail here – guaranteed high public expenditure on road building. These included:

- Attracting support from voters by catering for massive potential increases in personal mobility.
- The importance of maintaining, through the 1960s and 1970s, a sizeable indigenous car manufacturing industry (for employment and trade reasons) and a strong construction industry.
- Scepticism about the value of sustained high levels of investment in the rail network, as an alternative to road provision.

In the 1989 White Paper, the principal reasons for investment acknowledged by government (DoT, 1989a: Paragraphs 6–8), were:

- Helping economic development by reducing transport costs.
- Improving the environment by removing through traffic from unsuitable roads.
- Enhancing road safety.

Considering the scale of investment promised, it was a surprise to find that the methodology of the forecasts was not more robust. Yet in its *Eighteenth Report* (RCEP, 1994), the Royal Commission on Environment and Pollution criticised several of the assumptions behind them; for example, it was assumed that real incomes in Britain would continue to rise, and that the lifestyles of higher income groups would progressively spread more widely across the population. The assumption of 90 per cent car ownership implied that the ratio of cars per 1,000 population would increase from 331 in 1988 to between 529 and 608 by the year 2025. According to RCEP, this assumption was based on the 1990 level of car ownership in the United States, with its wealthier and much less dense pattern of settlement – hardly an appropriate yardstick for the United Kingdom. Despite such weaknesses, the National Road Traffic Forecasts (NRTF) were extensively used at local levels for modelling the impact of proposed improvements to the road network.

In the present context, the important point is that the NRTF were treated *as evidence*. The point was clearly demonstrated in the case of *Bushell and Brunt* v. *Secretary of State for the Environment* (1980), in which the House of Lords ruled that the NRTF were not challengeable at planning inquiries. Although the government stated that its traffic forecasts were not a target, and that it was not desirable that they should be met, they continued to be used as evidence of the need for specific schemes throughout the 1980s and early 1990s. As a result, planning inquiries were largely restricted to considering the route of a proposed road, and ruled out examination of alternative strategies that would remove the need for it. The official justification was that inquiries were intended to deal with objections, not with the formulation of policy, for which Parliament was the proper forum. However, as the RCEP commented:

This argument would be more convincing if . . . Parliament is regularly offered the opportunity of scrutinizing the road programme. . . . In our view, there is a need both for Parliamentary scrutiny of the broad thrust of policies and for opportunities for local people to question the policies as applied to their locality. The failure to allow the latter is symptomatic of a flawed policy. (RCEP, 1994)

Economic benefits

Ministers have for a long time required a cost-benefit analysis (CBA) to be conducted for major road schemes before giving approval. Guidance by the former DoT (1985) has had the effect of limiting CBA to three main classes of benefits:

- Journey time savings, which may accrue to the users of the new road and to other roads where congestion is likely to be reduced.
- Savings in operating costs on the road network as a whole.
- Accident costs savings.

These benefits are then compared to the costs, in two ways: first, in relation to capital costs, such as the acquisition of land and construction costs; and second, in relation to maintenance costs in the future. The appropriate methodology for CBA was the subject of extensive research in the 1980s (reviewed by Layard & Glaister, 1994) that made it possible, through the use of 'stated preference' and 'revealed preference' techniques, to arrive at numerical values for time-savings and accident reductions. In the light of subsequent updating, the figures currently used are around £10 per hour for working time saved and £5 per hour for leisure time, with £950,000 the value of a life saved. Even so, these numbers may appear somewhat arbitrary to non-experts.

The main point, however, is that the conclusions of CBA calculations were for a long time accepted as an important category of evidence in determining priorities for road investment. Fundamental criticisms of this approach were eventually made by RCEP (1994) and later by the Standing Advisory Committee on Trunk Road Assessment (SACTRA, 1994) on the grounds that CBA did not address the problem of induced traffic. In other words, there is a strong case for believing that the extension and improvement of the road network leads to an increase in the total amount of road traffic, as distinct from redistributing a pre-set level of traffic on to the enhanced network.

For example, the M25 motorway generated leisure journeys from the southwest of London to the north, with traffic flows at weekends much higher than predicted and congestion occurring around Heathrow Airport during the morning peak (7–10am). Many of the additional trips, as compared to the time before the M25 existed, have little or no economic value, and once congestion occurs it enters the equation as an economic cost in terms of time wasted, rather than as benefit. Despite such findings, which came from local authorities and pressure groups outside government, DoT's view was for a long time that any effect that the road programme had in generating additional traffic was of minor importance, and that its comparisons of forecast levels with actual levels occurring one year after the completion of schemes supported this interpretation. Use of the DoT's recommended method for conducting CBA has recently been replaced by a new approach to scheme appraisal based on qualitative judgements of five assessment criteria alongside quantitative calculations, where possible.

Apart from the limitations of CBA methodology, evidence of the relationship between road investment and economic growth is also unclear. Following Keynesian principles, the assumption was invariably made in postwar transport planning that new roads promote growth; indeed this was a central theme of the 1989 White Paper. Yet the evidence for these arguments was inconclusive to say the least. A study for the Department of the Environment by Parkinson (1981) revealed that the proportion of a firm's costs accounted for by transport is small – typically 5–10 per cent. Of this, 70 per cent is incurred at terminals and is virtually unaffected by transit times or road access. Thus, a 10 per cent cut in movement costs would reduce total production costs by around 2 per cent. Parkinson concludes: 'it is implausible that the fall in price which could result from this small reduction in transport costs is likely to lead to a significant increase in demand and output'. As a means of creating jobs, road building has also been shown to be relatively poor value for money. Pound for pound, it creates considerably fewer jobs than spending on other assets like housing and public transport (Vanke, 1988; German Road League/IG Bau Steine Erden, 1992).

Certainly the existence of an efficient transport system is essential for the growth of the economy. If goods cannot reach their markets in time and workers cannot reliably reach their jobs, economic output suffers. Yet the policy implications of this simple observation are apt to be misunderstood. Better road links may have the aim of opening up markets, but this does not mean that investment in roads is necessarily an effective lever for inducing economic growth. Traffic congestion on other parts of the network may cancel out the benefits of a particular scheme (Headicar & Bixby, 1992), while the evidence from work by Dodgson (1973) and others is that new roads may actually suck economic activity out of a region as easily as they stimulate it.

Nevertheless, while a variety of evidence from independent experts tended to cast doubt on the assumption that a general rise in movement signals greater economic activity at the micro-level, official policy was reluctant to accept this. In the 1996 Green Paper, the government at last conceded that many of its assumptions about traffic growth needed to be revised. The scene was set for the reforms promised in Labour's White Paper a year later. Interestingly, the idea that growth in car ownership is a proxy indicator of national prosperity, which appeared in the 1989 White Paper is repeated in 1998, although the evidence shows that levels of ownership in the United Kingdom, relative to the rest of Europe, do not correlate with other indicators like GDP per head.

Environmental benefits and accidents

On the question of the environmental case for road building, a serious challenge was raised by RCEP (1994) and others (Transport 2000, 1994). It was pointed out that bypasses, which tend to bring the most direct environmental benefits to towns and villages, accounted for a relatively small proportion of total public expenditure on roads through the 1970s and 1980s, while trunk roads and motorways (including motorway widening) were pressed through against heavy opposition based on levels of noise, pollution and loss of rural amenity that would result. In relation to accidents, the all-party Parliamentary Advisory Committee on Transport Safety (PACTS) found that 'many large schemes produced very small accident reductions . . . we believe that the small benefits that might accrue might be achieved by other methods for a fraction of the costs' (PACTS, 1993).

Discussion

By the mid-1990s, it was clear that the rather limited range of evidence, and the narrow interpretation put upon it inside government, were an inadequate basis for policy-making. In 1993, research by Phil Goodwin and his colleagues at the Transport Studies Unit at Oxford University demonstrated that even if the 1989 White Paper proposals were *fulfilled*, the problems of congestion would not be solved or, alternatively, that if the official projections of traffic growth were realised, there would be no possibility of increasing road space on a commensurate scale. The policy implication of Goodwin's work – dubbed 'the new realism' – was that since the supply of road space is not going to be matched by demand, demand must be matched to supply.

Up to that point, road construction had been identified with the belief that constraints on movement are undesirable, almost on principle. As a result, greater *mobility* tended to be confused with better *access* to destinations. Accordingly, policy-making emphasised the evidence of traffic growth as a justification for large allocations of public investment. As time passed, new road schemes had to be driven through in the face of growing local opposition, on the assumption that the government was thereby conferring generalised benefits on large numbers of road users and the national economy. Eventually, after witnessing police and bailiffs clearing protesters from the path of a new section of the M11 motorway in 1994, Brian Mawhinney, as Transport Secretary, recognised the need for a broader national debate on transport issues.

We can contrast the limited evidence used to support large-scale road construction with the precise records of road accidents and the extensive research into their causes. Although road safety may be improved by new construction projects (by removing accident 'black spots'), a wide range of other initiatives can be undertaken. On a number of these, the government has been slow to act because of anticipated negative public reaction and the lower priority (compared to new construction) given to the necessary expenditure. For example, the benefits of wearing seat belts were conclusively demonstrated during tests in the early 1960s, but Ministers did not feel that they could introduce a seat belt law until more than 50 per cent of the population were wearing them voluntarily, as a result of intensive public information campaigns (DETR, 1997). Again, while the introduction of experimental 20 miles per hour zones, starting in 1990, showed dramatic reductions (typically 60 per cent) in the number of pedestrians killed or seriously injured, it was at least five years before DoT would consider giving any priority to spending on these zones more generally.

In retrospect, it seems remarkable that the growth trends in vehicle miles and car ownership were elevated to a position where they received a dominant position over all other evidence, and indeed evidence about the effects of the policy itself. The contrast between evidence from official sources and that from independent professional and academic sources is also striking. For a long time, evidence from within, or commissioned by, the DoT was the only evidence admissible in policy-making. It was not until the 1990s, when organisations outside government – ranging from the RCEP to local pressure groups – successfully challenged the traditional direction of transport policy, that alternative evidence was given much weight.

Policy-making has, as a result, become more pluralist and arguably better balanced. While the barriers to a more evidential approach to transport policy seem to be coming down, the reasons can only be surmised at this stage. Changes in the political climate during the mid-1990s allowed evidence produced by bodies external to government to enter the decision process not only in transport, but also in other public policy arenas such as housing and welfare. The volume and quality of research outside government seems to have increased, as government's own research budgets have shrunk in response to public expenditure constraints, and as universities have been encouraged to undertake more 'applied' research relevant to policy-making.

Another factor may be that, during the 1990s, local authorities – despite the wide-ranging reductions in their powers – began to conduct practical experiments with alternatives to road building. Indeed, it is arguable that the initiative in forward thinking about transport issues was partially lost by central government in favour of local authorities. The widespread pedestrianisation of historic centres like York and Chester is one example, but innovative partnerships with bus companies to improve the appeal of public transport and experiments with community transport are others.

Conclusions

The conclusion from this brief review is that 'what works' in transport policy can be understood at more than one level of analysis. At the strategic level (and assuming that the policy objectives are established through appropriate political and consultative processes), deciding 'what works' will need a receptiveness to alternative perspectives and approaches that has not always been the hallmark of official thinking. If the goal is clear, there may be more than one way of reaching it, and this is especially important in the context of tight constraints on public expenditure. More research could be done on how political processes assimilate and use evidence, especially when it does not conform to popular views and beliefs.

At the tactical level of individual measures – whether constructing new roads or introducing limitations on the use of cars – it is clear that the government sometimes feels strong enough to pursue its course in the face of substantial local opposition, while at other times it is reluctant to force the pace. There does not seem to be much obvious correlation between these responses and what research or experimental evidence say about such issues;

57

nor, incidentally, with the size of the government's parliamentary majority. Public acceptability is often a more important criterion than whether the evidence supports a particular course of action. Nevertheless, the diversity of sources, from which evidence about 'what works' now comes, seems a positive feature of the present scene, and the contribution from locally driven initiatives can have a strong practical value. After a long period in which the use of evidence in transport policy has been restricted and confused, the mid-1990s saw a greater openness and clarity. Yet there is much more to be done before the full value of an evidence-based approach is recognised.

Note

1 This article was originally published in *Public Money & Management* 19(1).

References

Buchan, K. (1996). *For Whom the Shadow Tolls: The Effects of Design, Build, Finance and Operate (DBFO) on the A36 Salisbury Bypass*. London: Motor Transport Research Unit/Transport 2000.

Department of Transport (DoT) (1996). *Transport: The Way Forward* (Cmnd. 3234). London: HMSO.

Department of the Environment, Transport and the Regions (DETR) (1998). *A New Deal for Transport: Better for Everyone* (Cmnd. 3950). London: HMSO.

Department of Transport (DoT) (1985). *COBA 9 Evaluation Manual and Highway Economics Note 2* (Update). London: HMSO.

Department of Transport (DoT) (1989a). *Roads to Prosperity* (Cmnd. 693). London: HMSO.

Department of Transport (DoT) (1989b). *New Roads by New Means* (Cmnd. 698). London: HMSO.

Department of Transport (DoT) (1989c). *National Road Traffic Forecasts (Great Britain)*. London: HMSO.

Department of Transport (DoT) (1993). *Paying for Better Motorways* (Cmnd. 2200). London: HMSO.

Department of Transport (DoT) (1996a). *Transport Statistics, Great Britain 1996*. London: HMSO.

Department of Transport (DoT) (1996b). *Transport Report 1996*. London: HMSO.

Department of Transport (DoT) (1997). *Road Casualties, Great Britain 1997*. London: HMSO.

Dodgson J.S. (1973). 'Motorway investment, industrial transport costs, and sub-regional growth: A case study of the M62', *Regional Studies 8*.

(Dutch) Ministry of Housing, Physical Planning and the Environment (NEPP) (1993). *Second Dutch National Environmental Policy Plan*. Amsterdam: NEPP.

German Road League/IG Bau Steine Erden (1992). Quoted in *Going Green Report*. London: Environmental Transport Association.

Goodwin, P. (1993). 'Key Issues in Demand Management'. Paper presented at the Surrey County Council's Workshop on Demand Management.

Headicar, P. & Bixby, B. (1992). *Concrete and Tyres: Local Development Effects of Major Roads: A Case Study of the M40*. London: Council for the Protection of Rural England).

Interdisciplinary Centre for Comparative Research in the Social Sciences (ICCR) (1997). *Comparative Report on National Transport Policies* (Report of EU-TENASSESS project). London: ICCR.

Layard, R. & Glaister, S. (eds) (1994). *Cost-benefit Analysis.* Cambridge: Cambridge University Press.

National Audit Office (1998). *The Private Finance Initiative: The First Four Design, Build and Operate Roads Contracts* (HC 476). London: HMSO.

Parkinson, M. (1981). *The Effect of Road Investment in Economic Development in the UK* (Government Economic Service Working Paper No. 430). London: HMSO.

Parliamentary Advisory Committee on Transport Safety (PACTS) (1993). *Working Paper on Road Investment and Accident Reduction.* London: HMSO.

Royal Commission on Environmental Pollution (RCEP) (1994). *Eighteenth Report: Transport and the Environment* (Cmnd. 2674). London: HMSO.

Standing Advisory Committee on Trunk Road Assessment (SACTRA) (1994). *Trunk Roads and the Generation of Traffic.* London: HMSO.

Steg, L. & Tertoolen, G. (1999). 'Sustainable transport policy: The contribution from behavioural scientists', *Public Money & Management* 19(1).

Transport 2000 (1994). *Transport 21: An Alternative Transport Budget.* London: Transport 2000.

Vanke, J. (1988). 'Roads to prosperity', *The Planner* (December).

7. Cars in the Landscape: Some Undefined Questions for Transport Policy

REG HARMAN

This essay poses some fundamental questions about the constituency popularly referred to as 'motorists', and seeks to analyze how and why it is organised in the way it is. The author questions the primacy given to cars in transport policy and argues that the sheer volume of vehicles crowding on to British roads is changing perceptions of how the urban and rural landscape is planned and used. There is a case for the huge amounts of public funding allocated for road developments to be matched by stronger powers for local authorities to implement more cohesive strategies for managing the impact of cars on the landscape.

Transport has now secured a high place in the political agenda of the United Kingdom. Although education and health retain the top spots, transport secured a substantial rise in its budget commitments in the Chancellor of the Exchequer's Spending Review for 2002–03 to reflect the aspirations of *Transport 2010: The 10-year Plan* (DETR, 2000). Concern for transport briefly reached the Prime Minister's office, with the appointment of Lord Birt as a special adviser to guide long-term thinking, although his initial proposals failed to enthuse transport professionals (or anyone else) and the appointment turned out to be short-lived.

Two primary factors seem to have stimulated political concern:

- the lead given by the Deputy Prime Minster in the 1998 White Paper (DETR, 1998) with its major revisions to transport policy directions and mechanisms was followed by publication of *The 10-year Plan* for transport (DETR, 2000) and the passage of the Transport Act 2000, together with the range of accompanying guidance notes and other instruments; and
- the government's failure, despite these initiatives, to achieve any significant changes thus far to match public aspirations for transport which were raised substantially by the promotion of the new policies.

REG HARMAN is an independent consultant in the areas of transport policy and practice, and urban and regional planning. His principal interests include the interfaces between transport and spatial planning, and comparative studies of European development processes.

It is generally assumed that the government's major policy documents have identified all the key issues and have therefore set out measures to tackle them in a comprehensive way. Their major focus is on the use of cars – recognised as a very convenient means of increasing personal mobility and widening opportunities, but causing grave levels of pollution, danger, inefficiency and social inequity, especially when used to excess on crowded networks such as within urban areas. Current policies envisage people being persuaded to use alternative modes through major improvements in performance and some constraints on car use. The primary alternative to car use was seen to be public transport, while cycling and even walking have received some attention. These broad themes reflect similar concerns and policy directions across Europe, encouraged by a raft of European Union (EU) policy reviews and measures.

Leaving aside the severe difficulties the government has encountered in implementing its policies, largely through adopting inappropriate measures and showing insufficient political will, the question as to whether all the issues have really been defined and addressed remains. This question is the central theme for this chapter. How far have we seriously considered – or even understood – the implication of all that cars really mean to us? Cars and the roads on which they run now feature on our landscape in an all-pervading fashion – in the physical landscape of our towns, old and new, and our countryside; in the mental landscape of our personal attitudes and decisions; and in the political landscape of transport and related decisions. Of course, road freight movement and road-based public transport also contribute to the opportunities and the problems, but they remain a small part of total traffic (7.5 and 1.3 per cent, respectively, of total vehicle-kilometres in 2001).

Car ownership and use have grown at a considerable rate and scale, as some simple indicators will serve to show. Currently, there are about 24 million cars on the roads of Great Britain, equal to just over one car per household or one per 15 metres of public road. In the year after our monarch's Jubilee, it is useful to note that in 1952 there were 187,600 cars registered in Great Britain – equivalent to one for every 78 households or one for every 1.6 kilometres of public road. Thus car ownership, by one yardstick at least, has grown by 125 times. In practice, it is likely that a high proportion of the change to a much more car-oriented lifestyle took place in the first thirty years after 1952, as illustrated by reactions to the 1979–1980 fuel crisis (see Harman, 2002). Since the fuel crisis, the influence of car ownership and use has strengthened even more. There has been a steady growth in the car fleet, widespread provision for car use, and an everyday assumption by most people that transport is all about access to, and use of, cars.

It is sometimes alleged that changes in key aspects of society require a generation to achieve. If so, we have moved in one-and-a-half generations towards a commitment to lifestyles and landscapes where car ownership and use are socially and economically dominant. Because the scale of change has come about rapidly and insidiously, people's ability to appreciate fully the consequences, and hence to tackle them effectively, are still limited. Perhaps the much-remarked lack of real progress in implementing transport policies actually reflects a failure to identify the true impingement of cars on our landscapes and our lives.

The following sections set out four questions that do not feature in the 1998 White Paper or any other policy document. For each of them, some relevant issues are discussed and initial thoughts on appropriate policy responses are offered.

Who is the motorist?

The White Paper focused mainly on the disbenefits of excessive car use and the means by which people might be persuaded to use other modes of travel. In 1998, the government appeared keen to transfer a significant number of trips from car to public transport. However, its enthusiasm has clearly waned since then, as the difficulty of 'quick wins' in this field has become apparent for two principal reasons: the scale of change needed in facilities and infrastructure for alternative modes, and the opposition from motoring interests. The perception that the government was anti-motorist – following intense and complex debate over transport policies, including the fuel tax 'accelerator', which caused the September 2000 outcry over fuel prices (Rosen, 2002) – led to government worries that this might affect its electoral appeal. The election results of June 2001 hardly bore this out, however. Steps were nevertheless taken to ensure that policies were 'motorist friendly'. In this, the government was echoing the usual media references to 'the motorist' in relation to any capacity management or pricing policies that might constrain free use of the motor car.

In fact there are really two questions: Who is the motorist in relation to society as a whole? And is the motorist a cohesive categorisation? The media see 'the motorist' as an important player in society in economic and political terms. Over 32 million people, about 71 per cent of the population aged 17 and over, now hold driving licences, so those who use cars form a large and vociferous body. Because car ownership and use increase with income levels, car users overall consist of the stronger economic groups in society, who also exercise stronger roles in social and political areas, and so are more influential than lower income groups. Furthermore, views on behalf of motorists are regularly expressed by the Automobile Association (AA) and the Royal Automobile Club (RAC), both substantial and well-resourced bodies supported by large and articulate memberships. Thus a very large (non-political) constituency exists calling for better conditions for using cars, and it would of course be quite inappropriate for the government or any other decision-making body to ignore them. Indeed, it would be undemocratic to do so.

Taking account of the needs of those using cars should in no way imply the sort of completely *laissez-faire* policies advocated by some commentators (e.g., the motoring journalist Jeremy Clarkson). Indeed, this could prove counter-productive to optimising the effective use of cars. Good transport policy – especially related to effective spatial planning policies – will almost certainly need instruments that manage the use of cars within an overall framework designed to ensure effective access for everyone (see the contribution by Goodwin elsewhere in this volume). It is doubtful whether even the most assiduous motorist really wants public authorities to spend all available funds on new roads and related facilities only to achieve ever-larger traffic jams (as has been the *de facto* policy during some periods of the recent past). Excessive freedom on the roads also leads to inefficiency or worse. For example, driving or parking in ways that make less efficient use of road space may bring delays to all motorists, and hence the use of highway space needs to be managed. Driving at excessive speeds plays a major part in crashes and casualties, leading to personal, social and economic loss.

In fact, the constituency of motorists is by no means a cohesive one. Owners and users of cars may be categorised along a number of lines. One is that of socio-economic group (SEG). This includes, for example, established middle-class motorists, who can afford to pay more for car ownership or vary their lifestyle to reduce costs and gain better service. Generally, such people have the social and political strength to challenge proposals that might be seen to constrain their use of cars, although they are also more likely to appreciate where alternative approaches might benefit them. By contrast, there is a growing number of car owners in lower income groups who really need their car to save money or gain better access to jobs, schools and so on, and for whom the car forms a significant cost item. Anything that reduces (or keeps down) the cost of motoring is beneficial, and they will support such measures without necessarily being able to press an eloquent case, while opposing any steps that are perceived to worsen their freedom to drive.

Age is another category. Lower income motorists are likely to include high proportions of both young and elderly people. For younger motorists, the ownership and use of a car is an expression of maturity and freedom. Two pertinent factors have been shown up by studies in recent years. A report for the Chartered Institute of Transport (Solomon, 1998), based on surveys among sixth-form and university students, showed that three-quarters of all young people rated a driving licence as being much more important than the right to vote. A study by Bristow on a Transport Planning Society bursary (Bristow, 2002) revealed the (not surprising) picture that most advertisements for cars stress the characteristics of convenience, speed and attractiveness (see also the contribution by Steg & Tertoolen elsewhere in this volume). This matches the preference of young people for their cars to be distinctive, the higher proportion of older cars (young people cannot afford new ones), and the tendency to drive in a more impatient and lively style (the results of which are reflected in much higher insurance premiums).

By contrast, older motorists tend to drive more cautiously and, for this reason, may be less confident driving on motorways and other heavily used parts of the system. Yet many elderly motorists find their car vital to their continuing independence, enabling them to shop and take part in local activities, and visit friends, family and other destinations. Without this freedom, they may become seriously restricted in their activities, suffer a poorer quality of life, and need the support of public welfare services rather earlier (at an increased cost to the public purse). In addition, implementing policies to keep elderly people active in their own community often requires employed or volunteer carers taking less mobile older people out to facilities, which can be done only if they can drive and park with reasonable freedom.

How important is the car to transport policy?

The White Paper implicitly identified the car as the core means of movement. For example, it concentrated on attracting drivers out of their cars to use enhanced public transport: a simplistic image that has been used by the media in particular to misinterpret (deliberately or by accident) the wider thrust of transport policy. More specifically, the investment in *The 10-year Plan* was based on relieving congestion, but reduced congestion is primarily an improvement in transport by road vehicles and in supporting economic and social activity patterns based on such a lifestyle. *The 10-year Plan* is, in effect, addressing the needs of those using cars, thus maintaining the dominance of the car. Indeed, car ownership and use is built into the lifestyle of much of the population so much that car travel is the fundamental standard against which travel by *all* modes is measured. It is not surprising then that it has come to be the basis of most commercial decisions.

How far should this assumption form the basis of public authority decisions? There is a lot of high-level debate about provision for different modes in terms of major projects (e.g., road construction versus railway schemes) and about policy instruments (e.g., road pricing, public transport interchanges). However, implementation happens largely at the local level, and involves a range of public bodies and commercial companies. The government has partially recognised these factors, placing a major role for implementing transport policies on local authorities through the Local Transport Plan (LTP) mechanism, and through development planning (though the LTP process now seems likely to be watered down) and the emerging regional bodies. It also accepts the importance of the private sector, whose contribution is outlined in *The 10-year Plan*. Despite this note of realism, changes in practice have generally been slow and cautious, as central government seems nervous about any action that might be interpreted as 'anti-motorist'.

In consequence, car use retains its priority, so provision for it remains a major element in most plans and projects, despite brave words to the contrary. For example, major retail units based almost solely on car access continue to be developed, notwithstanding the emphasis of Planning Policy Guidance Note 6 (PPG6) on priority for existing town and district centres. Car-based supermarket developments continue to appear within urban areas, even though they can change the pattern of traffic in an area and become local congestion spots themselves. Strategies for existing town and district centres, of all sizes, continue to focus on attracting and maintaining car-borne users in practice.

Car access thus remains dominant in decision processes, while public transport, walking and cycling do not in practice receive the priority that policy documents claim. With local public transport outside London still provided on a largely commercial basis, and local authorities heavily constrained in their ability to provide adequate footways and cycleways, it is not surprising that increasing access by alternative modes remains very difficult. There are some worthy exceptions; but these only reinforce the general picture that most local authorities base their activities on the majority of people using cars for travel. Local authorities are also often persuaded by the arguments of commercial bodies who see (for the most part rightly) that car-owning customers produce most of the income they receive.

With funds for environmental and highway works remaining limited, the main result is seen in the shape of townscapes. Roads and parking areas tend to dominate, materials are basic (tarmac roads and galvanised steel barriers). Good pedestrian crossing places are limited. Detailed design and management are often poor (e.g., pavement repairs are patchy or omitted, overgrowing shrubs are not cut back, weeds proliferate). In consequence, many parts of towns – even in historic centres and 'leafy' suburbia – have an undue number of untended concrete spaces, open to the elements, giving them the feel of industrial areas, sometimes with a general tone of semi-dereliction. They are most unfriendly for people not in a car, especially women and older people and those on their own, and can become 'no-go' areas. This encourages those with a car to use it even where they might otherwise be happy to walk. For those without a car – especially the elderly and other people with some relative disadvantage – it makes their walk to the town or district centre less attractive and worsens their quality of life.

The issue of social equity was referred to in the 1998 White Paper, but it received little attention until 2001, when an inquiry was started by the government's Social Exclusion Unit (SEU). The final report (SEU, 2003) provided a useful review of difficulties in reaching services, and recommended assessment of accessibility as a key element in future local transport planning. However, the SEU failed to recognise the close link between car ownership and income, and hence the extent to which policies are geared to car use and thus favour the richer parts of society. Effective policies for social inclusion require denser urban development, better support for local facilities, and priority for walking, cycling and public transport; by implication, these involve appropriate restraints on the use of cars.

The emphasis on car use is also reflected in the different bases of decision making still in use for road development and public transport. Developments for train, tram and bus remain primarily driven by commercial objectives, despite the recent improvement in public funding resources and planning mechanisms. Different public bodies have different objectives (e.g., the multi-modal studies led by government offices in the regions have recommended a number of rail schemes as key elements in their strategies, but the Strategic Rail Authority has not given them any priority in funding). Funds available to local authorities for supporting development of walking, cycling and public transport are generally limited, as are their powers.

Great Britain also has a relatively low density of urban development compared to most mainland European countries: this makes walking, cycling and public transport less attractive, while car use becomes more valuable to users and hence gains more priority from decision makers. British development patterns and lifestyles show the same car-oriented focus as in the land-rich cities and districts of North America. Indeed, proposals for more concentrated development are often opposed by local interests because they are seen not to provide room for car use.

If transport measures are to address matters of economic and social policy effectively – especially those related to quality of life within the main urban areas where three-quarters of the population live, and also on trunk routes between those areas – then their appraisal should be set in the light of adopted public plans. The mechanism exists for this through the New Approach to Transport Assessment (NATA) and its Scottish equivalent (STAG), in which the implications for non-transport aspects, drawn from land use and economic planning strategies for the area, are tabulated on a consistent basis alongside transport factors. To date, however, operation of this process has been too narrowly geared toward financial and operational outcomes, while reference to land use and economic strategies is usually limited to general expressions of validity. The use of NATA is complemented by the Transport Assessment required under planning Policy Guidance Note 13 (PPG13) containing guidelines for new development schemes. This too seems so far to have not had a serious impact on local decisions. However, the principles of these processes provide considerable opportunity for effective integration of transport and land use planning in a practical and disciplined way at local level.

Where do we keep all the cars?

With the volume of cars now owned in Britain, it is not surprising that policies have been developed for parking (especially as every car trip requires space to park at each end of the journey). Constraining parking at destinations (e.g., places of employment, and retail and leisure complexes) is generally accepted as an effective form of traffic control, because if people cannot park easily at their destination, they may rethink the mode of travel, or even the choice of destination. However, local approaches differ widely, and few local authorities have taken the opportunity of exercising total control through Special Parking Zones (SPZs). Parking policies and standards appear in LTPs and in Local Plans, and overall guidance is given in PPG13, but these refer exclusively to new developments.

PPG13 also lays down guideline standards for parking provision in (new) residential developments, and this is now lower than it was as part of current policies. However, little attention seems to have been paid to the overall impact of housing a growing fleet of cars within the nation's residential areas. In fact, they are accommodated alongside the housing of people. The issue is compounded by the rapid formation of new households: current forecasts indicate that around 4 million extra households will be required within the next two decades, and thus a huge number of new dwellings need to be built (Prescott, 2003). The main problem is the speed of growth of car ownership: a good proportion of our housing and much of our street layout were designed before the days of mass car ownership. In the 1960s, parts of these were cleared out for redevelopment to the then current principles – largely inspired by the Buchanan Report (Buchanan *et al.*, 1963) – but since the 1970s the conservation trend has (rightly) seen the value of retaining older properties. Many of even the smallest old properties now serve as good modern homes. Of course, their owners adopt current lifestyles – which means owning and using a car.

This has a particular impact on the older terraced housing that still occupies much of our inner cities and other urban areas, largely dating from the Victorian and Edwardian eras. Because each house occupies a fairly narrow plot, rising car ownership has led to these streets seeing nose-to-tail parking, especially outside working hours, when most residents' cars are present. Often the streets are narrow, so that much of the parking is partly on the pavements, which are often narrow as well. This causes problems, sometimes serious, for anyone walking along the streets, not least the older and younger residents themselves. It also reduces the ability of people to fraternise along the street in the traditional way. Many local authorities have brought in limited redesign for some streets, involving environmental improvements and traffic management, but these often seem to have little effect. Overall, the residents of these areas tend to be in the middle to lower income groups, where people are still keen to acquire cars and to use them, and are sceptical about change.

The next swathe of house building occurred in the later 1920s and the 1930s, when numerous streets of semi-detached and terraced houses spread out across the fields surrounding most cities and towns. This was particularly the case in greater London, where vast estates grew up around existing small villages and towns, supported by expanding suburban and London Underground railway services and a network of new bus routes. Today these streets are filled with the cars of owner-occupiers, who tend overall to be at or above average income, and in consequence have a higher level of car ownership. Most of the semi-detached houses have a drive or front access, while the terraced blocks are usually served by a back access way, thus off-road parking is available in principle. However, for the streets of terraced and smaller semis, most residents tend to park in front and often on the street, especially where households have more than one car.

Cars standing in and around the property also dominate the residential developments built in the past two decades. Here design has assumed high ownership and use of cars, and the layout is planned around access by car, to the houses and from them to other destinations. There has been some evolution of design guides, but these tend to focus on enhancing the amount of greenness and, in more recent times, security. Houses tend to be smaller, because of higher land values, while there is more car parking adjacent to them. Roads off the main circulation system are often narrow and parking occurs on pavements here too. These design factors mean that walking and cycling are often difficult or at least involve long diversions, and public transport is not well provided for.

Thus in most residential areas cars are visually dominant and occupy a lot of space. This raises serious issues over the quality of life, as each resident finds his or her own lifestyle a little more constrained by the dominance of cars, and unable to influence the overall pattern. Furthermore, local groups are likely to oppose any development on the basis that it will add to traffic and parking problems: the outside influence is always seen as the common threat. Since no other body is in a position to act, this issue requires significant intervention by local authorities, primarily through major redesign in close and well thought-out collaboration with residents. Good models can be found, including the widespread use of Home Zones in the Netherlands, or the area redesign now on trial in the Ancoats area of Manchester (see *Planning*, 16 August 2002). The scale of the problem is very large, and so the scale of resources and powers needed to tackle it are too. There is a strong case for firm central government leadership on this.

Who manages the landscape?

In principle, the total fleet of cars forms a cohesive system with the total road network – they are one car-based passenger transport system. The national railway system, despite its perceived (and controversial) fragmentation under the Railways Act 1993, is seen to remain one system, with a few key players (usually Network Rail plus any relevant passenger train operating company) fully responsible for what happens on any part of the network. This is reflected in both informal comment and formal action – for example, the focusing of legal action after the few high-profile crashes of recent years. But who is responsible for the car-based passenger transport system?

A number of bodies have clear responsibility under the terms of the Highways Acts, other statutes, official guidance, and convention. These include:

- the Highways Agency (in England) and the relevant departments of state in Wales and Scotland, who manage the trunk roads systems;
- the local highways authority, responsible for all other roads within their particular area;

- district councils in the (English) shire counties, where they have agreed joint or agency roles with their county council;
- those local authorities who have taken responsibility for local parking control (through SPZs);
- local authorities through their responsibilities under the Town & Country Planning Acts; and
- the police, who apply the law, including infringements of traffic regulations.

Over them all is central government, providing guidance through the Department for Transport (public authorities' transport duties) and the Home Office (the police).

Thus there is a good range of responsible public bodies, but how effective are they in managing the system overall? This is where a serious gap appears to open up over several aspects. Two areas may be cited as offering clear examples of the problem. First, there exists a major role for local authorities to tackle parking in residential areas, especially in older areas of terraced housing. In doing this, they need to work very closely with local residents, perhaps through residents' associations. Since any scheme requires supervision to constrain those people who might ignore the rules (and hence cause problems), this also needs to involve the police (unless the local authority has taken powers to implement SPZs). The very limited extent to which this issue has been tackled so far bears out the serious limits to action which local authorities actually have. This reflects the constraints on both their real powers and on their funding. It also suggests an unwillingness to start a line of action that may cause local controversy, involve politicians' and officers' time, and require substantial funding to provide a satisfactory solution. This is likely to be compounded by the police, who are unlikely to be able to devote much staff time to development, and are unlikely to be able to assure the community that they would police it anyway (burglaries and street crime are usually seen as the key problems in most residential areas – carried out, of course, by unknown outsiders).

The second area is that of road safety and, especially, speeding. The total of national road casualties fell strongly from the mid-1980s to the mid-1990s, but has since remained static and is now starting to creep up again. The fall primarily reflected strong prosecution of drink-driving (which still continues). Today the major cause of road accidents lies in careless driving, especially at inappropriate speeds. The government has highlighted this at various times and runs occasional campaigns publicising the dangerous effects of driving at even slightly above the speed limit in certain areas. (A significant point, given that, although overall road casualty rates are below the European average, the United Kingdom has one of the highest levels of child and pedestrian casualty rates.) Local highway authorities also bring in some traffic calming measures (mostly cheap and crude humps rather the more sophisticated design measures found in Germany and the Netherlands). Yet speeds significantly in excess of the legally defined limits remains an everyday norm.

69

Recent road speed figures (DfT, 2002) show that over half of motorists travel at over 70 miles per hour on motorways with a horrifying two-thirds exceeding 30 miles per hour on restricted urban roads; in a good proportion of these cases, the excess is very substantial. Action can be taken through the use of roadside speed cameras, but the government has placed limits on their location and use.

The message that these two examples show is that ultimately there is no clear and sufficient responsibility for managing the use of Britain's road system by those who drive on it. There is no apparent integration between highway management, urban planning and railway regulation. Yet without such integration, how can the government's policies be implemented effectively? Ultimately, the government itself must set the pace, and incentivise and coordinate local authorities, public agencies and commercial organisations, if its policies are to be achieved. Yet, as a Dutch study of European transport policy implementation (Powell-Ladret, 2000) found, the United Kingdom has the most centralised decision-making process in Europe.

Conclusions

This chapter has tried to open up to debate some generally unconsidered issues that appear critical to the efficiency of travel and quality of life, especially in and around our urban areas. Above all, it has sought to identify the pattern and scale of ways in which the car has become dominant in the townscapes of our country, our personal lifestyles and our policies. National commitment to the car is immense, and yet the pattern and scale of its all-pervading influence are not fully appreciated. If the United Kingdom is to develop its transport systems in ways that are fair and effective for everyone (including those wishing to use cars) and that form an integral part of providing quality places to live, then:

- both transport and spatial development policies have to be applied on a more consistent and considered basis;
- higher levels of funding for transport, mostly from the public purse, are probably essential to real achievement;
- funding must be matched by powers to implement local strategies, especially for local authorities;
- while understanding of who will be affected and how is essential, decisions must be determined by overall economic and environment gain, not by groups with a vested interest; and
- responsibility for managing the highway system and all its users must be clearly established and accepted.

References

Bristow, A. (2002). *Could Advertisements for Cars Influence Our Travel Choices?* Available online at: www.tps.prg.uk/library.

Buchanan, C. *et al.* (1963). *Traffic in Towns* [Abridged edition of the Buchanan Report]. Harmondsworth: Penguin.

Department for the Environment, Transport & the Regions (DETR) (1998). *A New Deal for Transport: Better for Everyone*. London: HMSO.

Department for the Environment, Transport & the Regions (DETR) (2000). *Transport 2010: The 10-year Plan*. London: HMSO.

Department for Transport (DfT) (2002). *Transport Statistics Bulletin: Vehicle Speeds in Great Britain 2002*. Available online at: www.transtat.dft.gov.uk/tables/2002/vsgb/vsgb.htm.

Harman, R. (2002). 'Fuel tax protests and fuel rationing: An historical perspective'. In: G. Lyons & K. Chatterjee (eds), *Transport Lessons from the Fuel Tax Protests of 2000*. Aldershot: Ashgate.

Powell-Ladret, R. (2000). *A Thematic Comparison of Transport Policy Approaches in Europe*. Rotterdam: Dutch Ministry of Transport, Public Works & Water Management Transport Research Centre.

Prescott, J. (2003). *Sustainable Communities*. London: Office of the Deputy Prime Minister.

Rosen, P. (2002). 'Pro-car or anti-car? "Environment", "economy" and "liberty" in UK transport debates' perspective'. In: G. Lyons & K. Chatterjee (eds), *Transport Lessons from the Fuel Tax Protests of 2000*. Aldershot: Ashgate.

Social Exclusion Unit (SEU) (2003). *Making the Connections: Final Report on Transport and Social Exclusion*. London: Social Exclusion Unit.

Solomon, J. (1998). *To Drive or to Vote?* London: Chartered Institute of Transport.

8. Sustainable Transport Policy: The Contribution from Behavioural Scientists[1]

LINDA STEG AND GERARD TERTOOLEN

Publication of the British Government's White Paper on Transport, in July 1998, has raised public awareness of the problems associated with widespread car use. The authors argue that these problems, which largely result from the aggregated choices and behaviour of many individual car users, could be mitigated if the main determinants of car use and the underlying behavioural mechanisms were better understood. This chapter examines six strategies for changing social behaviour, and some important conditions for reducing car use. Examples are presented of how the insights gained can be applied in practice.

In many countries of the world, the popularity and massive use of motor vehicles are leading to problems of congestion, environmental quality, and quality of life in and around towns and cities. It is no longer feasible to resolve these problems through further road building or technical solutions alone, partly because the gains from such measures almost inevitably tend to be overtaken by continued growth of car use. Effective solutions require widespread changes in human behaviour and significant reductions in the volume of car traffic.

We start from the position that the problems arising from car use result from the cumulative effect of many individual choices and behaviours of car users. Behavioural scientists therefore have a part to play in contributing to the solution of these problems, and it is surprising that they have played a relatively minor role to date. Traffic and transport issues have conventionally been regarded as a challenge for economists and urban planners. These disciplines regularly make implicit assumptions about human behaviour and its determinants. A number of these assumptions prove, on closer inspection, to have limited validity and to be true only under certain conditions. To give some examples, economists frequently assume that humans behave rationally and will always choose the option with the highest utility.

LINDA STEG is a Lecturer in the Department of Psychology at the University of Groningen, The Netherlands. GERARD TERTOOLEN works for the province of Noord-Brabant, The Netherlands, on an innovative public transport project entitled 'Passenger Transport for Tomorrow'.

Yet people do sometimes make sub-optimal decisions, owing to lack of information or through the influence of habit. Moreover, technologists also assume that their innovations will be used in the way that was intended by the designer. This assumption is, unfortunately, disproved by experience. For example in the Netherlands, people who have installed energy-saving lamps are less inclined to switch them off when not in use; or they extend the use of energy-saving lamps to places that were not previously illuminated after dark, such as driveways and in gardens. Similarly, a driver whose car has been fitted with a catalytic converter may be inclined to use it more often because 'it is a clean car'.

Explanations of car use

The very widespread use of cars can be interpreted as a large-scale social dilemma, reflecting the conflict between individual and collective interests. From the individual's perspective, the advantages of car use outweigh the negative consequences, such as possible damage to the environment, safety risks and other problems. The negative contribution made by each individual to the sum total of environmental costs and risks seems negligible. Correspondingly, the individual may doubt whether his or her contribution to reducing damage and risks really makes any significant difference. The result is that individuals tend not to feel responsible for such collective problems and it remains attractive to act purely in one's own interest. A secondary point is that many people are pessimistic about other people's willingness to change. We could therefore interpret the current problems of car use as a summative consequence of the behaviour of many individual car users, each of whom is shifting what are considered to be negligible costs onto society as a whole.

Car use seems to have enormous advantages over alternative means of transport. On the one hand, these advantages are rationally perceived: they include speed, comfort, flexibility, radius of action and carrying capacity. On the other hand, subjective or emotional factors also play a role, such as expressing feelings of power or superiority, or deriving enjoyment from driving (Steg *et al.*, 2001). Car users can also express their personality through their choice of a car and the way they use it. The car has the potential to impress, while catering to feelings of self-worth. Steg *et al.* (2001) give an extensive overview of what they call such 'intrinsic motives' for car use. Their study shows that there are systematic differences between people, to the extent that intrinsic motives influence car use behaviour. Moreover, their studies revealed that intrinsic motives are more significant predictors of commuter car use than rational motives like speed and travel costs (Steg & Uneken, forthcoming). Advertisers take full advantage of intrinsic motives for car use; for example, cars are advertised by slogans like 'Go to the beach with your Spanish lover'. Policy aimed at reducing car use might well be more effective if it addressed these kinds of motives.

The advantages of car use encourage it to become a habit. People develop activity patterns and a lifestyle that are tuned towards the use of a car. Many other reinforcing factors in society help to support car use. Once car dependency is established (Goodwin, 1995; Steg, 1996), it is very difficult to alter habits and lifestyles. It appears that people will mostly reconsider habitual behaviour only when radical changes are introduced into the situation, causing them to re-evaluate the choices they have hitherto made automatically.

Strategies for reducing car use

Car use is strongly influenced by:

- The circumstances which determine the opportunities available – for example, the nature of the accessible infrastructure, the quality of alternatives (public transport), and the location of places where people are working, living, shopping and spending leisure time.
- The resources people have, such as the amount of money or time, as well as knowledge.
- Motivational factors, such as physical, psychological and other needs (see, e.g., Batra & Ray, 1986; Vlek, 1996; Vlek et al., 1997).

There is some evidence for thinking that behaviour resulting from rational processes can be changed more easily than behaviour that is habitual in origin.

Several key strategies for altering social behaviour have been proposed. Some of these are directed at changing the structure of the situation, while others are directed initially at changing individual preferences and choices. This essay describes four structural strategies and two cognitive-motivational strategies (see also Vlek & Michon, 1992; Vlek & Steg, 1996). The structural strategies are based on behavioural principles: car use can be made less attractive by 'push' measures, or the use of alternatives may be stimulated by 'pull' measures. Push measures restrict people's freedom of choice; pull measures do not. Each of these strategies is based on some, mostly implicit, assumptions about the determinants of behaviour and behavioural mechanisms. These assumptions need to be checked and validated before strategies can be successfully implemented.

Structural strategies

Car use can be reduced through financial/economic measures. It can be made more expensive and the use of alternative means of transport can be made cheaper. The relevant policy instruments include subsidies, discounts, taxes, fines and tolls. The assumption underlying such measures is that people's response will be rational, and they will choose the option with the highest utility at the lowest costs. However, this does not always happen, since feasible alternatives to car use must be available. Contrary to what policy-makers may think, financial considerations are not, in fact, the main determinants of car use. Research has demonstrated that people often evaluate comfort, speed and flexibility as the main advantages of car use and they are prepared to pay for these advantages (see, e.g., Steg, 1996; Tertoolen et al., 1998; Steg, 2003). Because car use is only partly determined by financial considerations, demand-price elasticities tend to be low. It is worth noting that during the world oil crisis of the mid-1970s, the substantial rise in fuel prices had only a marginal effect on car use. In the long term, people compensated for the rise in fuel prices by purchasing smaller and more economical cars (Mogridge, 1978). Radical rises in the costs of car use could possibly be an effective deterrent, but are unlikely to be easily achievable owing to lack of political or public support.

Car use can also be restricted through the provision of physical alternatives and physical changes. This type of strategy relies on directing traffic along certain routes, preventing it from entering designated areas, altering the geographical relationship of popular destinations and using technical apparatus to control traffic in various ways. Often this type of strategy is run in parallel with the promotion of alternative modes. The underlying assumption behind such measures is that behaviour is shaped by circumstances. However, individual preferences might be opposed to these changes. The effectiveness of physical rearrangements is limited to the extent that individuals have already exercised strategic choices about where to live or how to travel, and by the economic requirements of business and services (Owens, 1984). Exhaustive geographical reorganisation of origins and destinations of trips is possible only in the long term.

Technological innovations aimed at making cars cleaner to operate have led to substantial reductions in the emission of environmentally damaging exhaust gases. Technological innovations seem to offer a feasible and popular solution because they involve only a marginal limitation on people's freedom of choice. Correspondingly, while technological measures may be desirable (if not necessary), they are not sufficient to solve the fundamental problems of car use. In the first place, the effect of technological innovations tends to be overtaken by the continued growth in total car use. Thus, the benefits of technological improvements can soon be submerged by 'volume effects'. There is also a trend for new cars to be more powerful, heavier and therefore scarcely less polluting than older models. The implication is that technological innovations are effective only if used in a controlled manner and in association with other measures. Technological innovations may also have unwanted effects. For example, our research results have shown that the more people favour technological solutions to the problems of car use, the less willing they are to reduce car use and the more they reject measures aimed at this objective (Tertoolen et al., 1998; Steg, 1996). The range of contrary outcomes can, incidentally, include spending the money saved from using more economical cars or appliances on activities that are less friendly to the environment. Finally, radical technological innovations are not easily implemented in many cases: the introduction of electric cars, for example, requires a widespread adaptation or expansion of the infrastructure needed to keep them in service (Bilderbeek *et al.*, 1993).

A third type of structural strategy is legal regulation coupled with enforcement measures. Violations of the regulations – if detected – are usually met with some kind of punishment, fine or censure. The underlying assumption here is that laws and rules will be internalised by those affected. However, it is possible that people may resist, or elude, the implementation of the law on a wide scale, leading to the legislation or regulation being discredited and the practical effect being reduced to virtually nil. Effective regulation and enforcement are therefore crucially dependent on majority public support, or at least compliance. Such strategies also require an adequate organisation for supervision, monitoring and enforcement. On the other hand, applying a regulation and enforcement strategy may help to increase people's trust in the co-operation of others because there is some guarantee that their own willingness to comply will not be exploited by others who do not.

A fourth strategy, organisational change, uses physical changes in the choices available with changes in the financial and/or social pay-offs. Organisational change strategies are aimed at modifying and adapting the structure and functioning of institutions, organisations and lifestyles, so that they become more supportive of alternative, sustainable transport systems, modes and practices. The underlying assumption behind such strategies is that behaviour is embedded in and conditioned by institutions and organisations in society. There are, however, flaws with this assumption:

- The intended changes must be more or less uniform with the preferences of the groups being targeted.
- Organisations must be willing to fulfil their goals, implement their rules, and express their culture in a more environmentally friendly way. Environmental considerations will, however, almost inevitably compete with other interests, especially economic interests.

Cognitive-motivational strategies

The fifth strategy, provision of information, education and communication, involves increasing people's knowledge (e.g., of transport alternatives), heightening their awareness (e.g., of environmental impacts) and modifying attitudes, so that the inclination to adopt non-motorised forms of travel is strengthened. The underlying assumption is that people behave in a reasoned way and that behaviour can be modified by altering the perceived costs and benefits associated with particular choices. This assumption is by no means invariably true.

In the first place, feasible alternatives to car use must be available before providing information can have any effect. And because people's attention is selective, there is no guarantee that they will correctly perceive and process the information they receive. At the point when travel habits are being formed, people seldom consider consciously the advantages or disadvantages of different travel modes. Their choices become habitual, especially where the same journey is made over and over again (Aarts, 1996). Habitual behaviour helps to decrease the depth and complexity of the decision-making process, as well as reduces the scope for changing behaviour through persuasion (Verplanken et al., 1994).

Information, education and communications originating from governments have to compete with the mass-market advertising campaigns of the automobile industry among many others. The automobile industry spends huge budgets on stimulating the purchase and use of cars, while the money spent by government on promoting alternatives is only a small fraction of this (Steg, 1996). In public transport, professional marketing strategies are hardly being used. A main reason for this absence is the lack of knowledge about the backgrounds and motives of various target groups. A recent study into this topic revealed that it is important to distinguish traveller groups who are capable or willing to choose among different transport modes from travellers who are not (Tertoolen & Weggemans, 2002). Obviously, attempts to stimulate the use of transport will be especially effective if they are tuned towards the first group. The Dutch province of Noord-Brabant is currently planning and conducting further research on this, which is aimed at examining how different traveller groups could best be targeted to stimulate the use of public transport.

Government information campaigns are relatively ineffective if the choices and behaviour to be encouraged cost much money, time or trouble. Information campaigns, in short, rarely lead to sustainable changes in behaviour when it comes to transport. Moreover, if the behaviour to be changed has significant advantages to the individual, information campaigns may even have a contrary effect to that intended. For example, research has shown that the Dutch are generally very concerned about environmental issues, but this has not resulted in a reduction in car use (NEPP 2, 1993). The discrepancy between actual behaviour (car use) and environmental attitude may seem puzzling, but it has been well recognised in other contexts by social psychologists (Festinger, 1957; Cooper & Fazio, 1984). The phenomenon of 'cognitive dissonance' is an unpleasant psychological tension experienced when attitudes, or attitudes and behaviour, are (or threaten to be) inconsistent with each other. Inconsistency may be accentuated, for example, through mass media advertising. People are motivated to reduce cognitive dissonance either by reducing car use (behavioural change) or by reducing their environmental awareness (attitude change). Predictions from dissonance theory, supported by research, have shown that environmental attitudes are more likely to change than car use behaviour. One study showed that people who were relatively well environmentally aware, and who used their car very frequently, showed a reduction in their environmental awareness after receiving information about the (negative) environmental effects of their car use (Tertoolen, 1996; Tertoolen et al., 1998).

Cognitive dissonance may also arise when more specific attitudes towards car use are at issue (Steg, 1996; Steg & Vlek, 1996). These studies have shown that the more thoroughly people think about the problems resulting from motorised traffic, the lower becomes their awareness of the associated problems. By thinking over the problems of car use, people were confronted with a discrepancy: they perceive car use as a problem, but they are using a car themselves and are not willing to give up the enormous personal advantages obtained from doing so. Most people appeared to manage the sensation of dissonance by evaluating the problem of car use as being less serious than they had previously determined. Results also showed that especially those who had a relatively high awareness of the problem initially experienced a lower level of problem awareness after thinking over the issue. Respondents with a relatively low initial awareness of the problem scarcely modified their outlook at all. So cognitive dissonance especially arises when people have relative high problem awareness because in their case the discrepancy between attitudes (problem awareness) and behaviour (car use) is particularly acute. Nevertheless, the provision of information remains an important prerequisite for implementing other policy measures, because people must be informed about the need for such measures and about the nature and seriousness of the problems of car use. Eventually, however, this may help to raise public support for more direct policy measures that restrain car use.

A sixth type of cognitive-motivational strategy consists of social modelling and support. This is based on the observation that transport behaviour (and the underlying cognitive structure) is strongly determined by social factors such as norms and customs, comparison processes occurring in status and power seeking, and the public examples set by prominent members of society. In social modelling and support strategies, these factors are exploited – for example, by organising family, company or community support for the modification of people's attitudes, preferences and habits. They can be offered behaviour examples modelled by prominent figures in society and their trust in mechanisms of co-operation with others can be stimulated in order to achieve common goals. However, it appears that in most cases social factors only influence behaviour which is clearly visible by others. If the behaviour is more or less anonymous, social factors have relatively little influence.

Choice of change strategies

The first four ('structural') of the six strategies for behaviour change are generally more effective than the last two ('cognitive-motivational') strategies, but they are often not available or not easily implemented. Cognitive-motivational strategies are easier to design and apply, but their effectiveness is generally lower. In many cases, however, they are the only measures that government is prepared to adopt (Vlek & Steg, 1996). The combined application of several strategies linked to a consistent set of policy goals is likely to be more effective than the use of a single strategy. The choice of strategies should be based on knowledge of the determinants of that behaviour, and on the underlying decision processes or behaviour mechanisms.

Ideally, policy measures should be designed that are based on more than one strategy, and directed at several of the most important determinants of car use. For example, the introduction of electric cars requires the application of several strategies. These include expansion and adaptation of the infrastructure so that electric cars are widely available and places for recharging them are plentiful. In addition, people need to be informed and educated about the advantages of electric cars and about the way to use them. Financial and economic measures will also be needed to stimulate a widespread change from petrol or diesel fuels to electric traction.

Conditions for behaviour change

We can now review the scope for policy measures aimed at reducing car use and the necessary conditions that need to be fulfilled (Steg & Sievers, 1996):

- People should be informed about the collective costs and risks arising from expansion of motorised traffic, *and they must perceive this as a source of serious environmental and societal problems*. This requires, in the minds of the population, a clear characterisation of the problems and of the possible consequences of neglecting them.
- People must feel *responsible* for these problems and they need to be convinced that their own personal contribution to solving them will be significant.
- People have to balance the individual advantages that they derive against the collective disadvantages of car use and they must, again, be *convinced that the problems are worth solving*.
- Feasible *alternatives* should be available, either at a superficial (technical) or at a behavioural level.
- Selected strategies for behaviour change should be applied, in order to inform and motivate people, and to enable them to make actual use of alternative opportunities. Effective strategies require *clear policy objectives*, and a *solid and consistent application* thereof.
- Interventions by government need public and political support. People should be prepared to accept the need for, and the likely consequences of, policy measures against car use. Such success will depend, among other things, on the *legitimacy* with which they are perceived (which in turn is connected to problem awareness) and the extent to which the measures taken *conform with the existing norms and value patterns* (e.g., about the nature of freedom and justice) in society.

'Golden rules' for reducing car use

In the concluding section of this essay, we offer ten 'golden rules' or principles which should be taken into account when designing policy aimed at reducing car use. These principles are derived from current research on the psychology of car use behaviour. The first three principles are general, while the remaining seven are more specific and address psychological factors and processes. The principles are based on experiences gained by evaluating the effects of recent policy measures aimed at reducing car use in the Netherlands:

- *Policy should be based on a diagnosis of the main motives for car use.* An effective and efficient transport policy should be based on understanding the psychological determinants of car use and the behaviour mechanisms involved. This diagnosis should not only be aimed at detecting individual preferences towards travel behaviour, and car use in particular, but should also be aimed at analyzing opportunities, capabilities, needs and motivations.
- *Monitoring.* The effects of policy interventions should be clearly evaluated in order to assess the extent to which policy objectives are being reached. Public support for policy measures can be heightened by providing feedback about their effects.
- *Identify relevant target groups.* Generic measures, addressed to the population at large, may evoke unnecessary resistance because they force some people into a corner, or provide opportunities for some people that are not available to others (Steg, 1996). Target groups can be defined on the basis of similar motives, opportunities, abilities and demographic characteristics, or on the basis of trip purpose (e.g., commuting trips, work-related trips, recreational trips, shopping trips). The development of company travel plans or 'green commuter plans' are examples of targeting.
- *Influencing behaviour is more than a funny television spot.* Communication is but one means of influencing behaviour, and large-scale information campaigns are but one form of communication. Policy-makers should not merely transfer messages to the pubic, but should also listen carefully to public reactions and interpret motives, common means and preferences. Tailored information is generally far more effective than a one-size-fits-all approach, as often used in mass media campaigns. The widespread use of the Internet provides interesting new opportunities to communicate with the general public by use of tailored information campaigns. Such campaigns are in many cases especially effective to heighten people's awareness of problems and their awareness of possible alternatives to car use, and not to actually change car use behaviour.
- *Feelings are facts.* Not only the 'objective' (i.e., cognitive and rational) factors, but also the emotional and affective factors in car use should be taken seriously. Many drivers look down on bicycle use or public transport, and the privacy provided by the car plays a real and important role in car use behaviour.
- *Make smart use of cognitive dissonance.* The discrepancy between attitudes and behaviour may result in rejection of information, and may even make

the provision of information counter-effective. For example, when people receive feedback about the real costs of using cars, they may not reduce their own mileage, but may protest at government 'oppression' or 'exploitation' (Tertoolen *et al.*, 1998) instead. Cognitive dissonance, however, can also be used to influence behaviour. A change in behaviour can be brought about by reimbursing travel on public transport rather than private car for certain purposes: after some time attitudes may also be altered in line with the behaviour change that is brought about – provided, of course, that public transport is available, efficient and convenient, and provided that people change their behaviour voluntarily.

- *Individualise social dilemmas.* The individual's sense of responsibility for large-scale societal problems and their solution may be accentuated by reducing them to a more personal level. So public information might stress, for example, the deteriorating accessibility of jobs and services in a city or neighbourhood, rather than the global increase in car use and its environmental consequences and congestion. The effects of individual contributions to the problem can be made more visible and individual action can appear both more necessary and productive.

- *Habit and 'catastrophes'.* Travel behaviour is to a large extent habitual. People seldom respond to measures that simply provide alternative means of transport or to minor changes in the choices confronting them. Changes will, however, be more likely to occur when there is a minor 'catastrophe' – that is, a strong and noticeable change in the situation that provokes a reappraisal of existing behaviour. Examples of 'catastrophes' are a doubling in fuel prices or a radical drop in public transport fares, but they could include individual 'catastrophes' such as a change of dwelling or job. In these circumstances, people may reconsider their habitual use of cars.

- *Policy measures should correspond with relevant norms and values.* Support for policy measures is dependent on their perceived legitimacy which, in turn, is determined by the extent to which the measures correspond to existing norms and values in society, including notions of justice, fairness and freedom. For example, parking charges will be evaluated as more acceptable if good and secure parking places are provided. However, if fairness considerations are disregarded, behaviour will tend towards disobedience. It is crucial, therefore, to involve citizens in the planning and evaluation of the policy. The legitimacy of policy measures that restrict people's freedom of choice may be improved by consultation about the aim, necessity and effects of policy measures.

- *Explain the aim of policy measures as well as the intended effects.* Many of the problems associated with continued growth in car use are uncertain in their scope and difficult for ordinary people to understand. For example, many people cannot readily visualise what will happen if they continue to neglect the warnings about congestion and pollution. Clear images about possible futures, avoiding sensationalism and facilitating careful deliberation of future scenarios, is desirable.

In the Netherlands, attempts were made to apply these ten golden rules in several policy fields. The work was carried out within the framework of the so-called 'Policy Practice Test' (PPT) under the authority of the Ministry of Transport, Public Works and Water Management. The aim of PPT is to incorporate knowledge from behavioural sciences into actual policy-making. PPT is directed at all stages in policy-making, from the problem definition phase, through the design and implementation of policy measures, and the evaluation of effects with any accompanying adjustments. PPT has proved useful for policy-makers in several areas, including road pricing, car-pooling and maximum speed limits on highways (Weggemans *et al.*, 1996, 1997, 1998).

The message used in PPT is as follows. First, behavioural scientists and policy-makers defined or specified the important policy issues to be addressed. Second, behavioural scientists analyzed the policy area by applying theories and 'rules' as described in this essay to specific policy topics. The results were fed into practical advice that could be used to support or adjust the work of the policy-maker. For example, in the area around Rotterdam, in the west of the Netherlands, policy-makers were planning to carry out a large-scale mass market advertising campaign to encourage car-pooling. Psychological research had shown, however, that mass market advertising campaigns were unlikely to be effective in changing behaviour. The application of PPT resulted in advice to concentrate promotion on target groups and to inform these groups about car-pooling, rather than taking a mass market advertising approach. In this particular example, people living in a specific area were selected as a target group because the area appeared to offer realistic and workable alternatives to solo car driving. The process of disseminating information about car-pooling was guided by behavioural scientists and information was provided by a variety of ways (lessons in schools, advertisements, and free publicity in newspapers, as well as interviews and so forth on radio). The information campaign was combined with structural rewards for car-poolers: the car-pool area was equipped with more services and frequent car-poolers were offered free breakfasts. An information centre was opened to help potential car-poolers in the region. This strategy resulted in a successful car-pool programme and solo car driving declined from 84 to 80 per cent, while car-pooling increased from 16 to 20 per cent. The number of companies reporting that they encouraged car-pooling increased from 39 to 46 per cent.

Conclusion

Policy measures aimed at reducing car use need to be based on careful diagnosis of its main determinants. It is important to identify target groups and tune policy measures towards the main motives of those groups. Behavioural scientists can give a distinctive, innovative and useful contribution to policy-making, not only in the definition of the problem but also in the design, implementation and evaluation of policy measures. In the Netherlands, serious attempts are being made to involve social sciences more directly in transport policy and social scientists themselves are developing methods that enable policy-makers to utilise new understanding and knowledge of human behaviour. The emphasis is not only on generating new insights, but also on making effective use of existing knowledge in the policy process. Behavioural scientists cannot, however, offer simple and general recipes for behavioural change. Advice to policy-makers will always be a matter of made-to-measure strategies. The first results of this approach appear promising, but a great deal more work still needs to be done.

Note

1 This article was originally published in *Public Money & Management* 19(1) (1999).

References

Aarts, J.A.G. (1996). Habit and Decision-making: The Case of Travel Mode Choice. Doctoral dissertation, Catholic University of Nijmegen, The Netherlands.

Batra, R. & Ray, M.L. (1986). 'Situational effects of advertising repetition: The moderating influence of motivation, ability and opportunity to respond', *Journal of Consumer Research* 12(4): 432–445.

Bilderbeek, R.H., Korver, W. & Schot, J. (1993). *Technische innovaties in het personenverkeer en vervoer: een inventarisatie op zoek naar duurzame mobiliteit* [*Technological Innovations in Traffic and Transportation*]. Apeldoorn: TNO.

Cooper, J. & Fazio, R.H. (1984). 'A new look at dissonance theory'. In: L. Berkowitz (ed), *Advances in Experimental Social Psychology* 17: 229–266.

Festinger, L. (1957). *A Theory of Cognitive Dissonance*. Stanford, CA: Stanford University Press.

Goodwin, P. (1995). *Car Dependence: A Report for the RAC Foundation for Motoring and the Environment*. Oxford: ESRC Transport Studies Unit, University of Oxford.

Mogridge, M.J. (1978). 'The influence of the oil crisis on the growth in the ownership and use of cars', *Transportation* 7: 45–67.

NEPP 2 (1993). *Second Dutch National Environmental Policy Plan*. Amsterdam: Ministry of Housing, Physical Planning and the Environment.

Owens, S.E. (1984). 'Energy and spatial structure: A rural example', *Environment and Planning* A16(10): 1319–1337.

Steg, E.M. (1996). Gedragsverandering ter vermindering van het autogebruik [Behaviour Change for Reducing Car Use in the Netherlands]. Doctoral dissertation, University of Groningen, The Netherlands.

Steg, L. (2003). 'Factors influencing the acceptability and effectiveness of transport pricing'. In: B. Schlag & J. Schade (eds), *Acceptability in Transport Pricing Strategies*. Oxford: Elsevier Science.

Steg, L. & Sievers, I. (1996). *Milieuproblemen als sociale dilemma's: Factoren die van invloed zijn op het ontstaan van en mogelijke oplossingen voor grootschalige sociale dilemma's* [*Environmental Problems as Social Dilemmas*]. Amsterdam: Council for the Environment.

Steg, L. & Uneken, E. (forthcoming). 'Car use: lust and must'. In: J.A. Rothengatter & R.D. Huguenin (eds), *Traffic and Transport Psychology: ICTTP2002 Proceedings*. Oxford: Elsevier Science.

Steg, L. & Vlek, C. (1996). 'Car use as a social dilemma: Conditions for behaviour change in reducing the use of motor vehicle'. In: *Proceedings of the PTRC Congress. Part C: Sustainable Transport*. London: PTRC.

Steg, L., Vlek, C. & Slotegraaf, G. (2001). 'Cognitive-reasoned and affective-emotional motives for using a motor car', *Transportation Research, Part F: Traffic Psychology and Behavior* 4(3): 1–19.

Tertoolen, G. (1996). 'Free to move . . . ? Psychological resistance against attempts to reduce private car use'. In: *Proceedings of the PTRC Congress. Part B: Shifting the Balance Between Modes*. London: PTRC.

Tertoolen, G., Van Kreveld, D. & Verstraten, E.C.H. (1998). 'Psychological resistance against attempts to reduce private car use', *Transportation Research, Part A: Policy and Practice* 32: 171–181.

Tertoolen, G. & Weggemans, T. (2002). 'Reizigers onderscheiden: een gedifferentieerde benadering van (openbaar vervoer) reizigers'. In: *Collocium Vervoersplanologisch Speurwerk 2002: De kunst van het verleiden*. Delft: CVS (With summary in English).

Verplanken, B. *et al.* (1994). 'Attitude versus general habit: Antecedents of travel mode choice', *Journal of Applied Social Psychology* 24: 285–300.

Vlek, C.A.J. (1996). 'Collective risk generation and risk management: The unexploited potential of the social dilemmas paradigm'. In: W.B.G. Liebrand & M.D. Messick (eds), *Frontiers in Social Dilemmas Research*. Berlin/Heidelberg/New York: Springer Verlag.

Vlek, C., Jager, W. & Steg, L. (1997). 'Methoden en strategieën voor gedragsverandering ter beheersing van collectieve risico's' [Methods and strategies for behaviour change aimed at managing collective risks], *Nederlands tijdschrift voor de psychologie* 52: 174–191.

Vlek, C. & Michon, J.A. (1992). 'Why we should and how we could reduce the use of motor vehicles in the near future', *IATSS Research: Journal of the International Association of Traffic and Safety Sciences* 15: 82–93.

Vlek, C. & Steg, L. (1996). 'Societal reasons, conditions and policy strategies for reducing the use of motor vehicles: A behavioural-science perspective and some empirical data in OECD'. In: *Towards Sustainable Transportation: Proceedings of the International Conference Towards Sustainable Transportation*, Vancouver.

Weggemans, T.J., Tertoolen, G. & Veling, I.H. (1996). *Gedrag op maat [Made-to-Measure Behaviour]*. Rotterdam: Transport Research Centre.

Weggemans, T.J., Tertoolen, G. & Veling, I.H. (1997). *Gedrag op maat II [Made-to-Measure Behaviour II]*. Rotterdam: Transport Research Centre.

Weggemans, T.J., Tertoolen, G. & Veling, I.H. (1998). *Gedrag op maat III [Made-to-Measure Behaviour III]*. Rotterdam: Transport Research Centre.

9. Crossing London: Overcoming the Obstacles to CrossRail[1]

STEPHEN GLAISTER AND TONY TRAVERS

London's main transport modes are overloaded. An important part of the solution is CrossRail, a new east–west underground railway. It was agreed and fully planned all of ten years ago, but the obstacles to its construction are severe and have become worse as time has passed. While the value of CrossRail is clear and generally recognised, a large number of direct interests have both the incentive and the power to object to it as a specific proposal in an attempt to secure a better outcome for themselves. Many commercial, public and governing institutions will have to be persuaded to make a sacrifice in the interests of the project going ahead.

The economic case for CrossRail

In 1988, faced with a rail-crowding problem in central London, the British government set up the Central London Rail Study (CLRS) (DoT, 1989). The study concluded that an essential component of a solution would be a new east–west underground railway. Unusually for a new urban rail scheme, the benefits were estimated to exceed the costs. The government quickly gave the go-ahead for CrossRail. A full design was created and a start was made in 1994 on obtaining parliamentary powers. However, the London economy faltered in the early 1990s and, lacking strong government support, the Bill was allowed to fail and the scheme was dropped.

Strong growth returned in the second half of the 1990s, resulting in crowding on a scale that exceeded the problem of the late 1980s, and the economic case for CrossRail is now stronger than ever. The ratio of benefits to costs estimated in a government reappraisal of five years ago was 1:7 (DoT, 1996) – that is, the value of the time savings and congestion relief to rail users and road traffic was estimated to be 70 per cent higher than the cost of building the scheme. A further reappraisal in 2001 (RTSC, 2001) found that the benefit-to-cost ratio would now be between 2 and 3 (assuming no real increase in construction costs above the estimates of November 1999). CrossRail easily

STEPHEN GLAISTER CBE is Professor of Transport and Infrastructure in the Department of Civil and Environmental Engineering at Imperial College, London. TONY TRAVERS is Director of the Greater London Group at the London School of Economics.

meets the requirements for value for money that are applied to national roads that are likely to be built, and the economic return on road schemes is typically very high compared to many other public investments.

Obstacles to progressing CrossRail

Successive national governments, the Corporation of London (1999), London First, the London Chamber of Commerce, the Confederation of British Industry and, most recently, the Mayor of London have all voiced strong support for CrossRail. Yet, despite almost a decade of economic growth in Britain, it has not proved possible to start construction. How is it that such a strongly (and officially) supported project can be so difficult to progress? The answer lies in four distinctively British phenomena.

The Treasury and the Private Finance Initiative (PFI)

The Treasury is often blamed for a failure to agree funding for larger infra-structure projects in Britain. It would be simplistic and unfair to blame the Treasury for ministerial decisions made by successive governments. On the other hand, the Treasury can reasonably be accused of failing to react with enthusiasm to ingenious and enterprising public–private (or private–public) efforts to replace the country's deteriorating infrastructure.

For the CrossRail project, the Treasury has done little more than block efforts to proceed: they have certainly not provided assistance in finding private or public–private funding options. Doubtless, officials would argue it is not their job to help in this way. They see the problems as the need for a big subsidy, probable cost escalation (which even a public–private partnership (PPP) cannot insulate them from – as the Channel Tunnel Link experience demonstrated – see Glaister et al., 2000) and the risk that some of the cost of associated work on the national rail network will ultimately fall back to them. If, as is currently the case, the Treasury is seen as putting a stop to virtually all major projects – apart from ones that it can be persuaded to present as standard PFI-type schemes – it is unlikely that private capital will see much of a future in investing in Britain's infrastructure.

Reluctance of government to take a lead

The second difficulty is the need to put in place a mechanism actively to promote the project. Britain is a particularly awkward country within which to do such things. The British tradition has evolved differently. Recent governments have not been willing to take the responsibility for leading the construction or reconstruction of 'public' infrastructure. Arm's-length bodies, non-governmental organisations and, occasionally, private consortia have had to take responsibility for projects such as the Millennium Dome, the Channel Tunnel, the Jubilee Line Extension and the Channel Tunnel Rail Link. The government may have put up much or all of the cash, but the promotion and organisation of the projects have been left to others. As a result, many good projects are delayed for a number of years (some permanently) because of the difficulty of constructing an appropriate and effective administrative mechanism to deliver them.

Antiquated planning

Any one of the problems outlined above would provide CrossRail with difficulties. However, the most problematic of all (and the main subject of this essay) is the United Kingdom's slow, complex and often antiquated planning system. Major transport projects, such as new airports, railways and roads, inevitably have to pass through local and national planning procedures. Local authority planning decisions are subject to an appeal to central government. For larger projects, there is likely to be a full-scale inquiry. In the case of CrossRail there is an extraordinarily long list of enterprises procuring or providing transport services in the London region, each of which will have its interests directly affected by the project. In some cases, it will be a legitimate commercial interest that is affected, while in others it will be an administrative duty – or both.

The list of service providers, procurers and independent regulators affected includes:

- The Strategic Rail Authority.
- Transport for London (TfL).
- London Underground.
- Infrastructure providers for London Underground.
- Network Rail.
- Several train operating companies (TOCs).
- Heathrow Express Rail Link.
- British Airports Authority (BAA).
- Docklands Light Railway.
- Eurostar.
- London & Continental Railways.
- The Rail Regulator.
- The Health and Safety Executive.
- The Civil Aviation Authority.
- London Fire and Emergency Planning Authority.

Ten years ago there was reason to hope that a determined central government could have pushed the scheme through, as it did the Jubilee Line Extension. Many of the interests listed above existed ten years ago. However, it is clear that things have been made significantly more complicated by the privatisation of the national railway system, the creation of the Strategic Rail Authority and the devolution of London government. For instance, the TOCs on the Great Western, West Coast Main Line and several routes to the East of London all have valuable contractual rights to Network Rail's severely restricted track capacity. In many cases, these rights last for a number of years and the TOCs have built their commercial businesses on this basis. It is the Rail Regulator's job to protect those rights. The Regulator, who has been strongly critical of aspects of Network Rail's capacity to deliver, would only be able to agree to CrossRail trains being granted access to the rail network if satisfied that the TOCs' existing interests were being adequately protected.

CrossRail services will require track access agreements on several Network Rail zones, station access agreements for stations operated by TOCs, BAA, Network Rail (the main termini) and London Underground, and an access agreement with the tunnel owner. The safety case may require that the central London stations come under the control of one operator – and that would inevitably be London Underground and TfL. The tunnel owner might seek an agreement with Network Rail for the supply and maintenance of track and equipment. Accommodation would have to be reached with the several TOCs concerning transfer of (scarce) track access right and abstraction of revenues.

The contractual and commercial inter-relationships between these various bodies are too complex to analyze in full. The following is one illustration. The consulting engineering firm, Arup, has suggested that trains might run directly between Heathrow and Stansted airports (Arup, 2001), thus linking both airports to central London. To achieve this, CrossRail trains would require access to Heathrow and Stansted stations, Heathrow Express track, some of Network Rail's capacity currently assigned to Heathrow Express, and to TOCs such as Thames Trains, Great Eastern and WAGN.

Administrative bodies

In addition to rail service providers, funders and regulators, there are many governmental bodies involved in planning and developing major transport projects. The list includes:

- The European Union.
- Parliament.
- The Mayor of London (as planning authority).
- London Development Agency.
- Corporation of London and the London boroughs of Havering, Barking & Dagenham, Newham, Tower Hamlets, Camden, Hackney, Westminster, Kensington & Chelsea, Ealing, Hounslow, Hillingdon, Brent & Harrow.
- Association of London Government.
- Department for Transport (DfT).
- Government Office for London.
- Other government departments.

- Her Majesty's Treasury.
- Department of Trade and Industry.

Central government is by no means a single entity. The Treasury controls not only public finance, but also acts as judge and jury on public–private arrangements such as those proposed for the Underground. The DfT is in overall control of transport planning for England, but cannot proceed with many projects because the Treasury will not sanction progress. DfT is also responsible for local government finance. Many of the Department's London responsibilities (though not, e.g., London Underground) have been devolved to the Government Office for London (GoL).

DfT is also the sponsoring department for the Strategic Rail Authority (SRA), which now has overall responsibility for planning Britain's railways. The Rail Regulator is independent, but appointed by government to oversee competition and ensure economic regulation of the national railways. Even the government-appointed Civil Aviation Authority would have a locus in the discussion of CrossRail because of the growing need for additional ground access capacity at London's airports. A project such as CrossRail would be of sufficient importance to require the active involvement of all those central government bodies. Virtually any one of them could, potentially, field effective opposition to it, though none would be powerful enough to promote it alone. Such is the asymmetry of the risks facing the promoters of major projects in modern Britain.

Central government would be only part of the story. The Mayor of London, elected in May 2000, now has responsibility for the budget and policies of Transport for London (TfL), which he chairs. TfL is the agency charged with running much of the capital's transport and roads system, including the London Underground. The Mayor and TfL have pressed ahead with a Transport Strategy, Spatial Development Strategy and Economic Development Strategy (all required by law) for London. Each of these strategies inevitably relates to the future of railways in the capital.

The Mayor is scrutinised by the 25-member London Assembly, who have the responsibility (among other things) to oversee the Mayor and TfL's transport activities. London is also governed by 32 boroughs and the Corporation of London, which are, individually, the local planning authorities for the capital. CrossRail would run through a dozen London boroughs (possibly more, depending on the route) and would have profound implications for most of the others. Several more major rail projects have also been proposed and feature in the Mayor's plans. It is inevitable that a number of boroughs would come under pressure from their electors to oppose or change the existing CrossRail proposals. The boroughs' representative body – the Association of London Government – would have to be consulted separately from the boroughs. Even within London, democracy is complex and fragmented.

Other interest groups

Beyond the rail sector and government, the private sector also has a warranted concern about the capital's transport system. Representative groups include:

- London First.
- London Chamber of Commerce and Industry.
- Commercial landowners and developers.
- BAA.
- London City Airport.
- Thames Gateway partnership.

A champion for CrossRail

Added to the other obstacles to progress outlined above, the fragmented and uncoordinated governmental arrangements would be desperately off-putting to potential investors. It would also make it hard for investors to understand and assess the commercial risks in the project. This is a reason to search for a structure that encapsulates as much as possible of the scheme under one owner and promoter. The only hope for the success of CrossRail is that a powerful individual is appointed, in charge of a small team, with the sole task of promoting the scheme. The obvious location for this team is at the Greater London Authority, supported by the Mayor's considerable personal power and influence.

Recently, TfL and the SRA agreed to set up a Companies Act company, limited by shares half owned by each of the bodies, to promote CrossRail, the Hackney/Southwest line and other major projects. Central government has released substantial funding for the initial planning work. While this initiative could get the project moving, it needs a 'champion' as chairman of the company who has the resolute support of his or her chief executive. The new company will have to be aggressively focused on driving the scheme forward, and will need to resolve a number of potential sources of tension between its two parent organisations.

Considering the SRA first, it views the scheme as just one part of the rail network in the London area which is also, for example, expected to cater for the government's aspirations for growth in rail freight (SRA, 2001). While this is an entirely correct line for the SRA to take, it does mean that the CrossRail scheme could risk becoming ensnared in a tangle of other schemes around London, many of them needing to be completed first in the sequence defined by the grand plan. This tangle of schemes is a guarantee of interminable delay. Likewise, the SRA has a national focus. It is directly answerable to the Secretary of State for Transport and to Parliament, and it is natural that it should reflect national political pressures. This is illustrated not only by the attention it gives to rail freight, but also to non-London rail issues, in spite of the fact that the greater part of all rail passenger traffic in the United Kingdom is in the London area. At the moment, the SRA also faces many demanding tasks in connection with achieving the government's aspirations for renegotiating rail franchises and leading to a large increase in national rail expenditures under the government's 10-year transport plan. Inevitably, CrossRail will not, in practice, remain at the centre of the SRA's attention.

CrossRail cannot be delivered without associated work on Network Rail property at either end of the central London tunnel. The company has financial problems and has been severely criticised by the Rail Regulator. Network Rail will not be well placed for many years to undertake the additional responsibility for taking a lead on enhanced infrastructure in connection with CrossRail.

The other partner in the new joint company, TfL, has a different perspective from the SRA. It carries an unambiguous responsibility for strategic transport planning in London, and recognises CrossRail as the most important single major infrastructure project in the area. Arguably, however, this is a case where 'the best is the enemy of the good': it would be better to get on with providing CrossRail quickly rather than wait an unknown number of years so that it can be planned into a large and highly complex national rail network. Within the GLA, there is an argument that another scheme – the Hackney to Southwest London line – is more relevant than CrossRail to London's immediate needs, so it should take precedence. This argument has merit, but the reality is that the main, central part of CrossRail has been designed in great detail, while the Hackney scheme only exists in broad outline. Consequently, CrossRail is several years ahead of the Hackney scheme, so it is sensible for the new company to give clear priority to getting CrossRail started. To attempt to reverse the order would inevitably delay the first opening by several years, although there may be proponents of the Hackney scheme who would prefer it that way.

While the central tunnel of CrossRail is precisely defined, the lines of route at each end are not. Since the scheme was designed in the early 1990s, a great deal has changed. The airports have developed. The line of the Channel Tunnel Rail Link has been changed to bring it into North London via Stratford and it will carry domestic as well as Eurostar traffic. One of the first tasks for the new company will be to engineer an informed debate about the routes to the east. The process of reviewing these issues, bearing in mind the large number of interests, could descend into a protracted and inconclusive modelling and planning exercise. There are many powerful commercial interests involved, and finding a sensible and workable compromise, capable of being funded and sufficiently robust to survive the formal planning process, will require all the diplomatic skills of the CrossRail champion and the supporting team.

In this connection, the case of the Jubilee Line Extension to Canary Wharf and Stratford is instructive. It never showed benefits sufficient to match the costs and was strongly opposed by the Treasury, yet it was built. The promoters succeeded by creating a team that had strategic direction, good external political advice, tactical sense, as well as sound transport, technical, property and financial competence. Care was taken to respond to the concerns of objectors and to mitigate the adverse effects, but the most critical element was a political 'understanding' at a high level (i.e., in the Prime Minister's office) that allowed the promoters to defeat the many and powerful forces in opposition.

A procurement and financing structure

Even though the CrossRail scheme cannot be treated sensibly as a simple commercial venture, there are good reasons for wishing to involve the skills and disciplines of the private sector as far as possible in managing and providing the project and in providing the finance. These are essentially all to do with reducing the risks of inflated costs and other failures by transferring these risks to individuals with the ability to mitigate them. Maximum involvement of the private sector will make it more likely that the government in general, and the Treasury in particular, will agree to the scheme escaping the normal local authority spending-control devices.

CrossRail is in the public realm. It is primarily for the benefit of the London economy and the people that live and work in the capital. The public sector must therefore provide legitimacy and authority. It looks after the definition of public interest. It sets the objectives and the policy and regulatory framework. By contrast, the private sector (being financially committed to a result) is arguably more focused and less prone to dissipation of effort through the pursuit of public policy objectives not necessarily related to the project. The private sector has a vested interest in looking for ingenious and cost-effective solutions. It is often much better on implementation – especially contract preparation and supervision, and risk management. It can be more flexible in obtaining the right numbers of staff and skills necessary for each stage of the process. It is often better at marketing and persuading because it is less constrained by public sector protocols and better able to justify the resources.

This leads us to the conclusion that it is right that CrossRail should be promoted and financed by a body in the margins between the private sector, on the one hand, and TfL with the SRA, on the other. There is a rich history of precedents – public and private bodies that have successfully financed and constructed infrastructure and provided services. For example:

- The Metropolitan Board of Works provided London's excellent sewer system in the nineteenth century – one of many achievements of the great Victorian era of infrastructure engineering. It was a joint committee of the lower-tier local authorities, financed by borrowing.
- The Port of London Authority developed and operates the port of London. It was – and still is – a public trust.
- The London Docklands Development Corporation was a single-purpose enterprise, with bespoke powers and duties, created by central government in the 1980s.

- The British Broadcasting Corporation (BBC) and the London Passenger Transport Board in its original form in 1933 were examples of public corporations with special powers and duties to deliver or procure public services.

Funding CrossRail

In our view, it would be absurd to treat CrossRail as a purely commercial venture. CrossRail will be *public* infrastructure because it will run across one of the world's densest urban economies and will inter-relate with an extraordinarily complex pre-existing set of transport networks. As is typical of urban infrastructure projects, many of the benefits and costs of the scheme will not accrue to the direct users, but to others. This, in turn, has important consequences for public policy, pricing, regulation and appropriate sources of funding.

Though the finances of CrossRail are remarkably strong for a new urban underground railway, there is no realistic hope that it could be promoted only on the strength of fare revenues. There are four potential sources of financial support:

- Funding from Transport for London – although TfL's budgets are going to be under pressure by a multitude of other demands: not least the need to fund the repair and maintenance of the existing London Underground.
- Funding from central government – probably via the SRA, which may be able to help by setting minimum passenger service requirements under the franchises they negotiate with TOCs for services through the CrossRail tunnel, thus guaranteeing a minimum level of access charge income.
- Funding from private property interests – as much of the increase in property values will be diluted among a large number of owners of previously developed sites, the only way to recover a portion of this for the purpose of funding the scheme may be through some form of general taxation (see Travers & Glaister, 1994).
- A new funding instrument – for example, a mutually beneficial alliance between the promoter of CrossRail and the large commercial property interests that stand to gain from it. One such mechanism might be for the developers to invest using an agreement that concedes a charge over part of the value of their freeholds to be exercised in the event of a funding shortfall. This would have some of the characteristics of a club with the purpose of internalising the joint benefits.

The question arises as to whether funding for CrossRail should be distinct from that for other infrastructure schemes that London requires in the future (such as the Hackney to southwest London line), or from the scheme to rejuvenate the existing London Underground. If the Transport Commissioner for London were to succeed in introducing a structure within which capital can be raised by direct borrowing, then it would only be sensible for the financing of CrossRail to be included in part of that structure.

Parliamentary powers

A project such as CrossRail, which would pass through some of the most populous parts of the country, including a new tunnel under central London, must be planned in such a way as to pay attention to the interests of those who live and work along the proposed route. Opponents may put forward a number of arguments:

- Preference for a different route from any proposed (e.g., it should 'go round the north of central London and link up the main line termini').
- 'Not In My Back Yard' from residents and businesses.
- Lobbyists for a particular station.
- Opposition to any special business taxes.
- Opposition to a fares premium as a device to raise extra revenue.

The capacity of opponents to delay or even stop a major project is considerable. Terminal 5 at Heathrow Airport is a case in point. Fortunately, the government has now recognised that there is a problem. In reply to a parliamentary question on 20 July 2001, Secretary of State Stephen Byers made an outline announcement that: 'New measures will speed up major planning decisions and safeguard public debate' (DTLR, 2001). However, it will be several years before these proposals could be implemented. In the meantime, there are several procedures that may apply to the CrossRail scheme in terms of securing the necessary powers.

An order made by the Secretary of State under the Transport and Works Act 1992 (TWA)[2]

The TWA process is likely to take at least two years, including a six-week objection period after the original application is made, followed by a public enquiry, a report of the Inspector and the decision of the Secretary of State. A 42-day challenge period is in force after this decision is made. Generally speaking, the length of the public enquiry will depend on the number and nature of the objections. Terminal 5 at Heathrow has been subject to a public enquiry lasting three years. Consequently, the process of consultation and winning support pre-application is vital in shortening the process.

Alternative procedure under the TWA

This procedure is for schemes of 'national significance', and may be used at the discretion of the Secretary of State. Schemes that are considered of national significance must be referred to Parliament, followed by a public inquiry. A government minister must move a resolution for approval by both Houses of Parliament. After publication in the *London Gazette,* time would need to be made for both Houses of Parliament to debate a motion on the scheme. If either House voted against the motion, the Order could not be made. The voting can be whipped, but the more controversial the proposal the greater the need to lobby for support pre-application.

Private bill

The 1994 attempt to obtain powers for CrossRail was through the Private Bill process. The Parliamentary Committee hearing started in January 1994 and by May all of the evidence for and against the project had been heard and the Committee had come to a decision. This was as rapid a consideration as one could hope for. However, the TWA was enacted specifically to relieve Members of Parliament of the chore of sitting on Bill Committees and it is unlikely that Parliament would make any concessions on this.

Hybrid bill

This is a Public Bill that affects a particular private interest in a manner different from the private interests of other persons or bodies of the same category or class. The question of principle as to whether the scheme should be allowed is settled on the floor of the House, and once the Bill has completed its various stages, it goes for Royal Assent. One advantage is that timescales are more certain than under the TWA; another is that in order for the government to agree to the tabling of the Bill, the financial details would need to be worked out in advance with the Treasury. As a consequence, one of the main stumbling blocks to implementation (i.e., financing) will be overcome very early in the process. Room would have to be made in the government's legislative programme but, on balance, this appears to be the best current option.

Conclusion

The objectives of the 'Companies Act company' to deliver all aspects of CrossRail, jointly owned by TfL and the SRA, should specify a somewhat independent commercial remit while fully acknowledging the public interest and the requisite political accountability. A high-quality, expert team should be employed full time by the company in support of a strong chair and chief executive. This body would need to represent the Mayor of London, central government, the private sector (in particular those with direct interests in major infrastructure delivery) and, possibly, the London boroughs. It would either take direct responsibility for the management and procurement of CrossRail or, alternatively, procure the project from expert contract managers.

Consideration needs to be given to the extent of its powers. It could make sense to give it rights to provide a range of interchanges and to acquire and develop land in the vicinity of stations.

Most urgently, a physical scheme needs to be finalised with a view to starting the formal planning process at the beginning of 2003. The previous effort at pushing through CrossRail was defeated by lack of government support and the requirements of the Private Bill procedure. Next time, whole-hearted government support will be needed if the planning procedures are to be completed within a reasonable period. In the absence of new, improved government procedures, the Hybrid Bill procedure would be best (as used for the rapid implementation of the Channel Tunnel).

Central government should get a grip on itself and make a single individual responsible for Whitehall input to the project. This representative could sit on the board of the company, but would also have responsibility to ensure the Treasury, DfT, GoL, SRA and other central government entities act in concert. To use a cliché much loved by recent administrations, central government's efforts need to be 'joined up'. In a country as centralised at the United Kingdom, only a member of the Cabinet (and then one who was felt to be capable of delivering) would be of much use.

CrossRail is an opportunity to show that Britain and its capital city are capable of using their financial, business and democratic strengths to good effect. In the aftermath of rail privatisation, the Hatfield disaster, the struggle over the public–private partnership for the London Underground and the damage done by the national railways to Britain's international reputation, the time has come to show there is a better side to this country and its infrastructure.

Notes

1 This article was originally published in *Public Money & Management* 21(4) (2001).
2 We are grateful to Ashley Heller of TfL for his assistance in preparing this material.

References

Arup (2001). *London Regional Metro: Proposals for its Delivery* (15 January). London: Arup.

Corporation of London (1999). *CrossRail: A Report by the Corporation of London* (November). London: Corporation of London (Chapter 6 gives a list of the many beneficiaries from CrossRail).

Department of Transport (DoT) (1989). *Central London Rail Study*. London: HMSO.

Department of Transport (DoT) (1996). *CrossRail: Final Report* [the Montague Report]. London: HMSO.

Department of Transport, Local Government and the Regions (DTLR) (2001). *News Release 335* (20 July). London: DTLR.

Glaister, S., Scanlon, R. & Travers, T. (2000). *Getting Partnerships Going*. London: Institute for Public Policy Research.

Railway Technology Strategy Centre (RTSC) (2001). *A Reassessment of the Economic Case for CrossRail*. London: Railway Technology Strategy Centre at Imperial College, London/Corporation of London.

Strategic Rail Authority (SRA) (2001). *London East–West Study*. London: SRA.

Travers, T. & Glaister, S. (1994). *An Infrastructure Fund for London*. London: Greater London Group, London School of Economics.

10. *Railpolitik*: The Financial Realities of Operating Britain's National Railways[1]

JEAN SHAOUL

This chapter analyzes the context and financial performance of Britain's national railways under private ownership in the first half of the twentieth century and public ownership in the second half of the century, in order to understand the problems confronting the railways and the implications for privatisation. The evidence shows that Railtrack's collapse was inevitable: as a highly capital intensive industry, albeit heavily subsidised, the railway industry cannot generate the revenue to cover the full cost of the infrastructure and services, including the financial claims of the providers of capital, without jeopardising network performance. Privatisation could not resolve the external constraints and the consequent financial problems. The final section of the essay considers the implications of this analysis for the future of the industry.

Introduction

The privatisation of Britain's railways in 1996 was one of the last major privatisations carried out by the Conservative Government. The government claimed that privatisation would improve industrial performance by subjecting the nationalised industries to the discipline of the market, and yield benefits via greater efficiency from the ability of the new owners with their superior management skills to intervene and control performance (Moore, 1986a, 1986b; Redwood, 1998). Other benefits included:

- raising revenue and reducing the public sector borrowing requirement;
- permitting industry to raise funds from the capital markets on commercial terms without central government guarantee and as needed, rather than as part of the government's overall demand management plans that led to so much uncertainty;
- reducing central government's involvement in the running of the industry; and
- promoting wider share ownership, including that of workers' in their companies.

JEAN SHAOUL is a Senior Lecturer in the School of Accounting and Finance at Manchester University.

In its White Paper setting out its plans for privatising the railways (DoT, 1992a), the government said that it was determined to see better use made of the railways, greater responsiveness to the customer, a higher quality of service and better value for money for the rail-travelling public. The implications were very clear: passengers would be the main beneficiaries of privatisation as a result of competition and the new owners' ability to intervene and control activities and performance. The unstated assumption was that private sector management would overcome the structural constraints of the activity.

However, in October 2001, the Secretary of State for Transport felt compelled to put Railtrack – the debt-laden infrastructure company owning the track, stations and signals that had been dependent upon government subsidies throughout its short life – into administration, using his powers under the Railways Act 1993. He firmly ruled out re-nationalisation, saying that the government intended to set up a *not-for-profit* trust. To understand why Railtrack collapsed, it is necessary to review the history of the industry and understand the determinants of its financial performance. The railways are particularly interesting because they were nationalised after the Second World War in part at least because of their severe financial problems that were never overcome, even under public ownership.

History and background

As a highly capital-intensive industry linked originally to the extractive industries, railway finances were always precarious. Several railway lines folded within twenty years of opening and liquidations followed. Even the successful railway companies were rarely able to generate a rate of return on capital employed of more than 5 per cent. Most of the profits came not from running the trains, but from developing the land that lay alongside the tracks. When the First World War broke out, the railways, which occupied a crucial position in the economy and were major employers, immediately passed into the hands of central government under the Wartime Control Agreement between the government and railways. Although it had been widely expected that the railways would remain under government control after the war, the Railway Act 1921 consolidated the 120 railway companies into four new groups and returned them to private control. The amalgamation was seen as a means of bringing together the railway companies that had worked together closely in the past, and enable the weaker companies to get financial support and gain access to new capital thereby improving their equipment and operations. It would bring about economies of scale and eliminate competitive services (Bonavia, 1981a).

In the years that followed, the conditions of the transport industry began to change. While the railways dominated the long-distance freight market, road transport challenged the railways' position in the short- and medium-distance freight and the short-distance passenger market. However, with the slump in world trade in the 1920s, profits fell. British industries such as coal and steel, which were major customers of the rail freight business, shrank in terms of output. Since the government fixed the prices charged by the railways, they did not reflect the costs of providing the rail service. Without any relaxation of price and marketing controls by the government, which were not forthcoming, the railways had difficulty recovering operating expenses. Investment was therefore always difficult to finance and amounted to less than the depreciation charge during the interwar period. This, Bagwell (1968) argued, was equivalent to disinvestments of £125 million at current prices between 1920 and 1938.

During the Second World War, central government once again controlled the railways: it set the basis of payment for traffic carried and froze the charges. By the end of the war, there was a huge backlog of repairs and renewals. Gourvish (1986) and Bonavia (1981b) argued that most of the wear and tear on the infrastructure was the result of the intensive use of the network during the war and war damage itself, rather than under-investment before the war. When the war ended, the incoming Labour Government proposed that the railways would remain under government control.

The national railways under public ownership

Nationalisation was supposed to resolve both the external structural constraints and the consequent internal financial problems, and to promote a recovery for the industry through increased efficiency – ironically the self-same rationale that the Conservative Government used to justify privatisation fifty years later. According to Alfred Barnes, the Minister of Transport, the main objective of socialising the transport industry 'was to consolidate the various elements of transport . . . into a single whole which would operate as a non-profit making utility service at the least real cost to *trade, industry* and the travelling public' (Barnes, 1949; emphasis added). In other words, under public ownership, the railways would operate for the benefit of users (primarily industry), not the providers of finance. Lower transport costs would make industry more efficient and able to compete on world markets. Thus, it was not conceived as part of a socialist programme that sought to abolish production for private profit as others have noted (Millward, 1999), but as part of a series of national reforms to restabilise and promote the more successful (profitable) operation of capitalist enterprises in Britain.

In principle at least, public ownership means that some, if not all, of the claims on the surplus can be relaxed: the cost of replacing and enhancing productive capital, the return to the providers of finance (interest on loans and dividends to equity owners), and tax to the government. In practice, successive governments compelled British Rail (BR) to finance its capital investment with interest-bearing public debt rather than government grants, as was the case with some of the other state-owned enterprises. This, plus the pre-existing debt and the payments to the old owners, meant that breaking even was all but impossible. Yet no one seemed to have thought through the implications of these three forms of debt for a capital-intensive industry in the context of declining demand and the need for extensive investment. Continued growth of road transport meant that estimates of revenues were always over-optimistic. Income was insufficient to cover expenditure due to the effects of recurrent economic problems and pay rises. Repeated government intervention meant that investment was low relative to the requirements for capital expenditure on the infrastructure. Thus, despite nationalisation and reorganisation, the rail industry could not and did not break even.

British Rail was subject to frequent investigations, reorganisation and cuts in an effort to break even. Prices rose, lines were closed in the 1960s, and there were some partial debt write-offs in the 1960s and 1970s to reduce the burden of interest and a revaluing of assets downwards to reduce the burden of depreciation. However, this was insufficient to restore BR to profitability given the remaining accumulated debt. Preference was also given to the development of road transport for both the private car and road haulage, undermining receipts from the fare box. Pricing policy became a political football.

The introduction of current cost accounting in 1982 for all the nationalised industries and the requirement to make a 6 per cent return on capital employed placed an intolerable burden on the railways, given the age of the assets, and served as a financial ratchet to drive down labour costs in a bid to meet the government's targets. Thus by the 1980s, the form of the nationalised regime, far from resolving or compensating for the structural problems of the industry, was arguably more onerous than that of the private sector itself. It combined the commercial for-profit requirement with political control hostile to rail.

Financial performance of British Rail, 1976–1994

The railways' revenues came from several sources: fares from passengers, freight charges and government grants We will consider each in turn using the financial data from BR's annual report and accounts.

The passenger business was the largest of the three, accounting for 55 per cent of fare income in 1976. By 1994, with passenger income more than quadrupling, it accounted for 71 per cent of receipts as parcels declined and freight grew very slowly (Table 1). While passenger use and receipts rose, the increase did not keep pace with inflation, reflecting rail's declining share of a transport market that was rising overall.

The freight business was (and is) crucially dependent on the business cycle and the level and composition of industrial activity. Historically, rail's main freight customers were coal and steel, and their fortunes were inextricably linked. The move to super-pits close to power stations and the closure of small pits even though they were profitable reduced the need for transport. In the late 1980s and early 1990s, the privatisation of the state-owned gas, coal, oil and nuclear energy enterprises, and the liberalisation of the energy

Table 1. British Rail's revenues by sector (millions of pounds)

	Passenger	Freight	Parcels	Total revenues from fares	Government grants	Grants as percentage of revenue	Total revenue
1976	504	305	98	908	319	26%	1,227
1977	593	347	109	1,049	364	26%	1,413
1978	701	375	119	1,195	434	27%	1,629
1979	799	410	130	1,339	523	28%	1,862
1980	953	432	141	1,527	634	29%	2,161
1981	1,022	475	119	1,616	810	33%	2,426
1982	923	455	92	1,427	887	38%	2,358
1983	1,149	528	115	1,992	933	32%	2,925
1984–1985[1]	1,225	287	119	2,364	1,172	33%	3,536
1985–1986	1,332	528	126	2,250	895	28%	3,145
1986–1987	1,442	534	117	2,397	786	25%	3,183
1987–1988[2]	1,621	562	119	2,580	804	24%	3,384
1988–1989	1,802	579	124	2,789	606	18%	3,395
1989–1990	1,906	671	118	2,899	586	17%	3,485
1990–1991	2,056	663	114	3,076	605	16%	3,681
1991–1992	2,116	657	100	3,150	798	20%	3,948
1992–1993	2,153	634	88	3,115	608	16%	3,723
1993–1994	2,193	565	78	3,100	545	15%	3,645

Notes: [1]British Rail changed the year end: 1984–1985 (15 months); [2]British Rail changed year end: 1987–1988.
Source: Transport Statistics of Great Britain (various years); British Rail annual report and accounts (various years).

industry, freed electricity from dependency on coal. This, in turn, opened up the North Sea to the oil companies for the exploration of oil and gas that are moved by pipeline, further reducing BR's income. As well as changes in the composition of industrial activity, the railways have been affected by changing methods in industrial organisation. Just-in-time techniques, extended supply chains, multiple pick-up points to multiple drop-off points and the growth in superstores supplied from warehouses (Bagwell, 1968) are less suited to a fixed-track transport system and have led to the development of the road haulage and freight forwarding industry.

Similar forces destabilised the linkage between rail and parcels. The liberalisation of parcel and mail services, the ending of the state-owned Post Office monopoly and the entry of trans-national carriers cut BR's small but useful parcels income. Changes in communications technology (fax, e-mail, electronic data interchange, etc.) have further reduced the demand for certain types of services. In other words, BR's decline was bound up with two inter-related developments: changes in communications and transport technology; and the end of sheltered domestic markets for British goods and services that lay at the heart of the postwar programme of nationalisation and the restructuring of industry.

The third source of income – government grants – comprised the Public Service Obligation (PSO), intended to cover the cost of operating uneconomic lines kept open for social reasons; capital grants to offset the huge capital costs of the industry; railway level-crossing grants; capital grants; and pension funding grants. As a result of government policy in the 1980s that sought to make state-owned enterprises run on commercial lines, government grants fell in cash terms (without accounting for inflation) from 26 per cent of revenues in 1976 to 15 per cent in 1994, making BR the least subsidised railway system in Europe. In comparison to other European countries, the level of infrastructure spending on transport in general, and railways in particular, was low. The United Kingdom ranked 10 out of 18 European countries, with an average railway infrastructure spend as a percentage of GDP of below 0.3 per cent for 1987–1995 (European Conference of Transport Ministers, 1999). While France, Germany and Spain all have high-speed networks of more 1,000 kilometres, the United Kingdom had (and still has) virtually none: the legacy of years of under-funding. This in turn means that BR was generating most of its revenues from fares in the run up to privatisation. In short, although income from all sources trebled, this was much less than the rate of inflation, since BR was operating in declining markets and losing out to other forms of transport.

The inability to increase or even maintain income in real terms led to a focus on cost reduction to meet the government's financial targets. With the cost of external purchases low (30 per cent of revenues), labour was the main cost (Table 2). Between 1976 and 1994, BR shed more than one-third of its workforce. Whereas in 1976, there were more than 186,000 workers employed in the railway industry, by the time of privatisation, only 115,000 remained.

103

Table 2. British Rail's revenues and cost structure

	Total revenue (£m)	Purchase/sales	Labour costs (£m)	Labour/ revenues (£m)	Number employed	Average wage costs (£)
1976	1,227	0.23	919	0.75	186,833	4,919
1977	1,413	0.25	984	0.69	182,289	5,398
1978	1,629	0.31	997	0.61	182,198	5,472
1979	1,862	0.31	1,151	0.62	182,031	6,323
1980	2,161	0.34	1,345	0.62	178,059	7,554
1981	2,426	0.31	1,521	0.62	170,397	8,926
1982	2,358	0.23	1,762	0.75	161,407	10,917
1983	2,925	0.30	1,817	0.62	155,423	11,691
1984–1985[1]	3,536	0.33	2,376	0.67	147,219	16,139
1985–1986	3,145	0.30	1,949	0.62	142,757	13,653
1986–1987	3,183	0.30	1,968	0.62	166,989	11,785
1987–1988[2]	3,384	0.30	2,034	0.60	133,567	15,228
1988–1989	3,395	0.32	2,007	0.59	128,476	15,662
1989–1990	3,485	0.35	2,070	0.59	129,696	15,960
1990–1991	3,681	0.33	2,289	0.62	131,430	17,416
1991–1992	3,948	0.33	2,449	0.62	133,060	18,405
1992–1993	3,723	0.23	2,600	0.70	124,791	20,835
1993–1994	3,645	0.18	2,492	0.68	115,546	21,567
Percentage change 1976–1994	197%		171%		–38%	340%

Notes: [1]British Rail changed the year end: 1984–1985 (15 months); [2]British Rail changed year end: 1987–1988.
Source: British Rail annual report and accounts (various years).

This means that labour had indeed borne the brunt of cost cutting, as recommended by the Serpell Committee (Serpell, 1983). Labour productivity rose quite dramatically as valued-added per employee rose five-fold over the period. Wages rose, but less than the rate of inflation and less than those in comparable trades.

The failure to increase passenger receipts significantly meant that the cost-cutting never generated the necessary surplus, as the minority report on the Serpell Committee, set up to investigate railway finances, made clear (Serpell, 1983). While some throughput measures, such as average passenger train loadings declined, labour productivity as reflected in the number of train-kilometres per employee rose by 17 per cent between 1987 and 1994, the period for which such data is available, and was the highest in Europe (see Table 3).

At the very least, this challenges the claims that BR had poor labour productivity and was inefficient, and that private ownership is a necessary spur to efficiency. It suggests that private sector management has no monopoly on efficiency techniques and that ownership *per se* is not an important factor. From the perspective of this study, these findings are important because they suggest that privatisation was unlikely to yield further improvements in labour productivity without jeopardising service delivery, since productivity had already increased substantially and was higher than elsewhere.

It is pertinent to consider here the split of costs between track and train services since these were disaggregated after privatisation. After allowing for general expenses, about 50 per cent or more of costs were related to work on the infrastructure, signalling and property, with the rest related to train operations, including rolling stock. In other words, rail is a high fixed-cost industry, where much of the costs are associated with providing the network. In this, the railways are similar to other public utilities such as gas, electricity, telecommunications and water. The utilities, however, differ in that they supply an (almost) universal and essential service. It is therefore possible to devise methods of payment (monthly direct debit, prepayment cards, social security allowances, etc.) that spread the burden over time, allow cost recovery from consumers and do not require consumers to pay at the point of use. The railways, on the other hand, do not provide a comprehensive and universal service and largely charge their customers at the point of use. This in turns means that, in the absence of adequate demand, full-cost pricing is self-defeating. Thus the essential problem for railways and metro systems, in Britain and the world over, is that as capital-intensive industries, they cannot generate the revenues from fares to cover the full costs of their infrastructure, train operations and investment, as well as make a rate of return on capital employed.

BR made an operating profit before interest and tax in only 10 out of 18 years between 1976 and 1994. After 1983, the losses were so great that they almost cancelled out the profits in the good years. Interest charges took what little remained, with the result that in most years BR failed to break even.

Table 3. International comparisons of performance

	Train kilometres per member of staff		Average passenger train loading		Average freight train loading		Percentage support from public funds	
	British Rail	European average	British Rail	European average	British Rail	European average	British Rail	European average
1986–1987	2,990	2,162	95	131	244	296	0.21	0.67
1987–1988	3,127	2,233	97	130	253	296	0.22	0.67
1988–1989	2,928	2,133	96	143	268	302	0.14	0.72
1989–1990	3,422	2,301	92	144	217	311	0.12	0.70
1990–1991	3,289	2,320	89	144	268	322	0.14	0.68
1991–1992	3,106	2,424	86	139	316	323	0.16	0.52
1992–1993	3,205	2,527	86	143	315	324	0.20	0.56
1993–1994	3,463	2,220	83	130	267	319	0.18	0.59

Source: British Rail annual report and accounts (various years).

It was only because of asset sales in the late 1980s that BR was able to break even in 1983–1994. As a nationalised industry, BR was not liable for tax. Investment, predominantly in infrastructure as opposed to rolling stock, was only slightly higher than the depreciation charge until the late 1980s. In other words, there was little investment in the industry until the run-up to privatisation. Taken together we have a picture of an industry running to stand still in financial terms. Many of the workforce lost their jobs or saw their pay decline in real terms; passengers paid more to travel in overcrowded trains, particularly in the southeast; many travellers were forced to switch to road; the public at large suffered the social, environmental and public health costs of increasing road transport; while taxpayers paid for the diminishing rail subsidy and an increased expenditure on roads.

Crucially, with the loss of one-third of Britain's manufacturing base in the early 1980s, the disappearance of the mines and the loss of freight to road transport, industry no longer had a significant stake in the railways: nationalisation had lost its *raison d'etre*. Furthermore, as the rate of profit in industry as a whole began to decline (Armstrong *et al.*, 1984), the 40 per cent or so of GDP that did not provide a source of profit had to be opened up via privatisation, public–private partnerships and other policy instruments. Rail thus became a target for privatisation, but, as this analysis has shown, a reversion to private ownership would be even more onerous.

The form of railway privatisation

The government created a fragmented and complicated structure of more than 100 companies that comprised the main track and infrastructure owner, engineering service companies, franchise operators of train companies, operators for parcels and freight, rolling stock and leasing companies, and other suppliers of materials and services. This is described in the official documents (DoT, 1992a, 1992b, 1993) and has been extensively analyzed elsewhere.

The core of the privatised industry – Railtrack: the network owner – was to be sold by means of a public offering. Adopting measures used in the other utility flotations, the government removed the burden of debts and liabilities that had made BR so crisis ridden under public ownership: it wrote off more than £1 billion of its £1.6 billion debts before privatisation, and then gave a further £225 million debt relief at flotation to allow the Thameslink 2000 project to go ahead (NAO, 1998). It transferred £1 billion of its liabilities to the county councils. The pension fund, which had an asset value of over £585 million, was larger than the accrued liability, giving the infrastructure company, Railtrack plc, a pension holiday. The government allowed BR's £707 million tax loss to be transferred to the privatised company. It also priced the shares so as to value the company at £1.9 billion, less than half the £4.5 billion of the book value of the assets on a historic cost basis. The purpose of this was to ensure that Railtrack could deliver an appropriate rate of return

Table 4. Financial performance of the train operating companies

	1996	1997	1998	1999	2000	2001
Total revenues	2,908,338,000	4,462,195,000	4,405,164,000	4,722,986,000	4,480,291,000	4,562,581,000
Subsidies	2,000,000,000	2,200,000,000	1,829,000,000	1,586,000,000	1,418,000,000	1,214,000,000
	(69%)	(49%)	(42%)	(34%)	(32%)	(27%)
Number employed	46,845	44,577	37,108	36,392	37,095	38,234
External purchases/revenues	0.78	0.80	0.78	0.81	0.77	0.77
Labour costs/revenues	0.21	0.20	0.19	0.17	0.20	0.22
Average wage costs	£13,220	£20,450	£22,590	£21,690	£24,180	£26,740
Operating profit before interest and tax	3,478,000	−19,740,000	107,569,000	113,967,000	101,884,000	10,111,000
Operating profit before interest and tax/revenues	0.00	0.00	0.02	0.02	0.02	0.00

Source: Annual report and accounts (various years) of the 25 train operating companies.

to its shareholders, without the necessity for even higher fares, in the short term at least, which would have generated political uproar and jeopardised the privatisation.

For all the talk of competition, the government could not disguise the fact that the industry was a monopoly that would have to be regulated in order to ensure that customers were protected and that the industry invested and maintained levels of service. The regulatory functions were split three ways:

- Economic regulation of the infrastructure was to be carried out by the Office of the Rail Regulator (ORR). ORR would determine the track charges that the train operators would pay, taking into account Railtrack's costs and investment needs.
- The Railway Safety Regulator of the Health and Safety Executive, whose reports would partially determine the investment programme.
- The Office of Passenger Rail Franchising (OPRAF) would award 7-year franchises for passenger services to the train operating companies that required the lowest level of subsidy.

This fragmentation of the industry has important and interrelated implications. First, the relations between the different companies would be determined by extensive contractual arrangements. Second, all these companies would seek to operate economically so as to make a return on their capital employed in an industry that had not done so for decades under either private or public ownership. It was unlikely that this could be achieved under conditions where costs had already been cut without externalising costs: shifting the burden of adjustment onto their subcontractors' workforce. This would inevitably affect the coordination and coherence of a complex system, since all the hundred or so new business units needed to work in unison – though under different management and operating conditions. Thus, the form of privatisation made planning, implementation and accountability in the industry difficult, if not impossible.

The train operating companies (TOCs)

Table 4 shows the financial performance of the 25 TOCs, subsidiaries now of just a handful of companies. Their combined turnover in 2001 was £4.56 billion, more than double BR's total passenger revenues in 1993–1994 (Table 1). This was partly because fares on some routes rose faster than the rate of inflation and passenger numbers rose due to the expanding economy, but more importantly because subsidies were considerably higher than in the 1980s and early 1990s (Table 1) and accounted for 67 per cent of total income in 1996, declining to 27 per cent in 2001.

Most of the TOCs' revenues (80 per cent) went on external purchases, mainly charges for track access and train leasing, with most of what remained going on wage costs. Only after shedding nearly 20 per cent of the workforce and reducing average wage costs (relative to comparable grades in BR) were the TOCs as a whole able to make a profit. After making no profits in the first two years of operations, operating margins were 2 per cent, the same as in the years before privatisation for all the passenger services according to BR's annual report and accounts. This was despite subsidies higher than BR ever received. Furthermore, given that subsidies were set to decline to £0.9 billion in 2003–2004, the TOCs must either reduce costs still further or increase revenues by eliminating fare dodgers and attracting passengers.

Several points follow from this. First, since most of the TOCs' income went on charges for track access and rolling stock, it was their suppliers, Railtrack and the rolling stock leasing companies (ROSCOs), that were the main beneficiaries of the subsidies. Second, Table 4 shows only the *average* profits: many of the smaller franchises have been operating with heavy losses and declining subsidies, and have become the target of takeover bids which in turn has meant the emergence of private monopolies with less competition for the next round of franchise licences. Third, with an operating profit of just £11 million on a turnover of £4.5 billion for the year 2000–2001 for the TOCs as a whole and nearly half of them reporting losses before interest and tax, some at least now require extra subsidies if they are to continue operating. In December 2002, to cite but one example, the Strategic Rail Authority made £58 million available to one of the TOCs – Connex South East – in addition to its budgeted subsidy of £30 million for the year 2002–2003. This extra funding constitutes a substantial extra burden on the public purse.

Fourth, train operations are unlike commercial franchises such as MacDonalds, which sets exacting performance standards for its franchise holders. Rail performance targets were no more demanding than those set for BR in 1995. Thus no improvement was built into the franchise system, belying government claims that services would get better. Furthermore, performance indicators are no longer published in ways that permit direct comparisons with standards of performance prior to privatisation. OPRAF has developed new measures of punctuality and reliability for each of the franchise operators, published on a quarterly basis. Even so, the new performance data shows that punctuality and reliability have not improved for most of the TOCs. Even these results would not have been achieved if the train operators had not made extensive use of a loophole in the regulations that allows then to exclude from performance data days when they have 'serious problems' or extended their scheduled journey times. Taken together, this means that the private train operators are no more efficient in either financial or non-financial terms than their publicly owned counterpart.

Rolling stock companies (ROSCOs)

By 1999, the revenues of the three rolling stock companies had risen to more than £1 billion, equivalent to about a quarter of the TOCs' revenues. After the initial restructuring of the sector and the organisation of leasing arrangements, these companies had operating margins of more than 70 per cent and were generating a very healthy 24 per cent return on capital employed. Despite their profits, the ROSCOs have remained largely invisible. While the Conservative Government had set charges in a way that would encourage investment in new rolling stock, it established no regulation of the companies or ring-fencing of their finances to ensure that such investment actually took place.

Railtrack

Railtrack's revenues rose steadily after restructuring and privatisation (Table 5), with nearly all of its income derived from the track access fees paid by TOCs. The really striking feature is that passenger franchise receipts in 2001 were £2.5 billion, or 80 per cent of passenger revenues when BR ran both the infrastructure and passenger services (Table 1). This means that Railtrack was receiving nearly the same level of income to cover half its previous activities – managing the infrastructure – under the new regime as it did when it also ran the train services. With purchases and labour costs low, most of its remaining expenditure went on maintenance and renewals that were carried out by subcontractors. Until March 2001, Raltrack turned in operating profits and a rate of return on capital employed that pleased the City of London stock market. However, this apparently superior financial performance was not so much the product of new managerial efficiency as the result of track access charges set by the regulator, vastly increased govern-ment subsidies transmitted through the conduit of the TOCs and skimping on its main task: the maintenance, renewal and enhancement of the network.

Given the debt write-off and low tax burden, the largest claim on the surplus came from the investment programme. Total investment over the four years to March 2000 was £3.84 billion, after allowing for capital grants but before disposals and tax allowances. This was still less than either expected or required. According to the engineering consultants' report to the Office of the Rail Regulator, the Regulator could have reasonably expected network performance at the national level to show greater improvement (Booz Allen & Hamilton, 1999). Although Railtrack had failed to develop a comprehensive database of the condition of its assets, it nevertheless decided their life could be extended, thus allowing track quality to decline. While the lack of a con-sistent reporting methodology made it difficult to assess the condition of signalling and electrification assets, the Booz Allen & Hamilton report clearly stated that the rate of renewal of track and signalling assets would lead to a deterioration in long-term network performance. Finally, the consultants concluded, in a damning indictment of the government's claims about the benefits of the 'free market' and access to the capital markets, that:

Railtrack has no effective incentive to enhance and develop the network in an entre-preneurial manner [and] the performance regimes are structured to encourage focus on short run benefits rather than on long run considerations of asset condition and network capability. (Booz Allen & Hamilton, 1999: 21)

111

Table 5. Railtrack's revenues, subsidies, investment and financing charges (millions of pounds)

Year ending March	Operating subsidy to industry*	Total revenues: British Rail/Railtrack	Capital maintenance charges**	Operating profit before interest and tax	Capital investment	Interest charges	Debt	Debt to equity ratio	Return on equity
1976–1979 average	410	1,533	62		118	48			
1979–1987 average	873	2,819	341		198	75			
1988	804	3,384	529	108.5	343	66			
1989	606	3,395	369	107.0	424	31			
1990	586	3,485	750	−26.4	654	24			
1991	605	3,681	563	−46.4	772	54			
1992	798	3,948	527	−22.4	1,275	81			
1993	608	3,723	483	−94.3	1,488	96			
1994	545	3,645	543	23.0	1,128	121			
British Rail reconstituted as Railtrack, an infrastructure only company									
1995	2,060	2,275	1,272	305.0	401	141	2,192	1.48	0.21
1996	2,000	2,300	1,335	296.0	416	181	701	0.28	0.12
Railtrack privatised									
1997	2,200	2,437	1,371	339.0	484	39	1,009	0.38	0.13
1998	1,800	2,467	1,351	380.0	599	40	1,456	0.52	0.14
1999	1,500	2,573	1,328	471.0	1,653	81	2,384	0.74	0.13
2000	1,348	2,547	1,382	363.0	1,847	132	3,333	0.95	0.10
2001	1,214	2,746	937	−472.0	2,535	150	3,976	1.50	−0.18

Notes: Nominal values, unadjusted for inflation. * Operating subsidy paid to train operating companies towards the cost of the track access charges (paid to Railtrack) and the rolling stock companies for the lease of the trains. ** Railtrack's capital maintenance includes capitalised infrastructure expenditure.
Sources: British Rail, Railtrack, OPRAF and British Railways Board annual report and accounts.

The system of subcontracting engineering work led to little effective control as each party sought to place the responsibility onto others, so serving only to increase costs with little practical effect (Wolmar, 2001). By 2000, it was becoming clear that the cost of Railtrack's most important investment programme – the upgrading of the West Coast Mainline (WCML) – was spiralling out of control. Railtrack had already spent £2.1 billion on the project, originally costed at £2.5 billion, and the total cost was believed to be at least £10 billion. The project was more than two years behind schedule, necessitating compensation to the principal train operator on the route. Railtrack was therefore forced to increase its loans to finance the investment

At the same time, the failure to improve the infrastructure led to a decline in the 'health of the network' and was to have tragic consequences. A rail crash at Hatfield in October 2000, which killed four people and injured dozens more, was caused when a track, known to have been broken for months, derailed a London–Leeds express train travelling at 120 miles per hour. The crash replicated many of the features of two previous crashes that had highlighted the impact of fragmentation and privatisation on railway maintenance, and the fact that the tragedy could have been prevented if the recommendations of the Inquiry into the Clapham rail disaster in 1989 had been implemented.

The Hatfield crash caused such a political uproar that Railtrack could no longer pretend it was running a safe rail network. In danger of breaching its statutory duty to do so, it announced, without any warning, an emergency track replacement programme and more than 1,000 speed restrictions, plunging the network into chaos. This resulted in long delays and disruption to rail travel, compensation to the TOCs for late and cancelled services, a huge increase in Railtrack's maintenance costs of £644 million, a pre-tax loss of £472 million for 2000–2001, and the inability to raise funds from either its shareholders or the financial institutions.

Railtrack's financial collapse

By the end of 2000, Railtrack was in danger of breaching its banking covenants. With its very survival at stake, it appealed for additional public finance. In April, the government and regulators agreed to bring forward £1.5 billion of grant revenue from 2006 and the Rail Regulator accepted the need for an interim price review of access charges to consider additional post-Hatfield costs. Extra cash was made available to replace the broken rails and put in new safety systems.

Although never a financially viable or independent entity, and heavily dependent upon government subsidies, Railtrack continued to pay out dividends to its shareholders as though it were a normal private sector corporation. In May 2001, it announced dividend pay-outs of £124 million, despite making a loss and projecting a financial shortfall of £5 billion for the period to 2006 even after the April bailout. As its share price collapsed,

113

Railtrack was unable to raise cash from the Stock Exchange and requested another £2.6 billion in May and a further £1 billion in July. In September 2001, after announcing an interim dividend pay-out of £88 million, Railtrack asked for a further cash injection that could not have saved the company for long. The following month, the Secretary of State used his powers under the Railways Act 1993 to put the company into administration.

Conclusion

The failure of Railtrack, so soon after its privatisation, only serves to emphasise the problems of private ownership and finance in a capital-intensive industry. It was not an isolated incident: the government was later forced to step in when British Energy, the nuclear power generator, and the National Air Traffic Services partnership collapsed; it also had to rescue the Royal Armouries Museum and the Channel Tunnel Rail Link (CTRL).

While the government's case rested upon competition, efficiency and benefits to passengers, the real effect of privatisation was the redistribution of wealth to the new owners and providers of finance. Even this effect had more to do with the terms of the privatisation settlement, including regulation and the level of public subsidies, than any efficiency initiatives introduced by the industry itself. By focusing on concepts as ambiguous as 'efficiency' and 'customer services', the redistribution issue was made invisible in order to justify a deeply unpopular privatisation. The sale of the railways was part of a wider policy of privatisation that provided new sources of profit to replace those lost to British capitalism as a result of its economic decline in the face of globalisation. One-quarter of the top 100 corporations are now the direct result of privatising former state-owned industries, while many more have benefited from outsourcing by the 40 per cent or so of GDP that did not provide a source of profit.

What then are the likely implications of these conditions for the future of the rail industry? In October 2002, twelve months after Railtrack's collapse, the government handed over control to Railtrack's successor company, Network Rail, after paying out £1.3 billion in cash to Railtrack's parent company and ultimately to the shareholders. This included £500 million for the purchase of the company, £375 million for the purchase of the CTRL, and a cash injection of £351 million. With shareholders set to receive 252–260 pence per share, up from the expected 245–255 pence, compared with 280 pence when the company collapsed, they actually fared 25 per cent better than the Financial Times Stock Exchange (FTSE) 100 Index, owing to the 25 per cent slump in share prices since Railtrack's collapse and share suspension. The government is to provide Network Rail with £9 billion in grants and underwrite up to £21 billion in loans in order to reduce the company's interest charges. Network Rail has taken over Railtrack's £6.6 billion debts and taken out further loans of £3–4 billion in January 2003.

Since the Labour Government had ruled out re-nationalisation of the railways in its June 2001 election manifesto, the Secretary of State for Transport established a not-for-profit trust, made up of regulators, train operators, trades unions and passengers, which would raise finance in the bond markets, in order to run the rail network. This will lead to few fundamental changes in the operation of the industry. It will remain fragmented. It will still require huge subsidies to the TOCs to enable them to pay for the leasing of the rolling stock and for access charges to use the infrastructure, as well as capital grants to Network Rail for renewal of and investment in the infrastructure. Network Rail will continue to subcontract the maintenance, renewals and investment in the system. Despite the fact that the government will have no control over the company and its loans will therefore be scored as private sector debt, it is hard to disguise the fact that Network Rail is a *de facto* nationalised company where the beneficiaries are the banks, contractors, rolling stock companies and, to some extent, the train operators rather than the travelling public and the workforce.

A recent report estimated that Network Rail needed at least £50–53 billion up to 2010–2011 to cope with the projected freight and passenger growth and planned investment (James *et al.*, 2002). The Strategic Rail Authority will be forced to cut back on investment and drop many long-delayed schemes. The Rail Regulator has admitted that cost cutting, fare increases and line closures are under consideration. While branch lines account for 17 per cent of the 11,000-mile network, they take 64 per cent of the operating subsidy. Thus the new corporate structure is no more capable of resolving the financial problems of its predecessors – problems that are only set to intensify.

The source of the problem is not the management, regulation or lack of competition, but rather is systemic. There is insufficient value added, relative to the amount of capital invested in the industry, to meet all the numerous claims consequent upon private ownership – or indeed public ownership, if it seeks to emulate the financial dictates of private ownership. It can only be increased by raising fares and subsidies, which in the context of private finance, whether debt or equity, means subsidising the providers of finance. Privatisation, its particular form in the context of rail and its consequences, has increased the social, economic and political conflicts that were to some extent assuaged under public ownership.

The railways are a crucial component of a wider national and international transport system that is integral to economic and social development. As such, transport has come to be accepted by most people as a basic necessity and right for public ownership. This is understandable because transport is a capital-intensive industry, whose investment programme is not only expensive but entails a long lead time and an even longer payback period, if indeed it ever makes a return in purely commercial terms. While some routes or parts of the transport infrastructure may operate successfully on a commercial basis, not all – by their very nature – are able to generate revenues that cover the full cost of their supporting infrastructure and services. Policy-makers

115

have consequently viewed public expenditure for capital improvements and operating subsidies in transport systems – whether on sea, river, road, rail or in the air – as necessary for the overall productivity of the economy: investment that would not otherwise be made.

The experience of both publicly and privately owned regimes has been that it is impossible to provide efficient, safe, affordable and pollution-free public transport as long as it is a commodity to be sold for profit and run in the interests of the financial elite. What is required is a planned system of public transport, integrating all modes of transport – for both people and freight – that will end the over-dependence on private motor vehicles.

Note

1 An abridged version of the article was originally published in *Public Money & Management* 24(1) (2004).

References

Armstrong, P., Glyn, A. & Harrison, J. (1984). *Capitalism since World War II: The Making and Break up of the Great Boom*. London: Fontana Paperbacks.

Bagwell, P.S. (1968). *The Railway Clearing House in the British Economy*. London: Allen & Unwin.

Barnes, A. (1949). Memo to Cabinet Socialisation of Industries Committee, 23 May. In: *Treasury Correspondence and Papers: Socialised Industries (Control of Investment)*, T229/339. London: Public Records Office.

Bonavia, M.R. (1981a). *British Railway Policy between the Wars*. Manchester: Manchester University Press.

Bonavia, M.R. (1981b). *British Rail: The First 25 Years*. Newton Abbot: David & Charles.

Booz Allen & Hamilton (1999). *Railtrack's Performance in the Control Period 1995–2001: Report to the Office of Rail Regulator*. London: Booz Allen & Hamilton.

Department of Transport (DoT) (1992a). *New Opportunities for the Railways* (Cmnd. 2012). London: HMSO.

Department of Transport (DoT) (1992b). *The Franchising of Passenger Rail Services: A Consultation Paper*. London: Department of Transport.

Department of Transport (DoT) (1993). *Gaining Access to the Railway Network: A Consultation Paper*. London: Department of Transport.

European Conference of Ministers of Transport (1999). *Investment in Transport Infrastructure, 1985–1995*. Paris: Organization for Economic Cooperation and Development.

Gourvish, T.R. (1986). *British Railways, 1948–73: A Business History*. London: Cambridge University Press.

James, T. & Oxford Economic Research Associates (Oxera) (2002). *Funding the Railways: Looking Ahead I: Setting the Scene*. London: Rail Passengers Council.

Millward, R. (1999). 'State enterprise in Britain in the 20th century'. In: F. Amatori (ed), *The Rise and Fall of State-owned Enterprises in the Western World*. Cambridge: Cambridge University Press.

Moore, J. (1986a). 'Why Privatise?' Speech given to the annual conference of City of London stockbrokers Fielding, Newson Smith at Plasterer's Hall, London Wall on

1 November (HM Treasury press release 190/83). Reprinted in: J. Kay, C. Mayer & D. Thompson (eds), *Privatization and Regulation: The UK Experience*. London: Clarendon Press.

Moore, J. (1986b). 'The Success of Privatization'. Speech made when opening Hoare Govett Ltd's new City dealing rooms on 17 July (HM Treasury press release 107/85). Reprinted in part in: J. Kay, C. Mayer & D. Thompson (eds), *Privatization and Regulation: The UK Experience*. London: Clarendon Press.

National Audit Office (NAO) (1998). *Flotation of Railtrack*. London: HMSO.

Redwood, R. (1998). *Popular Capitalism*. London: Routledge.

Serpell, D. (1983). *Railway Finances* [the Serpell Report]. London: HMSO.

Wolmar, C. (2001). *Broken Rails: How Privatization Wrecked Britain's Railways*. London: Aurum Press.

11. Transport, Taxpayers and the Treasury[1]

DON RILEY

Land is a resource that is in limited supply. So also are resources like water, oil, air, aeroplane paths through the atmosphere and communication satellite orbits in near-space. The finite nature of these resources is reflected in the market price that individuals and organisations are prepared to pay for them. In what was originally a Viewpoint article for the journal Public Money & Management, *the author argues that the 'development gain' from installation of new transport infrastructure ought to be ploughed back into renewal of the infrastructure and improvement of public services.*

It is a common belief that regular increases in the price of land are generally a good thing for the economy, particularly for those fortunate enough to possess it. Now that a £1 million price-tag for a house in London is not uncommon, it is important to remember that the value of such a building may well be less than 25 per cent of the actual value of the land on which it stands. Moreover, the tendency for land values to increase is accentuated when people lose confidence in a government's promises to improve health services, education and transport infrastructure (despite voting for them to do just that) and so hedge their bets by moving to properties in 'good' locations. These are where the facilities are good for Billy's schooling, grandma's care and Dad's commuting journey to work.

The disadvantage is that when land values feed through into property price increases, we see headlines such as 'Key workers hit by house prices!' (*Daily Telegraph*, 21 August 2001). Just imagine the roar of censure if, instead of 'house prices', the headline had read 'drinking water prices' or 'petrol prices'. The utilities, or enterprises that provide such basic necessities – the 'infrastructure' of civilised living – are each also dealing with a limited resource, but competition keeps prices to a level that most people can afford. (In the case of oil firms, the prices are low enough to enable governments to add high taxes on top.)

Now let us examine the case of transport. In *Taken for a Ride* (Riley, 2001), I argued that the public is being misled by the Treasury into believing that, as

DON RILEY is Managing Director of DDS Ltd., London.

taxpayers, they have no alternative but to pay out of public funds for new railway and underground lines, or improvements to the existing system. Yet they do not, any more than if their tap water turned brown or low voltage dimmed their light bulbs: such facilities are fed by mega-expensive plants, mostly distant from London and even Britain, but situated on relatively cheap land. The difference to facilities which communities require to be local – such as schools, hospitals and transport (roads, undergrounds, trains or trams) – is that these require large amounts of land, the cost of which we keep driving up. This insane cycle is fuelled by the great myth that the benefits of transport provision cannot be captured in cash.

From my study of the property market in south London, I have been able to demonstrate how firms such as my own secured massive windfalls as a result of the extension to the Jubilee underground line. These gains are enough to have paid for the entire construction of the line. Even my small business received a bonanza greater than all the income and corporation tax that I (and my companies) have paid since I arrived in Britain from New Zealand nearly forty years ago. Building value increases that are based on solid refurbishment and expert craftsmanship are fine, but land value explosions are of no lasting benefit except to small numbers of individuals. In the twenty-first century, it is high time that politicians dropped their outdated dogmas towards revitalising our communities, large and small.

The 'property bubble' is a deceptive catch-all phrase for thousands of mini-bubbles generated by groups of commuters, people needing health care or families with children of school age who are, in reality, simply capitalising on what other unsuspecting taxpayers have invested in their patch through the various public expenditure programmes. The sane approach to providing infrastructure, especially transport infrastructure, is surely through 'recycling' or 'harvesting' the increases in land values so that every mini-bubble becomes sustainable, rather than bursting when failure of hope (and actual results) meets rising interest rates – as happened in 1990.

In city apartment blocks, all residents must pay for facilities they have available in common whether they use them or not. Their presence adds value to each flat, but the gym, crèche, infant school, caretaker's flat, lifts and parking space are paid for and maintained by shared capital from each flat. No one gets a free ride. This is analogous to the way common facilities of neighbourhoods (be they parishes, towns or boroughs) were originally provided. However, Parliament must first return responsibility to local democracy.

In the United States, land value gains are frequently captured through the creation of special tax districts. Elsewhere, privately run transport is often paid for by special levies during the building or refurbishment of a link. Whatever method is used, each offers a far simpler and more effective way forward than Public–Private Partnerships (PPPs) or the bond issues favoured by the London Mayor, Ken Livingstone. Politicians wrongly assume that services cannot be self-financing – that is why they say that taxpayers have to

119

provide subsidies and the services are 'public'. In the case of transport, those subsidies are enormous. Why can the rail system not pay for its own infrastructure, if it is an economically viable service? The answer is that it could do so, if it were allowed to retain the full value that it creates.

My conclusion is that Treasury meddling with the financing of transport should be shunted into history. Private Partnerships (PPs) work for us when we fly, boil a kettle or flush the loo: they could be made to work for transport. A policy of land-values-as-public-revenue would balance everyone's interests through the market and stimulate efficiency much better than endless subsidies backed by monitoring, performance regimes and targets. Under such a policy, I, like other swag collectors, would be queuing up to invest in the routes, trains and underground lines financed through a 'PP'.

Note

1 This article was originally published in *Public Money and Management* 21(4) (2001).

Reference

Riley, D. (2001). *Taken for a Ride*. Teddington: Centre for Land Policy Studies.

12. Past Abuses and Future Uses of Private Finance and Public–Private Partnerships in Transport[1]

STEPHEN GLAISTER

This chapter explains the origins of the Private Finance Initiative (PFI) and the way the policy has evolved under the present Labour administration into Public–Private Partnership (PPP). The author gives an assessment of the future prospects for the PFI/PPP in the transport sector. He believes that PPPs can make a considerable contribution towards efficient transport service delivery and this will be maximised if there is a better understanding of what the policies are seeking to achieve. Much of the action in the immediate future in transport PPPs will be with the local authorities, including the new Greater London Authority.

The idea of using the private sector to help with provision of public services is not new. National and local governments have always procured goods and services, under contract, from the private sector. The development in the United Kingdom of what we have come to know as the 'Private Finance Initiative' (PFI) was a process of adjusting the balance between in-house and private-sector provision. It began in 1981, when the National Economic Development Council believed a higher level of investment might benefit the economy and was worried that the system of External Financing Limits was hampering investment by nationalised industries. The policy has continued to evolve and, in its latest incarnation under the present Labour administration, has become known as Public–Private Partnership (PPP) (the history is recounted in Glaister *et al.*, 1998a: Chapter 8).

In practice, 'evolution' has meant, among other things, a gradual changing of the rules about what is and what is not allowable. In the 1980s and 1990s, the general trend has been in the direction of allowing market forces to determine outcomes, in place of administrative planning. In many cases, this has involved senior ministers giving firm redirection to the Treasury, whose job it is to implement current policies. These then become codified as the current 'Treasury rules'.

STEPHEN GLAISTER CBE is Professor of Transport and Infrastructure at Imperial College, London. He was a non-executive director of London Regional Transport from 1984 to 1993.

There has been a natural tendency for the Treasury to oppose these changes since they have implied a loss of their control over matters they controlled previously, usually in accordance with macroeconomic policy. A consequence of this long-running battle within Whitehall has been confusion among politicians, the general public and the private sector itself concerning what the PFI/PPP is all about and what it can and cannot realistically be expected to achieve. Much has been achieved, but the private sector has been led to waste resources evaluating abortive projects, engaging in competitive bidding and lobbying on projects that never came to anything or could have been executed at lower cost with less wasteful procedures. Also, blindness to commercial realities has led to false expectations of action on the part of the public.

Transport schemes have been at the centre of the aspirations of both the Conservative and Labour Governments for the PFI/PPP. This chapter reviews the experience and gives an assessment of the future prospects in the transport sector.

The motives behind PFI/PPP

There have been several, distinct policy objectives for PFI/PPP.

Public procurement

Much of what is now referred to as PFI/PPP is quite simply best-practice procurement of goods and services from private-sector providers. It is no more than clarity in specification of requirements, drafting of enforceable contracts with sensible incentives in them, and transparent and effective competition for their award. Examples are procurement of highway construction services, laundry services by hospitals, refuse collection and other competitive tendering exercises by local authorities, and the privatisation (not deregulation) of all of London bus service provision (reviewed in Kennedy *et al.*, 1995). Cost reduction is expected and often achieved, through specification of outputs to be delivered rather than the detailed specification of how they are to be produced, and through more efficient management of private- rather than public-sector activity in any or all of the construction, operation, maintenance and renewal.

A more subtle gain has come from integration of design with project execution and maintenance. This aligns the incentives on those responsible for the initial design and construction with those who have to manage and pay for operation and maintenance. In principle, this is an important remedy for the short-termism, endemic in capital-constrained budgeting by public authorities, which otherwise encourages cheap initial capital expenditures without due regard for the consequential adverse implications for the whole-life project costs. This was a consideration in the Northern Line trains procurement by London Underground and in the Design, Build, Finance and Operate (DBFO) contracts that have been used for some road schemes in the United Kingdom.

Risk transfer

It has always been recognised that a transfer of some risk to the private-sector provider is essential in order to create incentives to behave efficiently. Cautionary tales are to be found in some notorious open-ended cost-plus contracts for defence equipment that gave the supplier no incentive to be prudent or efficient. On occasion, there have been at least two misconceptions concerning risk. First, that transfer of risk is one of the primary purposes behind the PFI/PPP: an end in itself. Second, that if the private sector is to be involved then *all* risk must be transferred to it – with the consequence in some cases that the private sector has been unwilling to be involved at a cost of capital that was acceptable to the public sector.

Government now accepts that complete risk transfer may not be desirable. Sensible criteria for risk allocation include: creation of incentives on the private sector to behave efficiently; to maximise the private sector's ability to mitigate the costs of the possible future outcomes; and to place the remaining risks where the social costs of bearing them are least. Governments can bear some risks at less cost than the private sector because of their greater opportunities for risk spreading and risk pooling. This may be reflected in a lower cost of borrowing for the public sector, which may, in turn, be a consideration to set against efficiency gains from private-sector involvement. Note that sensible risk allocation may succeed in reducing overall exposure to risk, but a central issue is how best to handle irreducible risks – some of which may be straight-forward commercial risks, but some may be regulatory, policy or political risks.

The PFI/PPP process may make explicit risks that were previously unseen, not analyzed and not accounted for as part of the public sector. This transparency is a benefit though it may appear that the risks are being increased when, in fact, they are only being made more visible. For instance, traffic volume risk is inevitably considerable in a major road project and this will show up in the bids for privately financed schemes. Yet the taxpayer will remain blissfully unaware of the wastage that has occurred when a road conventionally procured within the public sector turns out to have been built with excessive capacity.

The market guide

Advocates of reducing the role of the public sector see advantage in using market tests of economic viability in place of bureaucratic planning. This is certainly a powerful argument where capital rationing causes governments

123

to under-invest in infrastructure projects for which there would be sufficient demand to render them *commercially* viable. Such advocates would also argue that to undertake projects that are a long way from being commercially viable would be to risk wasting national resources. In transport, as with other public goods and services, these arguments have some force, but they are often over-simplistic.

There are the familiar arguments for distinguishing between financial performance and economic benefit because of externalities like congestion and pollution. There are also conflicts between the desire to create commercially viable public infrastructure projects so that they can be funded at no cost to the taxpayer, and efficient use of that infrastructure from the public interest point of view. To make a new bridge commercially viable, the private owner must be assured of the right to charge tolls, yielding operating profits that can be used to fund the debt. These tolls may well be higher than the long-run avoidable costs that the public interest would require to be recovered, which implies inefficiently low rates of usage of a valuable facility. This is one of the classical arguments against using the private sector to *fund* public infrastructure (as distinct from *financing* it or being contracted to do the work).

Transparency

There have been several major benefits from PFI/PPP that are not always thought of as being part of the original intention. First, once a contract has been signed it becomes harder for the political authorities to meddle in the detail for reasons of expediency, unless they are willing to renegotiate. This does not preclude changes – which may be perfectly sensible – but it does make the cost of such action transparent. In turn, this should give the commissioning authority greater incentives to be clear about what it wants from the start and to take the trouble to get the contracts 'right'. It has been claimed that the British construction industry has developed a technique of bidding low in order to secure initial contracts in the expectation of making a profitable return through the claims lodged in respect of variations to the specifications during the project execution. The Jubilee Line Extension for London Underground may well prove to be an example of this.

Second, the PFI/PPP has, for the first time, created a mechanism whereby central government can commit firmly and credibly to a long-term spending programme. For instance, in the past, central government departments were never able to know their budgets for more than three years ahead at most, and real certainty only applied for one year ahead. Hence they were unable to make firm promises of the sizes of long-term capital expenditure programmes. The contracts under PFI/PPP are legally binding and can last decades. This has brought important stability to parts of the roads programme and the state funding of the passenger railway through the passenger franchise contracts.

124

Third, the process generates publicly auditable measures of quality of service delivery, enforceable by contract. Therefore proper records have to be kept to a standard that will demonstrate the facts when financial penalties are to be levied for under-performance. Litigation may occur. This has proved to be an important force for better performance – in some cases records were simply not kept in the past. This was one of the reasons that the service quality of buses in London improved substantially with the introduction of route tendering, even though unit costs were being rapidly reduced. Similarly, the volume and detail of publicly available data on the quality of passenger train services has increased under rail privatisation.

Misuses of the PFI/PPP

There have been several instances of the PFI/PPP being misused or even abused.

Evasion of spending controls

On occasion, PFI/PPP has been used as a device by a part of the government to evade its own spending controls. In the United Kingdom, we have highly centralised and prescriptive controls over spending by public bodies, including all spending by local authorities. The Treasury Rules have tended to be expressed in terms of limits on capital and revenue spending in the coming year or three years. If a PFI/PPP project can be constructed that converts an initial lump-sum payment into a fee to be paid over a number of decades, then more physical work can be purchased within the current annual budget limit – at the expense of committing the budgets of future administrations. The Treasury Rules are intended to control the amount of physical work being purchased in the interests of macroeconomic policy. So there is a clear conflict between the intent of these rules and the use of the PFI/PPP. The PFI/PPP has also created a new problem for the public accounts constructed on the 'pay-as-you-go' basis that seeks to control year-by-year outlays (see Treasury Committee, 1995). Examples of this phenomenon may include the expansion of the trunk road network under the PFI and the shadow tolling regime in the mid-1990s, and the Labour Government's PPP to fund catch-up investment in the London Underground.

Capture by special interests

The availability of funds under PFI/PPP in times of public expenditure constraint can create a risk of distortion of properly designed strategic public expenditure plans through pressure from special interests. A salutary example of this was the extension of the Jubilee Line in London. This scheme was never a part of a strategic plan for rail investment: it was not mentioned in the Central London Rail Study of 1989 that was jointly carried out by the government, British Rail and London Transport. Yet is has been the only major scheme to be constructed in London since then, even though its benefits were always estimated to be less than the costs. Meanwhile, two other rail schemes for London – CrossRail and the Chelsea–Hackney Line – were estimated to yield net economic benefits and were formally approved by the government. Yet they were never funded. This outcome was influenced by the fact that the private redevelopers of the major site at Canary Wharf in East London offered a contribution of £400 million (cash, undiscounted and over a period of years) towards a scheme that, at that time (1989), was estimated to have a present value cost of £1,000 million. The real value of this contribution will turn out to have been about 7 per cent of the out-turn cost of about £3,300 million, with the state paying the difference. It would be extremely hard to justify this kind of public expenditure as any part of a properly designed strategic transport plan for London, and it would undoubtedly never have happened without the influence of those making the private contribution.

A mechanism to obfuscate the public cost of investment decisions

On occasion the complexity and secrecy of PFI/PPP deals may have created the opportunity for hiding items of public spending from proper scrutiny. In the case of privately financed roads, government determination to protect the 'commercial confidentiality' of contracts has made scrutiny of value for money difficult.

Railtrack, a private company, was involved in solving the political problem of how to fund the inherently uncommercial Channel Tunnel Rail Link. The first of the two phases, now completed, was relatively straight-forward in both funding and engineering terms. Railtrack was able to commit funding with the help of a government guarantee of minimum revenues. There was also some manipulation of the cost of capital for the phase by government underwriting of the debt. On the day of the announcement of the funding plan for Phase One, and on several occasions subsequently, Railtrack threatened that it would only be able to complete the funding of Phase Two if it was granted a relaxation of the regulatory regime for the existing railway. The intention appeared to be to exploit the government's strong commitment to complete this project, in order to gain sanction for higher profits on the existing railway and thus cross-subsidise Phase Two, an uncommercial venture.

A smoke screen for inaction

In some cases, the appeal to the virtues of the PFI/PPP has had the effect – intended or not – of obscuring government inaction. In the case of CrossRail, it is hard to avoid the conclusion that the PFI hid the fact that the government was failing to deliver on a commitment to build it. It was appraised as a good scheme in terms of benefits in relation to costs, even though it was never going to be commercially viable – roughly speaking the incremental revenues would be adequate to cover the incremental running costs, leaving little contribution towards funding the capital costs. At various points in the early 1990s, the government first said it gave approval, then said it gave approval if it could be entirely funded by the private sector, and then if the capital could be half-funded by the private sector. This kind of 'market test' is not necessarily appropriate in the context of urban infrastructure because of scale effects, inability to appropriate benefits as revenues through price discrimination (particularly because of uniform pricing schemes like the Travelcard) and externalities. Yet the consequence was that the scheme was never started, though over £150 million was spent on preparatory work. This outcome may have pleased the Treasury – if they felt that there were higher priorities for limited public funds, then it was proper for them to take this decision – but government as a whole hid the decision from an expectant public through the appeal to the PFI.

Financing, not funding

Where projects such as shadow-tolled roads and prisons generate no cash revenues from users, they are fundamentally not commercially viable in the normal sense of user-payments covering costs. They can be made into profitable prospects for the private sector only by virtue of revenues paid by local or central government. PFI/PPP cannot, in itself, provide funding for such projects. It is self-evident that the funding must come from taxpayers. However, in the case of revenue-earning schemes people often seem to speak as if PFI/PPP can work magic. They appear to hope that a project that is not commercially viable, and that the public sector is unwilling to support, can be taken off the public sector's hands through PFI/PPP.

Only if the private sector can somehow generate sufficient revenue beyond the public sector, or reduce costs sufficiently, will this be true. In many cases, a project that is non-viable in one sector will be non-viable in the other; in which case it can come about only if there is some form of public subvention. This is the fundamental reality that was eventually conceded when several forms of state support were granted in order to allow Phase One of the Channel Tunnel Rail Link to commence. Similar concessions have now been made to enable Phase Two to be built.

The Private Finance Initiative is just what is says – financing – a way of converting between lump-sum capital payments and delayed cash flows, for a rate of return. The funding has to be found by one taxpayer or another in the end.

127

Table 1. Comprehensive spending review (transport) (millions of pounds)

	1998–1999 budget	1999–2000 plans	2000–2001 plans	2001–2002 plans
Motorways and trunk roads	1,350	1,407	1,536	1,580
Railways (domestic and international)	1,758	1,569	1,490	1,630
Local transport	523	598	695	987
Support for local buses	262	313	355	425
Transport programmes in London	599	436	128	157
Other transport	186	227	266	261
Total	4,678	4,550	4,470	5,040

The future of PFI/PPP in transport

Few doubt that the PFI/PPP will have an important role to play in the future. This section discusses which areas of the transport scene in the United Kingdom are likely to be the most active over the next few years. Table 1 shows parts of the outcome of the July 1998 Comprehensive Spending Review (Her Majesty's Treasury, 1998). This gives an authoritative overview of the government's intentions over the next few years.

Trunk roads and motorways

There is little in current policy that is going to prevent continuation of the growth in road traffic more or less in line with the growth in real incomes. Just to stop the growth would require an increase in fuel prices to the consumer of well over 10 per cent compound per annum, and therefore much more rapid increases in fuel (or other) taxation than is apparently regarded as politically feasible at present. The introduction of urban congestion charging outside London – if, and when, it happens – would alleviate the situation in the larger town centres, but it will do little for congestion in the suburbs and on longer distance routes. There are many communities that are pressing for 'their' by-pass and this pressure will increase. While it is virtually certain that substantial new trunk road capacity will eventually be built, it is unlikely that there will be any more toll-roads similar to the Birmingham Northern Relief Road, opened in November 2003. Other forms of PFI/PPP may be used for road schemes, involving less transfer of risk.

Railways

The figures for railways in Table 1 are surprising in the context of current policy on transferring road passenger and freight traffic from road to rail.

The fall comes about because of the rapid reduction in payments to the train operating companies (TOCs) under their contracts: between 1997–1998 and 2003–2004 they fell from £1,800 million to £660 million. The government has chosen not to plough these savings back into the railways. At the same time, there is severe pressure on rail capacity and, if transport policy aspirations are to be met, there will have to be more investment. Much of this investment will be commercially non-viable, so it will rely on new subsidy coming from somewhere – either from the Passenger Transport Authorities or from the proposed Strategic Rail Authority (for a fuller discussion, see Glaister, 1999). As in the case of motorways and trunk roads, the prospects are unexciting in the official financial projections, but the conflicting demands of transport policies may cause this to change.

Local transport

Local transport and local buses are both healthy growth areas: over 60 per cent growth in real terms in planned expenditure over the years covered by Table 1. This is consistent with the broader move to devolve powers to regional and local authorities, though some of the money is to contribute towards recovering a backlog of local highway maintenance. It is plain that there will be an expanded role for the local bus. This will involve physical works to highways, interchanges and other facilities as well as direct subsidies to the capital and operating costs of bus services. There will be many new opportunities here for PFI/PPP schemes with local authorities. Although some local authorities have been keen to build tramways for many years, they are a poor investment compared with cheaper, bus-based solutions. This has been recognised by the government (DETR, 1998a). A difficulty is that there will be a large number of relatively small schemes, which makes the administrative costs of the PFI/PPP prohibitive for the private sector if they are each treated as one-off schemes. Therewfore, there will be a renewed incentive to develop templates, bundles and portfolios of schemes.

London

Although the physical infrastructure, including the transport infrastructure, has been significantly under-invested in recent decades, this could change: the local population has high expectations of the newly created Greater London Authority.

Primary duties for the Mayor, who took office for the first time in May 2000, will be to create a Strategic Transport Plan and to approve the boroughs' own transport plans. However, formally speaking, the legislation gives limited discretion to the new Authority about how to spend its income. The volume of expenditure on transport, funded either by the Exchequer or by the Mayor, will be limited. The contracts for the provision of the commuter railway

129

services with the TOCs in the London area show a fall from £472 million in 1997–1998 to £21 million in 2003–2004. The Mayor will have the power to commission new activity *via* the Strategic Rail Authority, but only if he or she provides the corresponding funding. The plans for the PPP for the London Underground are dealt with elsewhere in this volume. The London bus system has been close to breaking even for some years. The only increased Exchequer funding is to be to the boroughs for road maintenance and infrastructure alterations such as bus priority schemes.

It seems that the Mayor will only be able to deliver on any promises that imply substantial increases in expenditure on transport by diverting funds granted for some other purpose (such as the police) or by creating new sources of funds drawn from the local economy. Powers were included in the London Government Act for the Mayor to introduce congestion charging and/or a workplace parking levy and a charging scheme has already been successfully introduced. It has become generally accepted that this will be an important source of independent income available to the Greater London Authority. The private sector has played an important part in providing the equipment and systems for administration and enforcement of such schemes. It has even been suggested (in an Edinburgh context) that, under a PPP, the private sector could be entirely responsible for a congestion charging scheme, including the employment of the enforcement officers. The enforcement and administration systems for the London Scheme are large and sophisticated, and electronic systems will be introduced onto vehicles in due course. This could become an extremely important new field for PFI/PPP, bearing in mind that whatever is adopted in London will be highly influential in what is ultimately adopted in the rest of the United Kingdom and around the world.

The London Underground PPP

This London Underground PPP is important, if only because of its size: the rejuvenation and maintenance of the existing Underground will cost of the order of £7 billion over the next 15 years. The particular PPP scheme announced by the government in March 1998 presents immense technical and political difficulties (Glaister *et al.* 1998b, 1999). The government saw it as vital to have the infrastructure contracts completed before the Mayor took power. The normal private sector cost savings have been compromised by assurances on terms and conditions given to all the present London Underground employees. There are worries about risks on the profit forecasts that are supposed to fund the payments under the PPP. More fundamentally, the concept of binding contracts concerning the centrepiece of any Mayor's transport strategy being fixed before he or she takes power is at odds with the democratic principles the new London government is supposed to represent.

130

Despite their complexity, the government's plans for the PPP were silent on how any new infrastructure is to be funded and financed. If the Mayor wishes to build new lines or increase capacity at stations, he or she will have to find the funds and somehow negotiate for the work to be executed in a way that can be fitted into the existing contractual regime. The considerable capital and maintenance expenditure on the London Underground over the next few decades (the £7 billion plus the value of any new schemes) will be administered by the new Greater London Authority. Partnerships with the private sector will undoubtedly be an important part of providing the services, even though it may not be under the PPP as currently envisaged. There may be important opportunities for the private sector to become involved in developing or redesigning the PFI/PPP for the London Underground.

New York has used commercial partnerships between the municipal authorities and the financial sector highly successfully to fund the rebuilding of a great deal of public transport and other infrastructure. The problems could be solved in London in a similar way, but only if there is:

- A clear statement of the Treasury's position and a credible commitment to a predictable level of grant.
- Creation of the institutional capacity to issue bonds backed by secure sources of income, some of which may be drawn from the local economy.
- A long-term investment planning regime.

If these requirements were met, then debt could be created and traded, and private finance would be in a genuine partnership with national and local government.

Regulation of London Underground

A central issue is the extent to which one can tie everything up in a long-term, binding contract. If one can, then an independent arbitrator and the courts could be used to settle disputes. They would make legalistic interpretations of what the contracts do and do not say and their implications, but there are complications, which in this case include:

- The long time scale of the contracts (thirty years) against a local economy that changes quickly.
- The existence of shared facilities.
- The public service characteristics of the 'output' at issue, together with direct and legitimate political responsibilities that will themselves change in nature quite frequently.
- The difficulty of defining and measuring the several dimensions of service quality with sufficient precision to be enforced by contract alone.
- The possible exposure of the London Underground business to the provisions of the Competition Act 1998 where it might be thought better to deal with a specialist regulator.

These features – and others – mean that it will not be sensible to attempt to write fully determinate contracts. For instance, there must be provision for periodic review of charges to allow investors a 'reasonable' return, and variation of duties and liabilities under the agreements.

As soon as discretion has to be exercised against a set of public interest criteria, then this is not the normal job of an independent arbitrator – it is economic regulation. It is an option to place these responsibilities with Transport for London or the Assembly with London Underground, but it is unlikely that this would be acceptable since they will themselves be parties to the contract with commercial interests worth billions of pounds. The presence of an *independent* regulator, bound by powers and duties set out in legislation *in advance*, may reduce the regulatory risks perceived by the private sector and thereby easing the way to the creation of the new arrangements (this issue is discussed further in Glaister *et al.*, 1999).

Best value

There is a new issue that those working on PPPs with local authorities will need to give attention: the introduction of the new 'best value' regime under the Local Government Act 1999. This will apply to all local authorities (and Transport for London is explicitly mentioned as one of the 'best value authorities') and so will have ramifications for PFI/PPP schemes for local authority clients throughout England and Wales. Under these proposals a best value authority will have to:

- Make arrangements to secure continuous improvement in local services.
- Consult representatives of local taxpayers.
- Publish an annual best value performance plan.
- Conduct reviews to the Secretary of State's specification and timetable.
- Audit achievement of the plans by authority's auditor, subject to Audit Commission inspection of compliance.

The Secretary of State may issue guidance and may specify performance standards and indicators, having regard to the recommendations of the Audit Commission.

In respect of the transport activities under the PFI/PPP, this could become an additional layer of regulation. For instance, where Passenger Transport Authorities (PTA) co-operate with the Strategic Rail Authority (SRA) in the provision of local rail services, there will be several sets of performance standards: those specified by the PTA and/or the SRA; the consumer protection requirements of the Rail Regulator; Passenger Charter standards; those set out in the performance regimes between the TOCs and Network Rail; and now the best value standards.

Competition Act 1998

The Competition Act 1998 may create a further complication in attracting private finance into transport. The structure of the privatised rail industry was fundamentally designed to create an industry driven through market forces, albeit with modification of price signals through twin regulatory regimes. This is also true of the deregulated bus industry. The Competition Act – through prohibition of anti-competitive behaviour and abuse of dominant position – clarifies the role that competitive forces are supposed to have in determining market outcomes. Unlike the old legislation, dominant undertakings will be subject to a system of law that is of direct and immediate effect. Any breach will render that undertaking liable to a fine.

Yet the concepts behind an 'Integrated Transport Policy' are essentially interventionist: attempting to achieve things that the market would not deliver on its own. There may be a fundamental conflict here. Some of the issues that may arise are:

- The acceptability of local dominance of local bus and rail markets by single commercial interests, in the interests of 'integration'. In particular, the concept behind Quality Partnerships between local authorities and bus operators involves exclusive rights to operate services. Furthermore, the same private companies will be providing both bus and rail services for some PTAs.
- The extent to which the Competition Act will constrain the use of integrated fare agreements intended to facilitate execution of unremunerative universal service obligations, through preventing competition so as to allow cross-subsidy. This is a return to an old debate concerning the use of quantity licensing to achieve cross-subsidy, swept away in the 1985 and 1993 Acts.
- To what extent are through-ticketing and other 'network benefits' consistent with the Competition Act?

Summary: The opportunities

Motorways and trunk roads do not appear to be promising prospects for PFI/PPP deals until, inevitably, fashion in transport policy changes to be more favourable to them. Railways are in favour with the government, but current spending plans do not match the aspirations – which would imply considerable expansion of rail capacity. Congestion charging and workplace parking charges may soon be introduced by the bigger local authorities, which will generate business in providing hardware and systems. Local authority expenditures on road maintenance, bus priorities, interchanges, other bus infrastructure and bus services (but not trams) will increase. It will be necessary to develop ways of bundling small PPP tasks in order to contain set-up costs. There may be fresh opportunities where local authorities have recently been granted more freedom to invest in their airports.

In London there will also be increased spending on traffic management – 'red routes', bus priorities and interchanges. The London Underground renewal will be a major opportunity, but the present proposal is unlikely to achieve very much. If the Mayor can secure discretion to issue debt and have a proper long-term capital plan for transport infrastructure in London, then there may be investment in heavy rail in London. Schemes include station capacity enhancements, CrossRail, the Chelsea–Hackney Line and Thameslink 2000.

The contribution that PFI/PPP can make towards efficient transport service delivery will be maximised if there is a better understanding of what the policies are seeking to achieve and, particularly, a more realistic appreciation that they cannot supplant the responsibility that the state has to provide the funding for those unremunerative activities it wishes to procure. The deal for the first phase of the Channel Tunnel Rail Link – though imperfect – sets important and welcome precedents.

Much of the action in the immediate future will be with the local authorities, including the new Greater London Authority. If more funding and discretion over capital budgeting is successfully devolved to them, then there is the prospect of more balanced and more mutually beneficial partnerships developing, in which the local authorities and the private sector each concentrates on what it does best: the local authorities giving policy direction, specifying what is needed, monitoring quality and value for money, and providing funding; and the private sector producing efficiently what is required, handling financial and management risks, and providing finance.

Note

1 This article was originally published in *Public Money & Management* 19(3) (1993).

References

Department of the Environment, Transport and the Regions (DETR) (1998a). Press notice, 3 December. London: DETR.

Department of the Environment, Transport and the Regions (DETR) (1998b). *Breaking the Logjam*. London: DETR.

Glaister, S. (1999). *What New Strategy for the Railways?* London: IEA and London Business School.

Glaister, S., Burnham, J., Stevens, H. & Travers, T. (1998a). *Transport Policy in Britain*. Basingstoke: Macmillan.

Glaister, S., Scanlon, R. & Travers, T. (1998b). *A Fourth Way for the London Underground*. London: Greater London Group, London School of Economics.

Glaister, S., Scanlon, R. & Travers, T. (1999). *The Way Out: An Alternative Approach to the Future of the Underground* (Discussion paper 1). London: London School of Economics.

Her Majesty's Treasury (1998). *Comprehensive Spending Review*. London: HMSO.

Kennedy, D., Glaister, S. & Travers, T. (1995). *London Bus Tendering*. London: Greater London Group, London School of Economics.

Treasury Committee, House of Commons (1996). *The Private Finance Initiative: Sixth Report, 1995–96* (HC146). London: HMSO.

13. Realising the New Opportunity for the Railways[1]

TONY BOLDEN AND REG HARMAN

Britain's railway system has a pivotal role in the implementation of the government's transport policies, which include effective integration with land-use development planning. A higher and more sustained proportion of public funds has already been allocated in order to achieve this role. The structure of the railway industry needs to take these policies into account. The new structure should also reflect general trends in European transport and railway policies, and its operation must be underpinned by a cohesive national system of management training and skill development.

The placing of Railtrack into administration on 7 October 2001 could be seen as an event waiting to happen. The railway industry may not have wished for further restructuring, yet it offered scope to set aright the fractious nature that the industry was portraying of itself. It also created one more opportunity for the industry to align itself more solidly with the needs of the government's transport and land-use planning policies. Indeed, the anguish caused by privatisation and the fragmentation of the industry in recent times has led to many calls for change, including those from Chris Green in his Sir Robert Reid Lecture to the Institute of Logistics and Transport (Green, 2001), Roger Ford (2001) in his articles in *Modern Railways* and Christian Wolmar (2001) in his book *Broken Rails*. The publication of the Strategic Rail Authority's (SRA) Strategic Plan in January 2002 (SRA, 2002) renewed public debate, as did subsequent events, including the SRA's latest and more downbeat Strategic Plan (SRA, 2003), published in January 2003.

This chapter offers a view of what form restructuring might take. It is evident, however, that such restructuring needs to adhere to certain key principles if the railway system is to play an effective role in achieving the government's transport policy aims. It must embrace:

TONY BOLDEN is now an independent consultant, having worked for many years in senior management positions for local and regional government bodies. He is a member of the Royal Town Planning Institute (RTPI) and the Institute of Logistics and Transport (ILT), and helps to advise them on transport policy and planning matters. REG HARMAN is an independent consultant in transport policy and practice and in urban and regional planning. His main interests lie in railway strategy, the links between transport and development planning, and comparative studies of European transport.

- The direction and implementation of the government's policies through its delivery of its part of the 10-year transport plan.
- Real integration with development planning.
- The major role that regional organisations and local authorities are expected to play.

Public policy and public funding

Transport 2010: The 10-year Plan (DETR, 2000a) heralded a major boost in funding for transport. The package of £180 billion in cash terms was designed to meet government policy aims set out in the 1998 White Paper *A New Deal for Transport: Better for Everyone* (DETR, 1998), including the reduction of congestion and pollution, better integration, and a wider choice for safe and reliable travel. The railways' share of that package was one-third, some £60 billion, made up of about £30 billion each from private and public sources. This indicated the importance that the government ostensibly places on railways in the overall picture. It also indicates that the railway system, in receiving such large amounts of public funding, must seek to implement wholeheartedly those public policies against which the funding is awarded. The £60 billion allocated to upgrade and expand the railway network is intended to enable growth of 50 per cent in passengers and 80 per cent in goods; both with much higher quality of services, as well as frequency and capacity.

The White Paper stressed the importance of integration between transport and other policy areas: notably land-use (spatial) planning. The 'daughter' documents that followed the White Paper addressed the policy and practice needs for particular elements of transport, but they also included revisions to several Planning Policy Guidance Notes (PPGs). These set out clear guidance on regional planning, development plans, housing, and especially the links between planning and transport: particularly important is the guidance on transport related to location and development planning, set out in PPG13 *Transport* (DETR, 2001; see also DETR 2000b). The report of the Urban Task Force (1999), chaired by Lord Rogers, picked out transport as a key element for regeneration of the United Kingdom's cities and conurbations to provide a high-quality living and working environment.

Achievement of the government's transport policies thus relies on action in the spatial planning field at all levels, as much as within the various fields of transport. What is common to both is that the major part of the implementation lies with local authorities, who in turn should work within guiding frameworks set up by devolved administrations in Scotland and Wales and the regional organisations in England. This includes the national strategies produced by the Scottish Parliament and Welsh Assembly; the regional plans produced by Regional Planning Assemblies, in association with Regional Development Agencies in England that incorporate Regional Transport Strategies; and the Local Transport Plans (LTPs) produced by Passenger

Transport Executives (PTEs) and local (transport) authorities in England and Wales, and equivalent policy documents in London and Scotland, all of which are required to coordinate with the development plans for the area.

There are some good working relationships between railway companies and local authorities, usually for specific projects; but, overall, the railway industry has maintained a distant and insular attitude towards local authorities and to both transport and spatial planning. The Strategic Rail Authority's Strategic Agenda (SRA, 2001a), its Strategic Plans (SRA, 2002, 2003), and the Network Management Statement 2001 produced by the erstwhile Railtrack (Railtrack, 2001) all mention regional planning in passing – they refer to the LTPs and some PTE initiatives, but do not appear to recognise the role of development planning at regional and local level. The Business Plan issued by Network Rail (2003) merely refers to 'regional and local agencies' without further definition. If anything, the restructuring under the Railways Act 1993 led to the many players in the industry spending more time in discussion and negotiation with other parts of the industry than in paying attention to the needs of outside bodies.

The railway industry needs to focus far more heavily on development planning, and on the role of regional and local authorities, for two principal reasons:

- Great Britain is a densely occupied country with a very large population, a high proportion living in urban areas. Development has spread out from the major cities, at lower densities, in parallel to far more demand for flexible movement enabled by the motor car. At the same time, the cities have remained a focus for many key activities. Sustaining this now, through appropriate development, including higher densities and appropriate locations, forms an essential part of government policy. Passenger rail travel has a huge potential for solving some of the critical problems of urban and regional development, and the national rail system should be geared to addressing this.
- Many existing suburban and regional railway stations are now badly sited in relation to residential areas or major destinations (offices, shops, health and education premises, main leisure venues). Integration of other transport modes to provide a convenient link to a wider catchment in the area is very poor in Great Britain; this applies to bus services and also to footways and cycleways. Whatever initiatives the railway industry may take to increase passenger numbers, there is no substitute for having far greater numbers of people living within close access to a railway station or denser groups of facilities located around it – or both.

Neither issue seems to be of fundamental importance to the government or to the railway industry. Yet both should be. Railway managers should be giving priority to something that puts them in a more competitive position in the travel market and offers them the chance of much greater revenue. The government should be interested because they are putting so much public money into the railway network, and they should be seeking a real return out of it in terms of a greater contribution to its aims for improved quality of life. They may also wish to provide the railway industry with access to more revenue so that they are in a position to fund continuing enhancements.

In November 2001, the SRA published *Land Use Planning and the SRA* (SRA, 2001b) as two complementary volumes: a policy statement and a guide for planning authority practitioners. These are concise and well focused, but have some limitations. For example, the SRA would not expect to be consulted on development plans, except over matters with specific implications for railway property or activities; and it would object to developments proposed on lines already congested. Yet it offers no vision of the railway industry seeking to play a much-expanded role in the nation. So does what seems like a useful step forward actually herald a real change in the SRA's approach?

In February 2003, the Deputy Prime Minister John Prescott published *Sustainable Communities* (Prescott, 2003). This set out a £22 billion strategy for housing development across England, with a major emphasis on promoting the development of communities as a whole and providing more affordable housing for key workers. The strategy's overall balance is driven by the increasing popularity of the south-east of England; so it aims at more residential development in four main areas – the Thames Gateway, Ashford, Stansted and Milton Keynes – while allocating funds for demolition and redevelopment in older, low value housing areas in the Midlands and the North. However, despite the implications for railways, it contains little more than passing reference to any transport implications. Furthermore, the SRA claims that it has no funds to provide enhanced rail access for the proposed development areas.

The shape of the railway system

There is one other and perhaps deeper principle that comes out of the government's transport policy: the significance of current land-use development patterns and of changes in railway operating over the years, especially for passenger travel. At present, we still envisage the railway system as providing a number of discrete passenger service types, whose origins go back to the so-called 'golden days' of railways. (For a truer picture of railway operations in that era, see Ahrons, 1951–1954.) Now we have:

- Intercity – for example, Virgin, GNER (images of streamlined 'Pacific' locomotives and named luxury trains).
- Regional cross-country (sturdy mixed-traffic engines and brief encounters in dusty buffets).
- London commuter routes (green Southern Railway electric trains).
- Suburban services in other cities (mud-coloured trains and smoky termini).
- Rural railways (quaint tank engines and friendly porters).

Yet the British railway system of the twenty-first century serves for the most part an urbanised country with overlapping movement patterns. Most passenger services are operated by multiple-unit trains, even the fastest long-distance ones, running at regular intervals and higher frequencies.

This fundamentally different situation from the early twentieth century ought to be reflected in current strategic thinking. The British railway system should be developing as a single nationwide transit system, albeit a multi-tiered one like the Dutch and Swiss systems. It should not remain hindered by the barriers of outdated concepts. Its programmes for system development and investment must address this principle, and the structure of the industry must be framed to enable this to happen. So it would be entirely inappropriate for the government to just put Railtrack onto a new footing as Network Rail while making more encouraging – or threatening – noises. There are several other critical aspects of the structure and approach for our railway industry that the government needs to address if opportunities are not to be wasted.

Railtrack and Network Rail

Obviously the management of the railway infrastructure forms the most immediate problem. One of the problems with Railtrack was its apparent remoteness from other bodies in the industry or in other relevant areas, notably local authorities. Few Railtrack managers engaged closely with local authorities and other organisations, even where they had an apparently crucial relationship. The desire to maximise profits, at the apparent expense of engineering expertise and proper project management, has not helped the industry. Even though it effectively depended on the government for the majority of its funding, Railtrack generally treated government policy as something irrelevant to its own activities.

Network Rail's position, as a not-for-profit trust directed by a board reflecting the key players in the industry, should provide a much better focus for cohesive management and maintenance of the network. Proposals for a more coordinated structure for the whole industry, such as those put forward by Chris Green and Roger Ford, are valuable but retain an essentially inward-looking industry. Network Rail needs to build the 'organic' two-way relationship that railways must have with economic activity and spatial development, at local and regional level (i.e., with the devolved and regional administrations and with the local authorities). So these bodies are equally important stakeholders and should also have seats on the new board. In this way, common cause may be established over many aspects at both high level and local action. The Network Rail Business Plan recognises the importance of stakeholders, but does not seem to see them as integral to its activities (Network Rail, 2003).

The establishment of Network Rail as a not-for-profit trust addresses another weakness in the initial Railways Act 1993 structure. In other European Union (EU) countries, rail infrastructure is managed by a public agency. In some countries that appear to have been most successful in integrated rail development (Sweden and the Netherlands), the track agency is established and run on very similar lines to the (trunk) roads agency. There was a Memorandum of Agreement between the Highways Agency (HA) and Railtrack, but its actual effects seem to have been remarkably limited. Railtrack's position appeared anomalous, especially in relation to the output from LTPs and multi-modal studies that are now being undertaken in selected areas to guide long-term transport investment.

Sometimes it expressed serious doubts over the feasibility of funding additional rail schemes, leading in some cases to their being dropped after initial stages. This is in marked contrast to trunk road proposals that have remained on the agenda – sometimes for a decade or more – until funding eventually becomes available. Putting Network Rail onto a similar working basis to the HA (i.e., with both as non-commercial bodies under government guidance whose prime function lies in managing the assets of a national network) should enable both rail and road infrastructure development to be placed on a similar basis. Indeed, they might with good effect be brought together to form one body: Strategic Infrastructure Agency (SIA).

The New Approach to Transport Assessment (NATA) (DETR, 2000b), which was adopted by the government in line with its White Paper commitments, should be used to undertake future assessment of rail schemes. This is also to be the basis for all assessments in Regional Transport Strategies, LTPs and the multi-modal studies. In Scotland, the same function is performed by the Scottish Transport Appraisal Guide (Scottish Executive, 2001).

Strategic Rail Authority: Strategy and regulation

The government has placed the role of developing and implementing the railway elements of national transport strategy on the SRA, set up in 1999 in 'shadow' form and formally established under the Transport Act 2000. The SRA is required by the Act (Paragraph 206) to 'formulate, and keep under review, strategies with respect to its purposes'. It produced the intended strategy, the Strategic Plan (SRA, 2002), in January 2002, after a prolonged gestation. This focused on the current problems and weaknesses of the industry. It set out a programme for priorities in spending the funds allocated by the government's *Transport 2010*, and primarily covered investment projects and the franchising of passenger services; largely existing commitments and proposals, with alternative approaches were not examined. Much of its attention was concentrated on short-term priorities, with medium-term schemes given much less coverage and the long term being almost completely passed over. In effect, the Strategic Plan sought to address change largely through current industry processes and potential railway franchises: a further indication of the rail industry's inward-looking mind-set and its remoteness from the other bodies involved in implementation of government transport strategy. Even on funding, the Strategic Plan left serious questions unanswered: especially the extent to which private funding, intended to meet half the investment capital needed, will actually be achieved.

141

In January 2003, the SRA published an updated Strategic Plan (SRA, 2003). This represents a significant change in focus from the previous plan, largely caused by continuing financial pressures on the rail industry, especially through much higher costs being incurred for infrastructure work. The revised plan envisages less traffic growth during the plan period, and also cuts back on investment intended during the decade. Instead, more attention is to be concentrated on reining back the costs of maintenance and capital schemes, improving performance and safety, and making better use of available capacity. The plan is aimed at demonstrating realism in the use of available funds, as a basis for achieving sustained or even expanded investment support under the next Government Spending Review. This realism includes serious cuts in programmes such as Rail Passenger Partnerships (RPP) and Freight Facilities Grants (FFG), which are essential for many local service and infrastructure developments, as set out in local authorities' LTPs and in the multi-modal studies. This excessive concentration on immediate objectives runs counter to the principle of a strategic approach, and suggests the risk of drifting back into the old and inefficient approach of action based purely on measures geared to short-term aims.

Network Rail's first Business Plan (Network Rail, 2003) declared that: 'Our ageing network is fragile and capacity is stretched.' It set out in depth the management plans for improvements over a number of key areas, including safety, performance, system capability, customer and stakeholder relationships, financial control, and business performance. A note of caution was also struck: '[I]t will take years, not months, to achieve what has to be done' – a clear indication that even restoring the railway's operational soundness requires medium-term planning.

The main questions facing the railway industry – and the country – concern the ability of the industry to contribute towards implementation of transport policy, and the scale and cost of possible options for this: setting these out does not depend on the structure of the industry; although its fragmented nature means that it needs to act decisively together. The rail strategy should focus on the future role, scale and funding of the railway system in this context. The SRA needs to take stock of the current issues, draw out a SWOT (strengths, weaknesses, opportunities, threats) analysis, and present its preferred options for future development – including the main plans, projects and funding requirements – in the light of this analysis. It needs to address the long-term future of the railway. What is it for? What should be its priorities? How do these relate to national and regional strategies in spatial and transport development? This, unfortunately, the SRA Strategic Plans have not done.

Such a strategic document could be relatively compact. It would set the industry's direction for a period of years, during which it would remain unchanged; it might well be presented to Parliament for approval. It would form the framework for a more specific investment plan (Rail Investment Plan – RIP), which should have a 10-year span and be subject to rolling reviews. The RIP would equate with the government's *Transport 2010* programme, the spending plans in the Scottish and Welsh strategies, the English regions' RTSs and the local authorities' LTPs (or equivalents). It would form guidance for potential investors bidding to undertake schemes, probably through public–private partnerships (PPPs), thus providing more confidence for achievement of the necessary private funding.

The SRA's role covers both development and management of the network. The activities of the Rail Regulator are primarily focused on regulating Railtrack to ensure fair competition among operators and good conditions for passengers, while allowing appropriate profits for shareholders. Now that Network Rail is a not-for-profit company, 'owned' by its operators and customers, this role appears largely redundant. So the regulatory function could be incorporated into the SRA, as part of its overall responsibility for fair conditions and adherence with national (and international) regulations and practices. The Civil Aviation Authority (CAA) offers a good example in – it combines both roles, even though the air industry is in the hands of many airline and airport companies, mostly private, and a lot of them based outside the United Kingdom.

Funding the infrastructure

To bring the railway system even more into line with the needs of national transport policy, changes to funding for the infrastructure would appear to be essential. Currently, most funding for infrastructure (and most of Network Rail's income) reaches Network Rail as payments for track access charges by train operators. Most passenger train operators' costs are met partly by revenue and partly by government grants under the franchise contracts delivered via the SRA. Around half the cost of running a passenger franchise concerns the provision of track at agreed charges. With Network Rail as a not-for-profit trust, simply responsible for managing the railway system, with the government able to determine much more of its direction, then this appears to be an unnecessarily indirect way of funding it. It would surely be far better for its primary funding to come direct from the government, perhaps via the SRA, with clear criteria set for its activities. Thus funding could be more directly judged against that for the HA's trunk road network (and Welsh and Scottish equivalents). Since establishment of track charges form a good element of the Rail Regulator's *raison d'être*, this appears to be another reason for winding up the position as a separate organisation. System maintenance also includes renewal, which may have some element of enhancement (the precise boundaries are difficult to identify), but what is important is that maintenance and renewal should be addressed as part of the same engineering regime. They should not be subject to different contractual rules.

Investment funding for major projects is, however, a separate issue – and should be properly managed by the SRA. This may well include funding from public sources (i.e., the government via the SRA, Welsh Assembly and Scottish Parliament, PTAs and local authorities, and possibly (English) regions in the future). It may also include private funds, from both investors and commercial companies. This would include train operating companies (TOCs), especially where they believe they have a real interest; and, indeed, this is eminently appropriate. These various funds are most likely to come together through some form of public–private partnership (PPP).

Rail passenger services: Funding and ROSCOs

Although subject to short-term direction by the government, the SRA at one point still seemed to want franchises for longer time periods, and for larger areas, than hitherto, so that franchisees could contribute heavily to major investment in the infrastructure. Currently, shorter franchises (seven years) are back on the agenda, but rail transport needs, emerging from LTPs and Regional Transport Strategies (including those proposed within multi-modal studies), may well not be the same as those that potential rail franchisees see as priority. These differences need to be reconciled and priorities listed as part of the proposed rail investment plan.

The SRA has continued to see the franchising of passenger rail services as its principal role (and has even assumed that its Strategic Plan would primarily reflect the ideas and views of franchisees). Certainly the licensing of passenger services will remain a substantial part of its activities and one that is indeed very important as the means of implementing government policy in this field. With a clearer view of what investment might be forthcoming, and how services might be developed, it might be more appropriate to remove the time dimension to franchises. This would allow for regular reconsideration of the principal objectives for each group of rail services. Refranchising might be geared, wherever possible, to match completion of stages of investment on the lines served, and the position of the incumbent operator would also depend on satisfactory adherence to laid down performance and customer care standards. This is in line with emerging EU policies on development of public services in parallel to transparency over public funding for them.

The franchises let in 1996 and 1997 were mostly based on the former British Rail (BR) divisions. Future franchises should be more closely matched to geographical circumstances. While some large rail service groups might emerge under the guidance developed by the SRA at national level (SRA, 2002), the principle of subsidiarity leads to arguments for putting much of the franchising out of the centre and into the hands of devolved administrations and regional agencies, the PTEs and the main local authorities. This already happens in other EU countries, notably France and Germany. South-east England would form a special case (as does the Ile-de-France in France): single guidance for the whole region would be appropriate, but this has to balance the interests of London and the neighbouring county (shire) authorities. Indeed, the resurrection of Network South East (NSE) as one operator might prove to be a suitable vehicle for this. Urban systems around the main cities should be the responsibility of the PTE or local transport authority; again, ensuring that the interests of the whole catchment area are taken into account. Development of some routes using light rail might form the optimum way forward, but this is effective only when integrated with local transport and land-use strategies. At very local level, especially for rural areas, micro-franchising of particular lines would provide a community focus (e.g., the Esk Valley line in North Yorkshire). Specialist services (e.g., airport express services), too, could form separate franchise operations.

The rolling stock leasing companies (ROSCOs) have been successful in providing new rolling stock, and that needs to continue at a pace. They could be expected to take a wider view of their role by becoming involved in financing new major infrastructure projects, especially where this might lead to new orders for particular rolling stock requirements.

Culture and management

Finally, it is important to return to the issue of culture. The management of the British railway system over the past half-century has, on occasions, been appalling. At other times, it has demonstrated good to exemplary performance in achieving significant gains in efficiencies, investment and traffic, despite an unjustified and uninformed poor public image and funding levels well below those of its European neighbours. This has been achieved primarily through a narrow concentration on running the railway – the 'focused' approach was common to railway executives long before modern management-speak coined the phrase. However, a conscientious and loyal workforce, from bottom to top, underpinned it: a culture in which successive generations of the same family worked on 'the railway', right into the 1990s. The railway companies formed the first 'modern' joint stock companies in the British economy; but BR was perhaps the last national 'family' business, in which a large corps of staff with shared expertise and standards remained dedicated to providing a sound level of public service. Most managers were either promoted from experienced supervisory and technical staff, or brought in through a management training scheme that had run effectively since the 1930s. A management development scheme brought quick promotion for the most capable, and useful guidance and placing for the rest.

The Railways Act 1993 broke up the national undertaking into a large number of companies with changing ownership and responsibilities, and different corporate cultures. This has removed many of the certainties within the industry, replacing many familiar working relationships by rules and schedules. Many of the senior managers and other personnel have retired or left, in some cases prematurely or disillusioned, before adequate replacements were available. Managers now work for different and sometimes competing companies – and move between them. They manage much more through systems and contracts, and rather less through leadership or a genuine belief in promoting a collective goal. At the same time, the need to achieve bottom-line commercial results makes them less aware of the wider context within which they work (Wolmar, 2001). Appropriate management and skill training is largely non-existent. The SRA is now promoting a Centre for Rail Skills to increase technical skills, and this initiative is one of several in the transport field where there is grave concern over shortages of skilled staff at all levels and across all functions.

Yet the current era offers a major new opportunity for the railway system, for more traffic and a better status over the long term. In order to optimise that opportunity, the management of the railway industry must understand and reflect the wider world in a way it does not do at present. So a major effort must be put into training managers and overseeing further career development. This must be an essential task for the SRA, whose main statutory duty (in accordance with the Transport Act 2000, Section 205) concerns promotion, development and integration of the railway network. The SRA will need to work closely with relevant professional institutes to ensure a common approach. It also needs strong support from the government. Only with this can the railway system be developed to work effectively within the new context. It is time to create a new ethos for the railway.

Conclusions

The government has given the national railway system a pivotal role in the implementation of its transport policies, which include effective integration with land-use development planning. These policies broadly reflect public opinion: people, by and large, see the need for better rail services. A higher and more sustained proportion of public funds has been allocated in order to achieve this role. People are now expecting real improvements on the trains and stations they use. However, the railway industry has followed its own inward-looking agenda. Railtrack and the SRA, in particular, have failed to engage in any meaningful sense with regional agencies and local authorities. Network Rail also appears too heavily focused on technical outputs. Yet these are the bodies that are charged with the major responsibility for putting the national transport policies into effect.

If these policies are to be successful, the structure of the railway industry must enable the industry to play an effective role and to use public funding to achieve the aims for which it has been granted. The structure should also reflect general trends in European transport and railway policies, and its operation must be underpinned by a cohesive national system of management training and skill development. We have consequently attempted to outline here some of the key matters that need to be embraced in any future reorganisation.

Note

1 This article was originally published in *Public Money and Management* 22(2) (2002).

References

Ahrons, E.L. (1951–1954). *Locomotive and Train Working in the Latter Part of the Nineteenth Century* (6 vols.). Cambridge: Heffer.

Department of the Environment, Transport and the Regions (DETR) (1998). *A New Deal for Transport: Better for Everyone*. London: HMSO.

Department of the Environment, Transport and the Regions (DETR) (2000a). *Transport 2010: The 10-year Plan*. London: HMSO.

Department of the Environment, Transport and the Regions (DETR) (2000b). *Guidance on the Methodology for Multi-Modal Studies* (2 vols.). London: HMSO.

Department of the Environment, Transport and the Regions (DETR) (2001). *Planning Policy Guidance Note 13: Transport*. London: HMSO.

Ford, R. (2001). 'Creation of a functioning railway', *Modern Railways* (September).

Green, C. (2001). 'Phoenix from the Ashes' (The Sir Robert Reid Lecture 2001). London: Institute for Logistics and Transport.

Network Rail (2003). *Business Plan*. London: Network Rail.

Prescott, J. (2003). *Sustainable Communities*. London: HMSO.

Railtrack (2001). *Network Management Statement 2001*. Available online at: www.railtrack.co.uk.

Scottish Executive (2001). *Scottish Transport Appraisals Guidance*. Edinburgh: Scottish Executive.

Strategic Rail Authority (SRA) (2001a). *A Strategic Agenda*. London: SRA.

Strategic Rail Authority (SRA) (2001b). *Land Use Planning & the SRA: Statement/Guide* (2 vols.). London: SRA.

Strategic Rail Authority (SRA) (2002). *The Strategic Plan*. London: SRA.

Strategic Rail Authority (SRA) (2003). *The Strategic Plan: Platform for Success*. London: SRA.

Urban Task Force (1999). *Towards an Urban Renaissance*. London: Urban Task Force.

Wolmar, C. (2001). *Broken Rails*. London: Aurum Press.

14. A Financial Appraisal of the London Underground Public–Private Partnership[1]

JEAN SHAOUL

This chapter examines whether the government's policy of Public–Private Partnerships (PPPs) in the context of London Underground is likely to satisfy the financial criteria for approving a partnership proposal: value-for-money (VFM), including risk transfer, and affordability. After analyzing the implications of the London Underground's cost structure for the PPP, the author looks at the methodology for appraising the PPP and concludes that the methodology cannot be relied upon to provide a sound decision-making tool for London Underground. The author demonstrates that the London Underground project is not affordable, and questions the appropriateness of the partnership policy in the context of vital capital-intensive industries.

The essential problem for London Underground, indeed railways and metro systems the world over, is that, as highly capital-intensive industries, they cannot generate the revenues from fares to cover the full costs of infrastructure, train operations and investment, and make a return on capital employed. This is despite the fact that London Underground's fares are among the highest in Europe. Full cost recovery would entail fares that would choke off demand, bring economic and social life in the capital to a standstill and be politically unacceptable. It is because of these basic realities that governments everywhere have funded capital expenditure, subsidised operating costs, and provided grants for the capital maintenance of their transport systems. Indeed, the financial difficulties of the National Air Traffic Services (NATS) public–private partnership (PPP) within three months of financial close, and the collapse within five years of the privatised national rail infrastructure company, Railtrack, despite subsidies running at triple the levels in the 1980s, provide further evidence for this assessment.

Now, however, under the government's policy of PPPs, the private sector is to take responsibility for London Underground's capital investment,

JEAN SHAOUL is a Senior Lecturer in the School of Accounting and Finance at Manchester University.

operational management and network maintenance. Not only is there a severe shortage of capacity on the existing lines, the rolling stock is old and the infrastructure is in need of considerable investment to ensure a reliable, regular and more frequent service. In addition, there is a backlog of essential maintenance estimated to be in excess of £1.2 billion.

Under plans announced in March 1998, the infrastructure is split into three sections and three private sector infrastructure companies were expected take responsibility for maintaining and refurbishing or reprovisioning the track, signals, stations and rolling stock in return for an annual infrastructure service charge (ISC) over the 30-year life of the project. London Underground will continue to run the passenger services, in effect leasing the trains and infrastructure from the infrastructure companies (Infracos). The Infracos thus have a concession to operate the infrastructure rather than owning it outright.

The government has in general justified its PPP policy, an umbrella term that includes the Private Finance Initiative (PFI), in two ways:

- Partnerships provide the mechanism for delivering the funding that the public purse could not or would not afford, and as such they are the only way of improving public services.
- They deliver greater value for money over the life of the projects because the private sector assumes some of the financial risks (and costs) that the public sector would otherwise carry.

As part of a process designed to allocate resources on a more rational basis, free from political interference or managerial preference, the government has put in place procedures designed to ensure that PFI/PPP projects only go ahead if they can satisfy two financial criteria: that they are demonstrably value for money and affordable – although it acknowledges that other non-financial considerations are also important (Her Majesty's Treasury, 1997). However, in the context of London Underground, by far the largest PPP project to date, the government has said that the PPP contracts would only go ahead if they can satisfy two criteria: they maintain or improve the current safety standards, and they provide superior value for money when compared to an alternative, publicly funded infrastructure operation. In other words, it has dropped one of the financial criteria – the affordability test. At the time of writing (April 2003), London Underground has been divided into four divisions and is shadow-running the proposed PPP structure. An agreement has been signed with two consortia to run the three concessions.

This chapter seeks to make a financial appraisal of the London Underground PPP. It examines the extent to which it satisfies the government's financial criteria for PPPs – value-for-money (VFM), including risk transfer, and affordability – and assesses the implications for the viability of the project.

London Underground: The financial context

This section briefly explains London Underground's financial performance, which has been more fully described elsewhere (Gaffney *et al.*, 2000), in order to understand the problems that confront it and the operational and financial implications of the PPP. London Underground's funding currently comes from three sources: fares, grants for maintenance and capital grants for investment.

Revenue from fares has risen since the 1980s, as demand and fares increased, peaking in 2001 at £1.3 billion before falling back to £1.2 billion as the recession began. This is a cyclical industry where demand varies with the economic climate. The number of passenger journeys rose by 25 per cent in the 1990s as Britain climbed out of the previous recession and fares rose well ahead of the rate of inflation, from 11 pence per passenger-kilometre in 1994 to 15 pence in 1999. The fares increase was necessitated in part by the withdrawal of all operating subsidies in 1994, and in part by the decline in maintenance grants from £398 million in 1994–1995 to £160 million in 1998–1999. Subsidies were set to disappear completely by 2001–2002, 'based on the assumption that the PPP will remove the need for government subsidy in respect of London Underground' (ETRA Select Committee, 1998). Hence fares had to rise to compensate for the withdrawal of subsidies and the fall in the already inadequate level of grants, although these have occasionally had to be increased, albeit in arrears, to ensure London Underground's financial viability. More recently, grants for maintenance have risen to double the previous levels (£293 million in 2001–2002 and £464 million in 2002–2003) despite the government's declared intention of phasing them out. While capital grants for investment increased, these were largely spent on new rather than existing lines.

London Underground was successful in containing labour costs (the main cost of running passenger services), which stayed constant or declined in real terms during the 1990s as 6,000 jobs (27 per cent of the workforce) were lost. While productivity increased from 0.278 million passenger-kilometres per employee in 1991–1992 to 0.423 million in 1998–1999, any further increase would be dependent upon additional investment. More importantly, no amount of increased productivity can release the resources to fund the necessary levels of investment as the nationalised railways showed (Shaoul, 2000; Shaoul & Gaffney, 2000).

London Underground is a state-owned enterprise with a very unusual financial regime. Unlike the former nationalised industries, it has no interest, dividend or tax obligations, and no statutory requirement to make a return on capital employed. Hence, it spends all of what remains of its income from fares and grants, after paying for purchases of labour, on capital maintenance. After providing for depreciation and capital maintenance, London Underground usually breaks even. However, for the financial years ending March 2001 and 2002, it made losses of £24 and £126 million, respectively –

the highest ever (despite the highest-ever level of maintenance grants) – in part at least because of the additional costs of restructuring and running it as four separate divisions (the three infrastructure divisions and passenger services) in readiness for the PPP. This means that London Underground's organisational structure was driven by the PPP before it had even established that the PPP was value for money or affordable, and has proved more costly than the previous arrangements.

The significance of this is, first, that under the *ancien regime*, where capital is a 'free' good, London Underground only broke even – courtesy of government grants – and, second, that since restructuring for the PPP, costs have risen, leading to the first-ever major losses. Consequently, without subsidies, bigger grants, higher fares or increased labour productivity, London Underground would be unable to afford any extra charges to cover the cost of the PPP. Nor could it service any debt if grants were replaced by interest-bearing loans – the option favoured by many opponents of the PPP such as the Mayor of London and Glaister *et al.* (2000).

The appraisal methodology

According to government guidelines (Her Majesty's Treasury, 1997), VFM must be demonstrated if a PFI project is to proceed. Alongside the options appraisal, there are other factors that need to be considered, such as affordability and any public service obligations. In the context of this scheme, other factors would include strategic issues relating to the division of responsibility for the network, the potential loss of flexibility and control, long-term partnership relationships, the contractual framework, the incentives in the performance specification and risk management. However, the weight that should be attached to each is unclear. This section considers solely the financial criteria of VFM and affordability.

Value-for-money methodology

While VFM is a colloquial term that has intuitive plausibility, its substantive meaning is ambiguous. In the context of public finance, it is associated with the 'three Es': economy, efficiency and effectiveness. The National Audit Office (NAO), whose role includes examining VFM across central government, has in practice for a variety of conceptual and methodological reasons, tended to focus more on economy than efficiency and effectiveness. VFM's meaning in relation to PFI/PPP is no more precise. It is assumed to be demonstrated by comparing the whole-life costs of the project as financed under conventional procurement methods (known as the 'public sector comparator' or PSC, discounted to yield a Net Present Cost or NPC) to the NPC of the project as procured under PFI/PPP. As well as the expected financial costs, the costs of some of the risks associated with the scheme are also included. The option with the lowest NPC is assumed to yield the greatest financial benefit. This section considers the suitability of discounted cash flow techniques, the choice of the PSC, and the risk transfer that lies at the heart of the justification for PFI/PPP.

The usefulness of the NPV approach, of which the VFM methodology is a variant, is severely limited by the assumptions made and options considered, as others have noted (e.g., Tribe, 1972; King, 1975; Ross, 1995). First, it is one of a number of methods of project appraisal used by the private sector because it is assumed to maximise shareholder or owner wealth. Thus its use in the public sector implies that the public interest is restricted to that of a shareholder, despite the fact that most public-sector organisations are not wealth maximisers in a financial sense. Indeed, London Underground has been in public ownership and run as a public service since the 1930s because it could not maximise shareholder wealth. Second, the NPV is not appropriate when capital is rationed, as it is in this case. Yet, the ostensible reason for the PPP is that the government has not, or will not, provide the cash that London Underground needs. Third, it applies only where the investment opportunity instantly disappears if not immediately undertaken. In practice, however, there is usually a time period over which the investment may be undertaken. Finally, many of the investments for London Underground are interdependent. As well as the formal assumptions of the NPV rule, which are not met in practice, there are a number of practical problems. A crucial aspect of the methodology is the choice of discount rate. Following Treasury rules, a discount rate of 6 per cent is used because it does not preclude the private sector (Her Majesty's Treasury, 1997). However, VFM comparisons are very sensitive to small changes in the discount rate (NAO, 1999a; Gaffney et al., 1999).

Although the NPV approach is used by some private-sector organisations in some circumstances, it is by not used in the majority of cases nor is it used as the sole criterion (McIntyre & Coulthurst, 1986; Pike & Wolfe, 1988; Drury et al., 1992). In part, this is because of the difficulty in predicting cash flows for very long into the future due to uncertainty. First, the implication of a 30-year contract between London Underground and the Infracos is that cash flows must be predicted for a 30-year period under conditions in which there is incomplete information about the status and condition of many of the assets. Whereas nearly all PFI projects are based on new builds, this one is based on old assets whose condition may not be known. That makes it even more difficult to be precise about what needs to be done, and whether and how it can be done, for example to ensure the outputs, such as the number of trains per hour on a given line. The lack of an asset register was one of the reasons that made it so difficult to determine and control the cost of maintaining and enhancing the privatised national railway infrastructure. Second, there is the additional uncertainty created by the new methodology, where London Underground is required to estimate the costs of meeting a defined level of performance, as opposed to estimating maintenance and renewal costs on the basis of expected or design life. Third, the level of performance is itself the function of travel patterns that can be expected to change over the life of the project.

The choice of the PSC is crucial to any VFM evaluation. VFM comparisons have traditionally been based on the convention that the costs of public-sector investment have to be met in the year in which they occur: in other words, the option for the public sector to spread costs over time through financing has been ignored. This is important because the discounted cash flow methodology favours options that defer expenditure over those which have high costs in early years, creating an artificial advantage for PPP options, where costs are spread over a period of 20–35 years. In this case, bond-financed public-sector options will also be included (PwC, 2000), partly because many opponents of the PPP had urged the government to retain the London Underground entirely within the public sector and finance the investment through bonds (Glaister et al., 2000). It also provides a fallback option if the PPP fails the VFM or safety tests. Thus testing the PPP against a public-sector option financed through borrowing, as well as conventional funding, could remove the inherent advantage the methodology gives to PPP, as long as a bond interest rate of 3.5 per cent is used, rather than the higher 6 per cent discount rate required by the Treasury.

As well as the financial costs of the scheme, the comparison also includes the costs of some of the risks associated with the construction and management of the scheme. Since some of the risks are to be transferred to the private sector, the PPP should provide greater VFM than a publicly financed alternative where the public sector bears all the risks. Thus all the risks associated with design, construction, finance, maintenance and operation of the scheme over the life of the project must be identified. Probabilities of their occurrence must be assigned and financial values attributed to their outcomes so that the amount of risk to be transferred to the private sector can be included in the public sector comparator. The more risk that is transferred, then the more expensive the PSC becomes relative to the PPP option. Risk transfer is the crucial element in establishing VFM because, as the evidence from the new hospitals to be built under PFI shows, conventional public procurement provides greater VFM until risk transfer is factored in, and even then the margin of difference is minimal (Health Select Committee, 1999; Boyle & Harrison, 2000).

However, the risk transfer methodology is far from proven. It depends upon the ability to identify and attach probabilities and values to a range of outcomes. Irrespective of whether and how much risk is actually transferred and to whom, it should not be forgotten that the main risks are those that arise from technical obsolescence, changing regulation and demand. The public sector will continue to hold these. Should conditions change during the 30-year contract, rendering parts of the facilities unsuitable or unpopular for any reason, London Underground could find itself locked into long-term contracts and payments that it would not be able to evade. The risk methodology does not address the question of the *additional* risks created by PPP. For example, the new organisational structure that separates the infrastructure from passenger services raises problems of planning, coordination and safety – the same issues that lay at the heart of recent accidents on the national railways. The publicly owned company will retain its statutory responsibility for safety (which has been declining almost continuously over the past seven years, as the serious injury rate per million passenger journeys has more than doubled), while the Infracos will be responsible for carrying out the work. In the absence of reliable mechanisms to monitor and enforce performance standards, the fragmentation of the system will have implications for the performance and safety of the London Underground that are not reflected in the comparisons between the different methods of financing the investment. Taken together, this means that financial modelling of this sort is fraught with difficulties, as the National Audit Office (2000) recognised.

Affordability

While a given project may exhibit VFM, it may not necessarily be affordable, resulting in cuts elsewhere and/or to the services to be provided under PPP. Thus, the criterion of affordability is crucial, but it is equally problematic. There is no recognised methodology or criterion for determining affordability, any more than there is for options appraisal. Logically, affordability implies identifying the services to be provided and comparing their costs against the current costs and services, and the overall budget.

Little attention has been paid to this issue, despite its importance. Indeed, while the NAO has carried out more than 20 evaluations of PFI/PPP, it has focused on the *ex ante* case for VFM to the virtual exclusion of affordability, in part at least because of its VFM remit under the National Audit Act 1983. Yet research on PFI in hospitals (Gaffney & Pollock, 1997; Froud & Shaoul, 2001) and schools (Edwards & Shaoul, 1999) has shown that affordability is a crucial issue. In the context of the London Underground PPP, the government has explicitly excluded the issue of affordability, preferring to rely on the sole financial criterion of VFM.

In summary, the methodology for establishing VFM in general, and for London Underground in particular, is subject to several limitations that constrain its usefulness. In any event, VFM is only one criterion among several. These include: affordability; the implications of the PPP structure for planning, coordination and safety; future investment to expand the network; democratic accountability; and stakeholder consent, including the wishes of those who will have to fund it – the passengers, taxpayers (both local and national), and the people of London. While the latter are outside the scope of this essay, they are nonetheless important.

The appraisal process

While the previous section examined the methodology for establishing VFM and affordability from an *a priori* perspective, this section examines the appraisal process adopted by London Underground to compare the PPP option against the various PSCs for each of the three partnerships. However, it should be noted that despite the fact that the London Underground PPP is the largest project of its kind, neither the output specification nor the business case setting out the VFM case and affordability have been put in the public domain for reasons of 'commercial confidentiality'. Thus this study is reliant upon secondary sources, such as the briefing notes put out by London Underground's financial advisors (PwC, 1999, 2000), a National Audit Office report (2000), an Industrial Society report (2001) and a report by Deloitte and Touche (2001). While the final decision to proceed with the project rests in part upon the VFM appraisal, the government's commitment to the PPP and the huge set-up costs of the project imply that it will deliver VFM.

The VFM case

The appraisal process is problematic in a number of respects: the assumptions about greater private-sector efficiency, the risk assessment, the assumptions underlying the bond-financed options and the period of comparison. London Underground's financial advisors, and government press releases, assume that the private sector will be able to make cost 'savings' on a £15 billion investment programme of about £2.5 billion, so the PPP will spend about £12.53 billion over 15 years (PwC, 1999). However, the government has not provided any evidence or justification to support this claim, nor has it explained why London Underground could not make similar savings. It bases this assumption on 'private sector efficiencies'. Yet the research literature, as it relates to comparisons between public- and private-sector efficiency, is not characterised by carefully controlled studies that explain the cause of any observed differences that may lie in a different regulatory and pricing regime, wage structure, social and legal obligations etc., as others have noted (Millward, 1982; Boardman & Vining, 1989; Ernst, 1994).

The record of the privatised rail and water industries are relevant here. In the national railways, services have declined, while infrastructure investment by Railtrack has not risen commensurate with need, expectation or commitments (Booz Allen & Hamilton, 1999). The water industry's 'efficiency savings' came not so much from lower operating costs, but from a lower level of capital expenditure on both renewals and investment than that predicted at privatisation (Shaoul, 1997). Indeed, the low level of renewals meant that the industry was running down the asset base in ways that threatened future delivery (Schofield & Shaoul, 1997). These 'savings' were partly the result of inflated cost estimates that provided the basis for price increases. More importantly from the perspective of the PPP proposals, while some performance targets were set for the water companies, many of them were not achieved (Schofield & Shaoul, 1997). They were also, in practice, difficult to enforce, as the failure of the public water supply to West Yorkshire in 1995 and leakages running at a higher level than pre-privatisation testify.

Thus, the 'efficiency savings' were made at the expense of consumers and the public at large and constituted *economy* not *efficiency*. Furthermore, both industries made more improvements in productivity and efficiency before privatisation, which suggests that the private sector does not have a monopoly on efficient management techniques. Yet London Underground and its financial advisors believe that private-sector operators can make similar savings in investment and maintenance expenditure, while still delivering the necessary standards of performance. Conversely, the NAO has made a similar point about private-sector efficiency assumptions in its criticisms of the tendency to underestimate public-sector efficiency in the VFM comparisons (NAO, 1998, 1999a, 1999b, 1999c, 1999d).

According to the Deloitte and Touche report, there have been a number of adjustments made to the PSC amounting to £2.5 billion. The first and largest (£1.17 billion) represents the expected failure of London Underground to meet the performance requirements, but this risk of failure was shown as an economic cost to passengers, although this is not the normal procedure as set out by the Treasury's *Green Book* (Her Majesty's Treasury, 1997). While it might be useful to compare the potential costs of the various options to passengers, and indeed any other stakeholders, costs to passengers are entirely separate from financial costs to London Underground and the two should not be confused. Furthermore, Deloitte and Touche found that many of the underlying assumptions were subjective and arbitrary.

As the negotiations proceeded, there was considerable 'descoping' of the project and changes to the contractual arrangements that had not been reflected in a similar downgrading of the PSCs' costs. Some of the numerous revisions to the PSCs involved performance adjustments that were extremely volatile, and there was considerable scope for double counting. While the costs had been subject to extensive simulations and sensitivity analyses, the 'expected value' or mean of each distribution was chosen even where the distribution was skewed, leading to a value considerably higher than the 'most likely' value.

The VFM comparison used three PSCs: a traditionally financed one, and two bond-financed options assuming different rates of interest, both of which produced better VFM results than the traditional PSC. However, the first bond-financed option, using a 6 per cent discount rate, incurs extra costs by not optimally timing the bond issues. The second bond-financed option used a lower discount rate that was cancelled out by adopting the theoretical concept of 'reputational externality' (the impact on the borrowing costs of other public agencies) and assuming a disproportionately high value for it. In other words, the appraisal process effectively dismissed the bond options.

Finally, the VFM comparisons are based upon a 30-year comparison of the financial costs and risks despite the difficulties in estimating costs over such a long period. Yet the contract, and hence the infrastructure service charge (ISC), will run for 7.5 years in the first instance. There will be periodic reviews every 7.5 years to 'give [London Underground] the opportunity to restate its performance requirements and allow the Infracos to put forward revised charges' (PwC, 2000: Paragraph 5.2.3).

Several points flow from this. The relevant period for VFM comparison purposes is 7.5 years, not 30 years. Furthermore, since the ISC will be determined by negotiation not contract, under conditions where there will be no alternative supplier, the Infracos will be in a position to dictate terms to London Underground. Despite this, London Underground chose not to use the first 7.5 years as the basis for the VFM comparison, although at least some of the bids were more expensive than the PSC for this period. Finally, the government has selected the preferred bidders for two of the three Infracos before completing the extensive legal negotiations – a procedure that may breach the European Union's procurement rules. In the absence of any 'competitive tension', this could lead to any PPP VFM advantage being whittled away.

The affordability case

Under the concession agreements, London Underground will pay a basic ISC, which will be fixed for the first 7.5-year period but 'stepped up' every time major enhancements are delivered. The ISC is to be subject to periodic renegotiation (not regulation) at 7.5-year intervals, and will depend upon the amount of work to be carried out under the concession agreement and the PPP's costs, including the cost of capital. Due to assumptions about private sector 'efficiencies', London Underground's financial advisors (PwC, 1999) estimate that the Infracos will spend £12.53 billion not £15 billion, over the first 15-year period on basic maintenance and investment. Since PricewaterhouseCoopers (PwC) expect rail receipts to rise by 40 per cent over the 15-year period, most of this would be funded directly by fares, leaving £2.44 billion to be borrowed.

The Infracos will need to set the ISC to cover their costs: maintenance and investment in the network, dividends on shareholders' capital, debt service and repayment of principal where the annual 'cost of capital' is estimated by PwC at 10 per cent. There is therefore a shortfall equivalent to the interest and dividend payments in each of the 15 years. Estimating debt repayment conservatively – and excluding bidding costs and advisors' fees, and using PwC's estimate of £900 million for investment and maintenance – the Infracos' total costs will come to at least £1,075 million in year 2 (see Table 1). Since PwC estimates that London Underground's 'free cash' after the cost of train services will be about £540 million, this leaves it with a shortfall of £535 million. Furthermore, there will be a similar gap, depending upon the investment profile, every year. While the amount of free cash in previous years can also be estimated using London Underground's annual accounts as the gross operating margin, plus depreciation and the government's maintenance grant, the results are similar.

157

Table 1. Estimate of London Underground's infrastructure charge and funding gap in Year 2 of the proposed PPP

PPP	Millions of pounds
Annual infrastructure costs	900
Debt-financing costs	110
Repayment	65
Total costs	1,075
Minimum infrastructure service charge	1,075
Operating cash flows	540
Funding shortfall	535

Source: Estimated from PwC (1999).

In reality, this £535 million per year funding gap is likely to be very much higher, since these calculations depend upon several contradictory assumptions:

- London Underground assumes that income will rise by 40 per cent over the 15 years, but since fare increases are to be pegged at no more than 1 per cent above inflation after 2001–2002, this can only be achieved by increasing the number of passengers. London Underground assumes that the capacity will exist to absorb the increase in passenger numbers under conditions where the network is already overcrowded.
- According to the contractual framework, availability of train services has been set at 95 per cent of current performance (Industrial Society, 2001), so it does not appear that any extra capacity has been built into the project. Alternatively, setting the benchmark at 95 per cent of existing performance guarantees that increased demand will generate incentive payments that will erode any extra rail receipts.
- London Underground does not seem to have considered the impact of any recession during the 15-year period on passenger numbers. A similarly rosy view of air-traffic volumes, even before the tragic events of 11 September 2001, was a major factor in destabilising the National Air Traffic Services (NATS) PPP (Shaoul, 2001).
- Finally, PwC assume that the cost of operating passenger services will decline, even though the new organisational structure has resulted in additional costs.

Thus, even on the most conservative estimates, it does not appear that the PPP is affordable. While the bond-financed option is cheaper, it is still unaffordable. Such an affordability gap implies an annual government grant at least double the present level. Moreover, if the estimates of revenues and costs turn out to be optimistic, this could rise even further. If, on the other hand, the government contribution does not rise, then Transport for London, which will ultimately be responsible for London Underground, will have to raise the additional finance. Alternatively, the Infracos would have to resort to further loans with their concomitant costs, increasing the relative attraction of the publicly funded options. These same issues lay at the heart of Railtrack's collapse that has in turn led to the bidders' bankers raising the cost of finance by one-eighth of 1 per cent, further increasing the costs of the PPP (*Financial Times*, 26 October 2001).

Additional credence is given to this analysis by several factors. First, the PPP project has been 'descoped': less risk is to be transferred than originally intended, and changes to the contractual arrangements have been made that favour the Infracos (Deloitte & Touche, 2001). Second, the original report (Gaffney *et al.*, 2000) establishing an affordability gap has never been rebutted. Third, the government has said that it will reinstate the maintenance and renewal grant for the duration of the contract. Given the additional costs of private-sector finance and of the operation of the newly restructured London Underground, this can only mean that the higher level of grant required is largely the result of using the private sector to finance and operate London Underground and the consequent restructuring of its operations. Finally, if the government has promised to reinstate the grant to help make the PPP affordable, then in all probability the affordability gap is very much larger than that indicated by this analysis.

Conclusions

The evidence presented in this essay has identified problems in the appraisal methodology and processes that raise doubts as to whether the procedures are sufficiently robust in terms of both their design and operation to ensure that sound decisions will be made. At best, the VFM comparisons are only the predicted costs. This in turn means that the VFM test is best at measuring economy, not efficiency or effectiveness. It is worth considering how useful such appraisals have really been in practice. The NAO noted that some projects had over-estimated their VFM and turned out to be more costly than their business cases suggested (NAO, 1999a). Numerous information technology PFI projects have failed – some of the most well known include the Benefits Agency and the Passport Agency projects – and contracts have proved difficult to enforce. While information technology projects are very difficult to get right, the relevance here is that the projected PFI costs were lower than under conventional public procurement. This was in part, if not wholly, because of the risk transfer. In practice, it was the public sector and the public at large that bore the risk and the costs.

While the government excluded the issue of affordability, this analysis has shown that the London Underground project is not affordable. The payments to the Infracos can only be met by some combination of public subsidy and cut backs in passenger services. Furthermore, signing a 30-year contract that is renegotiated every 7.5 years would be tantamount to signing a blank cheque to the Infracos. Far from ensuring the financial stability of the London Underground, the PPP will only jeopardise its future, leading to some combination of increased fares, job losses, service cut backs, subsidies, delayed investment and, ultimately, bail-out.

While London Underground will always require subsidies, bail-outs in such circumstances are necessitated by the increased costs of the PPP over normal financing methods. Nor can it be assumed that the Infracos can run London Underground without incurring extra costs that could lead to their defaulting on their financial commitments. In such circumstances, even if the contract were terminated, London Underground would have to continue to service the Infracos' debts as the bail-outs of NATS (NAO, 2002) and the Royal Armouries Museum (NAO, 2001) testify. The stage has been set for recurrent financial crises. In short, by any normal financial criteria, irrespective of safety and any other considerations, the project would not be allowed to proceed.

This raises a more fundamental issue. As with any policy instrument that is so central to government policy, there is a tension between promoting the use of partnerships and ensuring that it is only used in ways that meet the objectives of greater efficiency and value for money. If a policy measure such as PPP, particularly where it does not have broad popular support, is to win acceptance, it needs to find expression through the actions and activities of government departments such as the Treasury (Broadbent & Laughlin, 1999). However, such championship raises issues about a possible conflict of interest if the same public agencies both promote and control these projects (Freedland, 1998), particularly where there is a lack of publicly available finance for conventional public procurement – itself an explicit government policy choice.

Finally, this analysis demonstrates why the capital-intensive public infrastructure industries, and other public-sector activities that provide vital public services on a universal and comprehensive basis, have been in public ownership not just in Britain but all over the world. They are simply too risky and/or not cash generative enough for the private sector. The private-sector partners, and more particularly their financial backers, far from assuming risk under the PPP, are set to receive income streams guaranteed in one form or another by the public sector, while the government, Transport for London, London Underground, the workforce and the public carry the risk. At the same time, the government would in effect surrender the control of public finance, policy and decision making to the capital markets, while the public agencies retain the responsibility for service delivery. As such, this marks a major development in public policy. Taken together, these findings constitute a powerful indictment of both the project and the policy, and raise questions about the appropriateness of the policy for public infrastructure projects that provide essential public services.

Note

1 This chapter is based on an article published in *Public Money & Management* 22(2) (2002).

References

Boardman, A.E. & Vining, A.R. (1989). 'Ownership and performance in competitive environments: A comparison of the performance of private, mixed and state-owned enterprises', *Journal of Law and Economics* 32(1): 1–33.

Booz Allen & Hamilton (1999). *Railtrack's Performance in the Period 1999–2001: Report to the Office of the Rail Regulator*. London: Booz Allen & Hamilton.

Boyle, S. & Harrison, A. (2000). 'Private finance and service development'. In: J. Appleby & A. Harrison (eds), *Health Care UK, Autumn 2000*. London: King's Fund.

Broadbent, J. & Laughlin, R. (1999). 'The Private Finance Initiative: Clarification of a further research agenda', *Financial Accountability and Management* 15(2): 93–113.

Deloitte & Touche (2001). *London Underground Public–Private Partnership – Emerging Findings: Report for Transport for London*. London: Deloitte & Touche Corporate Finance.

Drury, C., Braund, S., Osborne, P. & Tayles, M. (1992). *A Survey of Management Accounting Practices in UK Manufacturing Companies*. London: Association of Chartered Certified Accountants.

Edwards, P. & Shaoul, J.E. (1999). 'Lessons of Pimlico', *Public Finance* (29 October–4 November): 16–18.

Environment, Transport and Regional Affairs (ETRA) Select Committee (1998). *London Underground, 7th Report, 1997/98* (HC 715–1). London: HMSO.

Ernst, J. (1994). *Whose Utility? The Social Impact of Public Utility Privatization and Regulation in Britain*. Buckingham: Open University Press.

Freedland, M. (1998). 'Public law and private finance: Placing the Private Finance Initiative in a public law frame', *Public Law*, 288–307.

Froud, J. & Shaoul, J. (2001). 'Appraising and evaluating PFI for NHS hospitals', *Financial Accountability and Management* 17(3): 247–270.

Gaffney, D. & Pollock, A.M. (1997). *Can the NHS Afford the Public Finance Initiative?* London: Health Policy and Economic Research Unit, British Medical Association.

Gaffney, D., Pollock, A.M., Price, D. and Shaoul, J. (1999). 'PFI in the NHS: Is there an economic case?' *British Medical Journal* 319: 116–119.

Gaffney, D., Pollock, A. & Shaoul, J. (2000). *Funding London Underground: Financial Myths and Economic Realities*. London: Listen to London.

Glaister, S., Scanlon, R. & Travers, T. (2000). *Public–Private Partnerships and Investment in Transport*. London, IPPR Commission on Public–Private Partnerships.

Health Select Committee (1999). *Department of Health Expenditure 1999: Minutes of Evidence*. London: HMSO.

Her Majesty's Treasury (1997). *Appraisal and Evaluation in Central Government (The Green Book)*. London: HMSO.

Industrial Society (2001). *The London Underground Public–Private Partnership: An Independent Review*. London: Industrial Society.

King, P. (1975). 'Is the emphasis of capital budgeting theory misplaced?' *Journal of Business, Finance and Accounting* 2(1): 69–82.

McIntyre, A.D. & Coulthurst, N.J. (1986). *Capital Budgeting Practices in Medium Sized Businesses: A Survey*. London: Chartered Institute of Management Accountants.

Millward, R. (1982). 'The comparative performance of public and private enterprise'. In: Lord Roll (ed), *The Mixed Economy*. London: Macmillan.

National Audit Office (NAO) (1998). *The First Four Design, Build, Finance and Operate Road Contracts* (House of Commons Paper 476, Session 1997/98). London: HMSO.

National Audit Office (NAO) (1999a). *The PFI Contract for the New Dartford and Gravesham Hospital* (House of Commons Paper 423, Session 1998/99). London: HMSO.

National Audit Office (NAO) (1999b). *Examining the Value for Money of Deals under the Private Finance Initiative* (House of Commons Paper 739, Session 1998/99). London: HMSO.

National Audit Office (NAO) (1999c). *The Newcastle Estate Project* (House of Commons Paper 104, Session 1999/2000). London: HMSO.

National Audit Office (NAO) (1999d). *The PRIME Project: The Transfer of the Department of Social Security Estate to the Private Sector* (House of Commons Paper 370, Session 1998/99). London: HMSO.

National Audit Office (NAO) (2000). *The Financial Analysis for the London Underground Public–Private Partnership* (House of Commons Paper 54, Session 2000/01). London: HMSO.

National Audit Office (NAO) (2001). *The Department of Culture, Media and Sport: The Renegotiation of the PFI-type Deal for the Royal Armouries Museum in Leeds* (House of Commons Paper 103, Session 2001/02). London: HMSO.

National Audit Office (NAO) (2002). *The Public-Private Partnership for National Air Traffic Services Ltd.* (House of Commons Paper 1096, Session 2001/02) London: HMSO.

Pike, R.H. & Wolfe, M.B. (1988). *Capital Budgeting in the 1990s*. London: Chartered Institute of Management Accountants.

PricewaterhouseCoopers (PwC) (1999). *London Underground PPP: Briefing Document*. London: PricewaterhouseCoopers.

PricewaterhouseCoopers (PwC) (2000). *London Underground PPP: Methodology for Preparing the Public Sector Comparator*. London: PricewaterhouseCoopers.

Ross, S.A. (1995). 'Uses, abuses and alternatives to the net present value rule', *Financial Management* 24(3): 96–102.

Schofield, R. & Shaoul, J. (1997). 'Regulating the water industry: By any standards?' *Utilities Law Review* 8(2): 56–70.

Shaoul, J. (1997). 'A critical financial analysis of the post-privatization performance of the UK water industry', *Critical Perspectives on Accounting* 8: 479–505.

Shaoul, J. (2000). 'On the wrong track?' *Public Finance* (3 November).

Shaoul, J. & Gaffney, D. (2000). 'Fantasy funding: London Underground and the PPP', *Public Finance* (7 April).

Shaoul, J. (2001). 'NATS debt model fails to take off', *Public Finance* (30 November): 18–20.

Tribe, L.H. (1972). 'Policy science: Analysis or ideology?' *Philosophy and Public Affairs* 2(1): 66–110.

15. Regulatory Control of the Track Access Charges of Railtrack plc[1]

JOHN STITTLE

Railtrack plc, floated in 1996, was the private-sector owner of Britain's railway track, signals and stations. Its major source of revenue came from track access charges, which individual train operating companies (TOCs) paid for use of the infrastructure. Since many of these TOCs received substantial subsidies to assist in paying their track access charges, Railtrack was in effect being heavily subsidised. In October 2001, the government decided that these arrangements were no longer viable and placed Railtrack into administration. This chapter explains how the level of indirect subsidies to Railtrack had become excessive, and raises crucial questions that need to be addressed in settling the future shape of the railway industry.

The privatisation of the British railway industry in 1996 was not typical of many of the earlier privatisations of other industries. There were two major differences affecting in this privatisation:

- The organisational and legally determined structure of the newly privatised railway meant that the network would be fragmented in a complex myriad of separate trading entities.
- The structure of the privatised industry would mean that some component companies of the rail industry would still require support for both revenue and capital expenditure in the form of central government subsidy.

The form of privatisation, and the subsequent determination of rail companies' income stream and levels of profitability, must also be placed in a political context. The organisational structures and financial control mechanisms in the privatised railway network are largely the products of the prevailing political climate at the time of privatisation. Many of the railway's established financial systems were subverted, and became more subservient to powerful and overriding political or regulatory objectives.

Railtrack plc became the owner of Britain's track, stations and signals. At the centre of the regulatory control of Railtrack were two key factors: the value of the company's assets (or, in practice, a proxy measure) and its

JOHN STITTLE is Fellow in Accounting in the Department of Accounting, Finance and Management at the University of Essex.

Administration

On 7 October 2001, as a result of a petition by the Secretary of State for Transport, Local Government and the Regions, Stephen Byers, the High Court agreed to put Railtrack plc into Railway Administration. Under the provisions of the Railways Act 1993, and with the government refusing further subsidies (Ford, 2001: 19), the High Court believed that Railtrack was insolvent. Railway Administrators were given the legal duty to manage the company and keep the rail network operational; they were also charged 'to agree the terms on which the licensed activities currently undertaken by Railtrack would be transferred out of Administration as a going concern'.

Railtrack's major funding difficulties can be directly traced to the Hatfield rail crash in October 2000. The accident was largely attributed to Railtrack's management failings and neglect of its infrastructure. The resulting introduction of the National Recovery Plan (to rectify this neglect), and the compensation payments to the TOCs, were reported to have cost at least £733 million by 31 March 2001 (Railtrack, 2000–2001). The company's financial difficulties were further compounded by major cost over-runs on capital programmes – for example, upgrading the West Coast Main Line, originally costed at £2.3 billion, had soared in excess of £7 billion (Grant, 2001).

Mr Byers indicated that the public interest obligations of Railtrack would, after Administration, be better achieved through the formation of a not-for-profit company without shareholders. He added that unless and until the track access charges were revised, the regulatory regime for the charges implemented for 2001–2006 would continue to apply.

---

permitted rate of return. These two variables were vital in establishing the level track charges imposed on Railtrack's major customers who are the train operating companies (TOCs). The level of revenue generated by the track access charges (TACs) therefore fundamentally affected Railtrack's total income stream.

Theoretically and politically, the high degree of regulation should have provided a more efficient railway infrastructure within clearly defined objectives and constraints. In practice, many of these objectives and constraints were considerably modified in Railtrack's favour.

Background

The United Kingdom's Transport Act 1993 laid the foundations for the eventual privatisation of the national railway network. The effect of this legislation was to fragment the former state-owned British Rail into more than 100 separate trading companies: the largest being Railtrack plc. TOCs paid Railtrack an annual fee, in the form of TACs, for the use of the track, stations and signals. The level of the TACs and Railtrack's overall profitability was determined by applying a rate of return to the regulatory asset base.

The level of the TACs charged by Railtrack was regulated by the Rail Regulator, Tom Winsor, who was required to examine the methodology and levels of the TACs every five years. The first regulatory regime, introduced on privatisation in 1996, expired in April 2001, and a new regulatory regime operates from 2001 to 2006. In addition to the Regulator, the rail industry is also supervised by the Strategic Rail Authority (SRA).

In contrast to some of the activities of other privatised state industries, Railtrack was a monopolistic supplier of its assets and services. The TOCs were compelled to use Railtrack's assets and pay its TACs. This monopolistic position is a key reason for the high degree of regulation. Railtrack did not receive revenue subsidies directly from the government, these being channelled via its customers, the TOCs, which operate passenger and freight services. Railtrack plc had an annual turnover of £2.54 billion (Railtrack, 2000–2001), over 90 per cent of this revenue originating from the access charges.

The level of the TACs was not only crucial for Railtrack, but also for the TOCs. Many of the TOCs would be unprofitable if they were required to pay the full level of TACs, so the majority of companies in effect receive substantial subsidies from the SRA. The TOCs were due to receive, in total, £913,028,000 in subsidy in the 2000–2001 financial year ('Shadow' SRA, 2000). When the TOCs pay track fees to Railtrack (or its successor Network Rail), they are, in effect, including a large proportion of state subsidy in these payments. Accordingly, both Railtrack and Network Rail have been substantial, although indirect, recipients of state funds.

The level of TACs needs to be determined so the Regulator can fulfil his statutory obligations. Under the Railway Act 1993, the Rail Regulator's main statutory objectives are to:

- Promote . . . and protect . . . railway services; promote use of the network; promote efficiency and economy on the part of persons providing rail services.
- Provide incentives to Railtrack, operators and funders to ensure the efficient utilisation of the network.
- Ensure that Railtrack is practical, cost-effective, comprehensive and objective in its operation. (ORR, 1999b)

Most of these objectives will be met only if the revised TACs are established at the appropriate level. It is within the framework of these objectives that the revised TACs can be assessed.

Income generation: Track access charges

Control over the level of the TACs was important in achieving the Regulator's objectives of providing a financial incentive for Railtrack 'to ensure efficient utilization and development of the network' (ORR, 1999a). However, in developing greater incentives, there was a major difficulty with the nature of

Railtrack's cost structure. It is reported that over 90 per cent of its income arising from the TACs comprises fixed costs (ORR, 1999a).

The Regulator believed that this situation constituted little incentive for Railtrack to increase capacity and accommodate additional services. Nevertheless, a key component of his objectives was to provide adequate financial incentives for Railtrack. Determination of Railtrack's cost of capital determined its permitted return on capital and hence had a direct relationship to the level of track charges. In establishing the level of the revised TACs, it was essential that this cost of capital was set at a level that delivered greater incentives for Railtrack (or its successor) as operator of the infrastructure.

In the Regulator's opinion (ORR, 1999a), the first TACs regime for 1996–2001 was unsatisfactory in terms of meeting his statutory objectives. He noted: 'These [1996–2001] arrangements have failed to deliver the improvements which were intended.' In other words, the Regulator recognised that the initial TACs failed to generate operating, efficiency or financial benefits. Moreover, the situation was unlikely to improve owing to the use of a dubious, if not totally inappropriate, methodology in calculating the asset base to determine the revised TACs for 2001–2006. During the consultation period leading up to the announcement of revised TACs, the Regulator continually revised his economic and accounting assumptions in Railtrack's favour. The earlier problems in calculating its asset base were compounded by the use of an excessively high return on capital and undemanding efficiency targets.

Structure of TACs

The revised TACs did not meet with Railtrack's approval. The company alleged that the initial TACs were unsatisfactory, since there was little or no incentive to encourage growth in train operations because most of its costs were fixed (Railtrack, 2000–2001). The revenue benefits of permitting additional services to operate on its tracks would largely accrue to the TOCs instead. Therefore, any revised structure of charges needs to be modified to encourage additional cash inflows as a result of potential growth.

Railtrack's TACs were based upon usage charges (reflecting the cost of running an extra train on the network), charges for electricity for traction purposes and fixed charges (comprising over 91 per cent of costs). Even very small changes in the variables affecting the level of these charges has a significant effect on the level of charges in terms of net cash flows payable by the TOCs (ORR, 1999a).

As part of the TACs methodology, Railtrack could pass operating (variable) costs directly onto the TOCs as part of the level of the TACs. (Levels of actual TACs can be subject to some variation between TOCs and vary on different rail lines depending on the track quality, availability of train paths, and peak or non-peak hour usage.) The fixed charges represent the residual revenue requirement, after deducting the expected revenues from variable charges and other sources, such as property income. This approach is also based on a default mechanism. Fixed costs are, in effect, a remaining balance, the cost of which is simply passed on to the TOCs. However, this approach does not help to fulfil the Regulator's statutory objectives. It neither encourages traffic growth nor provides a viable basis for future capital investment growth, though it is modified by a requirement to apply the Regulator's efficiency savings.

The first TAC regulatory controls were introduced at the time of privatisation in 1996. However, the Regulator (ORR, 2000a: 1) later accepted that Railtrack was 'privatized in a hurry, with inadequate attention paid to . . . the regulatory and contractual matrix'. He also conceded that the initial TAC regime did little to remedy Railtrack's 'weak financial structure and gave it little or no incentive to invest' (ORR, 2000a: 1). The first TACs were rapidly issued for the impending Railtrack flotation. They were brief and poorly structured. Railtrack's 'outputs which . . . [it was] . . . expected to deliver were not clearly defined or monitored' (ORR, 2000a: 1). Additionally, there were 'insufficient incentives' for Railtrack to provide appropriate network enhancements and a failure to provide investors 'with the confidence to continue to provide finance for new infrastructure projects' (ORR, 1999a: 1).

Essentially, the first round of TACs were established to cover operating costs, current cost depreciation and a return on capital. The operating costs comprised costs of 'infrastructure maintenance, day-to-day operating costs and external costs such as rates and electricity' (ORR, 1995: 9). These costs were to be subject to annual efficiency savings of 3 per cent per annum. Current cost depreciation was based upon replacing the assets in a 'modern equivalent form'. The pre-tax return on assets (valued at current cost) was to be 8 per cent per annum, in line with other 'public sector trading organizations' (ORR, 1995: 9).

Establishing revised levels of TACs

The first stage of calculating the TACs was to determine Railtrack's 'activity level' expenditure, required 'to operate, maintain and enhance the network to deliver' the rail network in (what is termed), 'a steady-state' condition. In effect, this expenditure was the amount needed to maintain the rail infrastructure in its present condition, without any capital improvements or additions. In his earlier proposals (ORR, 2000a), the Regulator believed that, over the 5-year review period (2001–2006), the total maintenance, renewal and operating 'steady-state' expenditure would amount to £15.7 billion. Further pressure from Railtrack caused the Regulator to increase the amount to £16.1 billion, most of which was directly passed on to the TOCs. This did not encourage cost control.

The only publicly available evidence to support the higher figure came from engineers (consulted by Railtrack) who believed that it was a reasonable estimate (Booz Allen & Hamilton, 1999). Not all such estimates have been published, but the Regulator, apparently, accepted most of them. Not only

167

was the expenditure set in the upper ranges, but the efficiency savings applied to the total figure also appeared lenient in comparison with other regulatory regimes in other industries.

Efficiency savings

Against the increased allocation of £16.1 billion for direct costs over five years, the Regulator insisted on efficiency savings. He assumed net savings of 2 per cent overall (ORR, 2000b) in the first year of the new controls, followed by 3 per cent for the next year, 4 per cent per year in years 3 and 4, and 5 per cent in the last year. This implied an average equivalent constant overall cost reduction of 3.1 per cent per annum.

Although the Regulator conceded that there 'is substantial scope for improved efficiency', the target was still rather low compared to other privatised utility companies. Other Regulators (e.g., in the water and electricity industry) have applied at least 3 per cent per year efficiency savings (OFWAT, 1999), and in the early years of their privatised existence even higher savings were achieved. Certainly in the early years of the revised TACs, the efficiency savings did not appear unduly onerous. In his draft report (ORR, 2000a), the Regulator was working on the basis of a simple average efficiency saving of 4.2 per cent each year. Pressure from Railtrack seems to have reduced this figure by nearly 25 per cent. Probably, the need for greater investment led the Regulator to be rather reluctant to demand higher efficiency savings. His explanation was that 'the rate of investment in enhancements to the railway is likely to put significant upward pressure on Railtrack's costs and this will tend to reduce the net cost reductions which can be achieved in the short term' (ORR, 2000a).

Cost of capital

The Regulator had a difficult balance to achieve in setting Railtrack's rate of return. The cost of capital had to be low enough so the monopolistic supplier could not exploit its position; and it had to be high enough so that the company's shareholders received an adequate return on their investment. The Regulator stressed (ORR, 2000a) that in considering the appropriate value for the cost of capital, he had 'to discharge his duties . . . [so] . . . not to make it unduly difficult for Railtrack to finance its relevant activities'.

In the same report (ORR, 2000a) on his conclusions from the periodic review, the Regulator particularly stressed that the cost of capital would be up to 1 per cent higher than the electricity and gas industry because of 'differences in the underlying risks'. The nature of these differences and risks, and just how they differ for Railtrack, was not explained. The Regulator did highlight that the cost of capital and the permitted return were set to accommodate 'the need for Railtrack to raise substantial new finance, including equity' (ORR, 2000a: 39).

Most of the information about investment plans appeared vague in detail and timing. Although the Regulator noted that (ORR, 2000b) the Regulatory Asset Base (RAB) would increase by a total £1.656 billion over the period 2001–2006, many of the future investment schemes gave an overall appearance of only very generalised intent. For example, the schemes included vague items such as 'station modernization facilities', and the politically sensitive investment areas of 'train protection'. Other projected enhancements to the rail network (not included in the RAB) totalled £6.56 billion, but no meaningful breakdown was given.

In order to determine Railtrack's regulated return on assets, the company's cost of capital has to be calculated. The weighted average cost of capital determines the allowed rate of return on the RAB. The Regulator has three factors to take into account: the cost of debt, the cost of equity and assumed level of gearing.

Cost of debt

Railtrack's cost of debt had two components: the 'risk-free rate' and a company-specific premium. The Regulator originally used index-linked government bonds as the base measure for the risk-free rate – these bonds have virtually nil risk of default and largely eliminate the inflation risk. At the time of the Regulator's proposals, the redemption yield for index-linked gilts with maturities of five years ranged between 2.2 and 2.5 per cent. Railtrack regarded this figure as too low, and wished to use a longer-term average rate. Over the period January 1986 to April 1998, this rate ranged from 3.5 to 3.8 per cent. (These figures were obtained by the Rail Regulator and they ceased at 1998. This latter date was the last possible date by which they could be incorporated into the draft discussion document for the 2001–2006 track charges. The final TAC document was based on these figures.) In the revised TACs, the Rail Regulator (ORR, 1999b) stated that it was his intention to set a forward-looking cost of capital 'since this will better reflect what Railtrack has to pay in the capital market'. The Regulator used a range of 2.25 to 3 per cent to take account of the recent variability of the risk-free rate.

In addition, there was also a debt premium to consider. In his December 1999 review, the Regulator suggested a premium up to 1.5 per cent over the existing rates. Later, in the October 2000 review, the Regulator generously accepted Railtrack's objections that the original premium was too low and proposed that the real cost of debt, in total, should be between 4.5 and 4.75 per cent. (These figures imply a premium of a seemingly excessive 1.5 to 1.75 per cent over the assumed risk-free rate.) In relative percentage terms, this new debt premium represented a large increase of 25 per cent over the initial debt premium. Considering the monopolistic nature of Railtrack's business (supported indirectly and by relatively secure state aid), the risk of debt default was low – it appeared that the bondholders in Railtrack plc (in contrast to the shareholders) would not lose a great amount. Indeed, when

169

Railtrack was superseded by a new not-for-profit company, Network Rail (see below), the bondholders were quite reasonably compensated. Additionally, the Regulator sweepingly assumed that future debt rates levels would remain relatively high.

Cost of equity

The Regulator originally proposed estimating the cost of equity using the Capital Asset Pricing Model (CAPM), which is used in other regulated industries. The general CAPM determines the cost of equity by applying the equity beta value to the equity risk premium and then incorporating the risk-free rate of return. Under CAPM, the risk of equity is generally reflected in the equity risk premium. This premium (for holding equity) is the market return in excess of the risk-free rate. The Regulator did not want the company to use the historical equity risk premium, but preferred the risk premium currently demanded by investors in providing equity. In the water industry, the Regulator used a premium between 2.75 and 3.75 per cent (OFWAT, 1999). Using CAPM, the Rail Regulator believed that a higher equity risk premium between 3 and 4 per cent was appropriate for Railtrack. In response, Railtrack said that a range of 3.35 to 5 per cent should be used. Railtrack claimed that this higher figure was needed because the recent general stock market equity risk premium was at an historically low figure.

In order to identify a narrower central range for the cost of capital, the Regulator proposed to focus on a range of 3.25 to 3.75 per cent for the equity risk premium – a figure that is similar to the values assumed by Ofgem, the Regulator for gas and electricity (ORR, 2000b). Railtrack claimed that its equity risk premium should be higher because the scale of the task of operating the rail infrastructure is large and has increased since privatisation. The Regulator agreed, but said it did not affect the forward-looking risks affecting the company. Additionally, Railtrack claimed that the risk of capital expenditure 'overruns' in the rail industry was higher than other utilities, but provided little justification or evidential support for this argument. Given the importance of investment, the Rail Regulator agreed that the assumed cost of capital would be sufficient for Railtrack to obtain the investment it needed.

Assumed level of gearing

The equity beta depends on the overall level of gearing, since additional gearing increases the variability of equity returns. (Identifying the equity beta allows a company's specific share price to be compared with general systematic stock market changes. For example, an equity beta of 0.75 will imply that, if general market equity prices increase by 1 per cent, then Railtrack's individual equity price will increase by 0.75 per cent and vice versa.) The previous Rail Regulator, John Swift, had assumed an equity beta of between 0.75

and 0.85, based on Railtrack's low historic level of gearing. Railtrack believed the appropriate range for its beta was 0.8 to 1.0. If the equity beta used by the former Regulator is taken into account to include a gearing level of 50 per cent, the result would be an adjusted equity beta in the range of 1.2 to 1.35. Compared with other privatised former utilities (some of which are in a more competitive trading environment, such as companies in the gas and electricity supply industry), this adjusted beta factor appeared rather high and unduly advantageous to Railtrack.

In response to representations from Railtrack, it became apparent that the Regulator had accepted many of the company's demands to increase the overall cost of capital. In the October 2000 TACs review (ORR, 2000b), the Regulator was still concerned about Railtrack's ability to raise new finance 'without undue difficulty'. In part, continual fear of deterring new investment seems to have been behind some of the reasons for the Regulator's lenient treatment of Railtrack. The Regulator proposed a pre-tax real weighted average cost of capital between 5.9 and 7.9 per cent, after initially suggesting a range between 7.0 and 7.5 per cent. This latter figure was 0.5 to 1.9 per cent higher than that proposed by Ofgem.

The Regulator considered that his position had been weakened by the intervention of the Competition Commission in the water industry. A referral to the Commission by Mid-Kent Water plc and Sutton and East Surrey plc (13 September 2000) increased the cost of capital even further. Comments from the Commission, although not legally binding on the Regulator, were indicative of the findings that might be made about Railtrack if reference were made to the Commission. The findings of the water industry case were that the cost of capital was to be determined at the upper end of the water companies' demands (Competition Commission, 2001).

Arguments in the case centred on the determination of the risk-free rate. Although this was based on gilts which had experienced falling yields, the Regulator agreed (with Ofgem's view) that the longer the present relatively low yields on index-linked and conventional gilts persisted, then 'the more persuasive becomes the argument that these lower yields are not simply a feature of shorter term market conditions' (ORR, 2000b). In practice, adopting the Competition Commission's views of the cost of capital would increase Railtrack's estimated cost of capital by 0.46 per cent.

The Regulator's final position was that Railtrack's real pre-tax rate of return should be 8 per cent. This was intended to allow Railtrack the scope and incentive to invest in new projects. On 13 March 2001, however, the SRA announced that it was considering taking over responsibility for Railtrack's new investment programme. It noted: 'Many felt Railtrack could assume leadership of the industry. It did not' (SRA, 2001). If implemented, Railtrack would have been relieved of a large investment programme and, correspondingly, a substantial risk. This reduction in risk would impact upon the 8 per cent return, which could fall substantially, perhaps as low as 5 per cent, reflecting the transformation of Railtrack into a maintenance company.

Regulatory Asset Base (RAB)

It was in Railtrack's interests for the RAB to be stated at the highest value, since it formed the basis for calculating the permitted return on capital. Throughout the negotiation process with the Regulator, Railtrack attempted to obtain the highest valuation. It tried to capitalise the largest amounts of assets possible instead of classifying them, for example, as maintenance costs or repairs, which would mean that those items were treated as 'one-off' expenses and written off to the profit and loss account.

The Regulator originally regarded the use of tangible fixed assets as the basis for the RAB as inappropriate. In his December 1997 review, it was reported that: 'the current cost value or replacement cost of existing assets . . . is considerably higher than the market value of Railtrack at the time of flotation [and this] . . . is not an appropriate basis on which to value Railtrack since this would over-reward the shareholders at the expense of their customers' (ORR, 1997: 59).

The Regulator initially believed that the value of equity should be rebased at the close of the first day's trading, so that shareholders would be remunerated for any deliberate political under-pricing which had occurred in order to ensure the success of the flotation. Railtrack, on the other hand, believed that its share price at or near flotation was not a fair measure because it did not compensate for the perceived risks associated with flotation that it considered were greater than other privatisations. It argued that the RAB should include an uplift on the first day's trading value, both for consistency with other regulators and for the alleged higher risks at privatisation. It believed the appropriate date for the initial value of the RAB was at the close of trading after the 1997 general election, when the share price was £6.52 rather than £3.90 at the close of the first day. Railtrack believed that these assumptions implied a RAB of £4 billion. By contrast, on his assumptions, the Regulator concluded that Railtrack's RAB was £2.54 billion (value at 20 May 1996), which represented an uplift of 5 per cent on the value of equity over the offer price.

In the July 2000 periodic review, the Regulator noted that Railtrack now wanted the RAB revalued (at 2000 price levels) to £6.86 billion, but the Regulator ultimately decided on £5.11 billion (ORR, 2000a). Additionally, the Regulator used a 15 per cent uplift – a level at the top end of expectations. Although the Regulator did not concede all of Railtrack's demands, the concessions that were made appeared arbitrary.

The level of the uplift, in principle, was finally confirmed in the October 2000 review. Again, as a result of pressure from Railtrack, this RAB was increased by further enhancement expenditure that would be made over the next control period of £1.52 billion. By March 2006, this core RAB would increase to £7.9 billion (ORR, 2000c). This was a net total increase of £1.2 billion since the July draft conclusions. In his final draft conclusions (ORR, 2000b), the Regulator accepted the proposed 15 per cent uplift largely to accommodate the under-pricing of shares because of the perceived high degree of political risk. The permitted return subsequently applied to this RAB value would determine the overall profitability levels of Railtrack's regulated activities.

Conclusions

The key determinant of Railtrack's income was the level of TACs. Although the revised TACs presented major concerns, there were some benefits. The revised 2001–2006 TACs were more clearly defined and better structured than the earlier 1996 TACs. The 1996 calculation of the regulatory asset base using the complex (and contentious) accounting methodology of modern equivalent assets was seemingly disregarded. Additionally, current cost depreciation based on modern equivalent assets were dropped. Efficiency savings were more explicitly targeted and publicised.

Despite these limited improvements and benefits arising from the revised TACs, both the permitted return and the value of the RAB seemed excessively high and the efficiency savings too low. There was no evidence that the new charges would provide greater incentives for Railtrack to invest more heavily in the future, an original objective of the Regulator. The Regulator's statutory objectives in establishing the level of TACs were explicit. The TACs were to be set to ensure that Railtrack 'is cost effective, comprehensive and objective in its operation [and promoted] efficiency and economy' of the rail network (ORR, 1999b). However, the revised TACs provided little evidence that these objectives would be fulfilled. Likewise, there was no reason to assume that the TACs would meet the other major objective of providing 'incentives to Railtrack . . . to ensure efficient utilization of the network' (ORR, 1999b).

The level of the TACs was largely dependent upon three key variables: the cost of capital, the regulatory asset base and, to a slightly lesser extent, efficiency savings. In many instances of decisions involving these three variables in the revised TACs, the Regulator conceded many of Railtrack's demands and interpretations. There were very few instances where the Regulator's control mechanisms were strongly directed against Railtrack despite the company's protestations. Nor would it appear that the revised TACs assisted the Regulator in fulfilling his statutory obligations and objectives. As a consequence, the government was eventually faced with having to support the TOCs through higher subsidies to enable the TOCs to bid and operate their franchises. The final outcome of the revised TACs was a degree of misallocation of public resources with an excessively high level of public funds being needed to support a private-sector company.

Update on recent developments

On 3 October 2002, with strong encouragement from the government, Network Rail Ltd. reached final agreement to purchase the infrastructure company,

Railtrack plc, from its parent company, Railtrack Group plc. Network Rail agreed to pay Railtrack Group £500 million for its equity interests in Railtrack plc and assume responsibility for around £1.7 million of Railtrack's existing debt. Network Rail also agreed to pay £80 million for the rights to operate, manage and maintain the Channel Tunnel Rail Link, along with the concession to manage St Pancras station in London (ORR, 2002a).

Although the Rail Regulator had earlier established the TAC for the period 2001–2006, he had inserted a contractual provision (ORR 2002b) into each franchised passenger train operating company's agreement enabling him 'to initiate an early review of access charges' if he considered that there is a material change in circumstances and if it is 'unduly difficult for persons who are holders of network licences to finance their activities'. In the light of these two conditions, the Regulator consulted with the SRA, the Department for Transport and other interested parties in the rail industry about reviewing the TACS. After receiving 'widespread support', the Regulator indicated that the TACS would be reviewed for implementation from April 2004. Further information about the level of these revised TACS has not yet been provided.

Acknowledgement

The author is grateful to two anonymous referees for their helpful comments on an earlier draft.

Note

1 A version of this article was originally published in *Public Money & Management* 22(1) (2002).

References

Booz Allen & Hamilton (1999). *Railway Infrastructure Cost Causation* (Consultants' Report for ORR). London: Booz Allen & Hamilton.

Competition Commission (2001). *Mid Kent Water plc and Sutton and East Surrey plc*. London: Competition Commission.

Ford, R. (2001). In: *Modern Railways* 58(638): 19.

Grant, S. (2001). In: *Modern Railways* 58(638): 26.

Office of the Rail Regulator (ORR) (1995). *Railtrack's Access Charges for Franchised Passenger Services: The Future Level of Charges: A Policy Statement*. London: ORR.

Office of the Rail Regulator (ORR) (1997). *Review of Railtrack's Access Charges: A Proposed Framework and Key Issues: A Consultation Document*. London: ORR.

Office of the Rail Regulator (ORR) (1999a). *Periodic Review of Railtrack's Access Charges: The Incentive Framework: A Consultative Document*. London: ORR.

Office of the Rail Regulator (ORR) (1999b). *Periodic Review of Railtrack's Access Charges: Provisional Conclusions on Revenue Requirements*. London: ORR.

Office of the Rail Regulator (ORR) (2000a). *Periodic Review of Railtrack's Track Access Charges: Draft Conclusions, Vol. 1*. London: ORR.

Office of the Rail Regulator (ORR) (2000b). *The Periodic Review of Railtrack's Access Charges: Final Conclusions, Vol. 1 and Vol. 11*. London: ORR.

Office of the Rail Regulator (ORR) (2000c). Press release, 20 October. London: ORR.

Office of the Rail Regulator (ORR) (2002a). *The Proposed Acquisition of Railtrack plc by Network Rail Ltd: A Statement by the Rail Regulator*. London: ORR.

Office of the Rail Regulator (ORR) (2002b). *Network Rail: Interim Review of Access Charges – A Statement by the Rail Regulator*. London: ORR.

OFWAT (1999). *Draft Determination of Future Water and Sewage Charges 2000–2005*. London: OFWAT.

Railtrack (2000–2001). *2000 Annual Report and Accounts*. London: Railtrack Group plc.

SBC Warburg (1996). *Railtrack Share Offer Prospectus*. London: SBC Warburg.

Shadow Strategic Rail Authority (SRA) (2000). *Annual Report 2000*. London: Shadow SRA.

Strategic Rail Authority (SRA) (2001). *A Strategic Agenda*. London: SRA.

16. Delivering Better Transport? An Evaluation of the Ten-year Plan for the Railway Industry[1]

GERALD CROMPTON AND ROBERT JUPE

In July 2000, the British government published Transport 2010, *its 10-year plan to improve the nation's transport. This chapter reviews the proposals to improve the railway system, and examines their likely effects on investment by the railway companies and on passenger safety. The plan is analyzed in the context of the structure of the privatised railway industry and its regulatory bodies, with particular reference to the performance of the now-defund Railtrack. The authors conclude that the government was over-confident in believing that a defective privatised structure could deliver the expansion it wanted. The situation is unlikely to improve unless the rail industry is restructured and its ownership structure simplified.*

The Labour Government, elected in May 1997, was not expected to approve of the railway structure hastily established by its predecessor. In opposition, Labour had resisted the privatisation of British Rail (BR) until 1996, but, in government, it took the view that this system could be made to work with more forceful regulation. What remained was to supply a new goal of planned expansion of the network in order to increase rail use in the context of an integrated transport system. A new mechanism was also needed to supply strategic leadership for the industry, and to oversee the implementation of the new government's vision.

Transport was not given priority during the Labour Government's first term, and progress was slow. An ambitious integrated transport White Paper was issued by the newly created Department of the Environment, Transport and the Regions (DETR, 1998). The White Paper's comprehensive range of 11 subsidiary documents covered road and rail, but also included waterways and walking. Legislative priorities, however, meant that the long-awaited Transport Bill became law only in Autumn 2000. In the meantime, a Strategic Rail Authority (SRA) was established in shadow form in early 1999, gaining

GERALD CROMPTON is a Senior Lecturer in Business History at Canterbury Business School at the University of Kent. ROBERT JUPE is a Lecturer in Accounting at Canterbury Business School at the University of Kent.

statutory basis more than two years later. The SRA was the government's chosen instrument for implementing its growth strategy. In broad terms, *Transport 2010*, the government's 10-year plan, defined its agenda. The project required the co-operation of everyone in the industry, but the government's hopes were dependent primarily on the performance of the SRA for strategic direction, and on Railtrack for infrastructure investment.

Another change intended to add direction to the government's transport strategy was the enhanced role given to Passenger Transport Executives (PTEs) by the Transport Act 2000. PTEs have, since their inception in 1968, had powers to provide financial support to rail passenger services in conurbations outside London. This role was enlarged to include responsibility for implementing an integrated transport strategy. PTEs are co-signatories to five passenger franchise agreements, and have been able to develop some new train services (SRA, 2002: 7).

The 10-year plan aimed to improve all types of transport, in order to 'tackle congestion and pollution' and 'to create prosperity and a better environment' (DETR, 2000: 9). Its features included:

- A 50 per cent increase in passenger use.
- An 80 per cent increase in rail freight.
- Installation of new train safety systems.
- Modern trains.
- Modernisation, and increased capacity, on the west coast and east coast main lines.
- A high-speed Channel Tunnel Rail Link.
- Improved commuter services in London and other cities.

This essay examines the transport plan in the context of the performance of the privatised railway system.

Analysis of problems with privatisation

Transport 2010 provided a cogent analysis of the weaknesses of rail privatisation. It drew attention to the 'years of under-investment', which produced 'an outdated and unreliable network' (DETR, 2000: 42). It also emphasised that privatisation 'created a fragmented system where reducing public subsidy, not improving or expanding services, was the priority'. This system had a number of major weaknesses (DETR, 2000: 42):

- There was no framework for strategic planning of the industry as a whole.
- Most franchises were held by the train operating companies (TOCs) for only seven years, thus inhibiting long-term planning and investment.
- Performance standards were generally based on low historic norms.
- The industry structure did not anticipate the need for significant investment to cope with sharply increased passenger and freight traffic.
- There were no incentives for private companies to invest in expansion.

In the late 1990s, confidence in the privatised system declined substantially. Even previous supporters of privatisation became alienated. The *Economist* concluded that privatisation was a 'disastrous failure', incorporating 'political cynicism, managerial incompetence and financial opportunism'. Atomisation of the system had generated 'perverse' incentives and radical changes were needed (*Economist*, 1999a). The accident near Paddington in October 1999, when over 30 people died, increased support for this position and contributed in part to a poll result that month that showed over 70 per cent of voters favoured Railtrack's re-nationalisation (Travis & Wells, 1999).

This declining confidence was hardly surprising, given that John Major's Conservative Government had introduced a system with 'features which are not currently possessed by any other European railway' (Nash, 2000: 161). Supporters of the fragmented structure claimed that it resulted from European Union Directive 91/440, requiring railway infrastructure to be separated from operations. However, 'separation' was mandatory only as an accounting mechanism, and not an organisational split (Wolmar, 2001a: 65). It was only the United Kingdom that privatised the infrastructure and 'adopted a comprehensive policy of subcontracting out the supply of . . . rolling stock and the renewal and maintenance of infrastructure to the private sector' (Nash, 2000: 162).

Strategy for improvement

Despite the fragmented system, the key change introduced by *Transport 2010* was financial rather than structural – the need to increase public funding in order to expand the network and increase passenger and rail freight use over ten years (DETR, 2000: 45). There was a halt in the planned decline in subsidy to the TOCs. The Conservative Government 'set subsidies for the train operators at sharply declining rates, with . . . payments reducing by £2–300 million per year from the initial level of £1.8 billion in 1996/97' (Wolmar, 2001a: 113). Instead, £11 billion of revenue support for train operators was planned. In addition, the SRA would administer a new £7 billion Rail Modernisation Fund to encourage investment, and capital payments of £4 billion were intended for Railtrack to fund renewal schemes.

Implications for infrastructure investment

Private-sector investment

There was still a heavy reliance on the private sector to deliver infrastructure investment. The plan argued that: 'The private sector – usually Railtrack or train operators – will carry out the investment in new infrastructure. The Government will need to provide substantial financial support' (DETR, 2000: 44). Close textual analysis reveals strong similarities between this approach and that of the Conservative Government's privatisation White Paper, *New Opportunities for the Railways*, which stated:

The Government wants to ensure that Railtrack continues to invest to maintain and improve the network. Investment will largely be financed from charges to operators ... the Government is also ready to provide direct support for investment. ... Railtrack will normally have the lead responsibility for promoting major investment. (DoT, 1992: 10)

The 1992 document did not indicate exactly how investment in the railway might increase. Harman (1993: 23) thought 'significant expansion of infrastructure, and hence of the network, seems highly unlikely'.

Interface costs and cash leakages

The structure of the privatised system had major implications for railway finances and railway investment. These may be summarised as 'interface costs' and 'cash leakages' (Harris & Godward, 1997: 107). Interface costs arise because many companies are involved in a supply chain, and so there is upward pressure on prices as each company aims to make a profit on its contribution. One important architect of rail privatisation argued that the new system would improve economic efficiency. While accepting that the new rail charges would 'increase costs overall', he argued, curiously, that the changes would not have 'any significance for customers or franchisees' as costs were simply being reclassified and increased public subsidy would support the required return on assets (Foster, 1994: 23). While possibly valid in a narrow sense, this view ignored the planned decline in subsidy and the effect of cash leakages and under-investment on the railway system.

A dramatic example of interface costs is represented by the Rolling Stock Leasing Companies (ROSCOs). Virtually all their income is from the TOCs, whose revenue is supported by subsidy. In 1995–1996, the ROSCOs generated pre-tax profits of £331 million, which represented a phenomenal return of 41 per cent on an £800 million turnover. By 1997–1998, pre-tax profits had risen to £387 million on a turnover of £797 million – a return of 48 per cent. This amazing performance might be ascribed to efficiency gains. The *Economist* (1999a: 86), however, noted that the cautious BR engineers had, before privatisation, over-estimated maintenance costs, the firms' 'chief operating expense'. Some rationale might have been found for these interface costs had they led to a major increase in infrastructure investment. In practice, however, there were major leakages in the form of profits and dividends. Railtrack paid out dividends totalling £709 million between 1995–1996 and 2000–2001, representing 41 per cent of the total operating profits of £1,700 million generated over six years (Railtrack, 1995–1996 to 2000–2001). Such payments were highly significant, both in terms of the size of the leakages, and in the opportunity cost in lost investment. In theory, Railtrack and its senior management were

179

meant to be incentivised by the rate of return on capital allowed and bonus schemes (Foster, 1994: 21–22).

Railtrack's investment plans

In practice, however, 91 per cent of the access charges paid by the TOCs were fixed and so gave 'little incentive for Railtrack' to increase network capacity (Stittle, 2002: 50). Following the Regulator's complaint of a £700 million maintenance underspend at the end of 1996, Railtrack's licence was amended to strengthen its duties to maintain, renew and enhance the network (Wolmar, 2001a: 99), but the enforcement issue persisted.

Railtrack was required to publish an annual Network Management Statement (NMS), a key document detailing plans to maintain and improve the network. The initial NMSs were thin affairs, labelled 'a disgrace' by the first Regulator, John Swift QC (Wolmar, 2001a: 215). The 1998 NMS announced that £17 billion would be spent over ten years 'to regenerate the railways', but this earned a Regulator's rebuke deploring the 'very few commitments to deliver significant improvements' (Harper, 1998a). The investment 'plan' was further undermined by Railtrack's Chief Executive, Gerald Corbett, who emphasised that the programme depended on the Regulator's satisfactory review of access charges as 'profits are good for the industry and . . . our investment programme' (Walters, 1998).

This combination – ambitious projects conditional upon a generous regulatory regime – became Railtrack's mantra. Its 1999 NMS offered £27 billion of expenditure over ten years, but only guaranteed £5 billion of maintenance expenditure. This approach was repeated with the 2000 NMS, which indicated expenditure of £52 billion over 12 years. However, Corbett conceded that Railtrack had 'stayed on a profit . . . agenda for too long. We have now . . . the public service obligations agenda' (Walters, 2000). This conversion aimed to reinforce the case 'that funding would have to come from elsewhere . . . the NMS merely set out aspirations . . . that were increasingly dependent on government subsidy' (Wolmar, 2001a: 215).

Transport 2010 increased rail's financial support, but gave mixed signals to Railtrack. The Rail Modernisation Fund, administered by the SRA, allowed the industry to 'formulate a long-term investment programme' (DETR, 2000: 45). It also accepted the need for capital payments to Railtrack. In 1999, however, management consultants commissioned by the Regulator reached the disturbing conclusion that 'there has been a decline in the . . . network assets'. Their report highlighted inadequate maintenance, poor safety standards and a decline in the railway system (Elliott & Smithers, 1999).

Railtrack's maintenance policy

A major investigation by the National Audit Office (NAO, 2000a) into maintenance and renewal expenditure by Railtrack drew attention both to the problems of inadequate expenditure, and to the regulatory framework's limitations. The NAO's report emphasised the consequences of a low track renewals rate with, for example, the number of broken rails increasing by 25 per cent to 937 in 1998–1999, compared to 755 in 1997–1998 and Railtrack's forecast of 600 (NAO, 2000a: 6). It also stressed that there had been regulatory problems, and that 'much still needs to be done to provide a fully effective regime' (NAO, 2000a: 8).

The inadequate rail maintenance was not accidental, but stemmed from Railtrack's adoption of 'Project Destiny'. This project was based on 'targeting replacement of assets only when . . . needed rather than at set time intervals' (Wolmar, 2001a: 167). The attempt to save on expenditure provided the context for the Hatfield crash in October 2000, which 'nearly brought Britain's railways to a halt' and brought Railtrack 'to the verge of bankruptcy' (Wolmar, 2001a: 1–2). Cracks in rails were spotted in 1999, but due to a series of blunders, the rails were not replaced (Wolmar, 2001a: 2). Railtrack, lacking an asset register, could not establish whether there were more broken rails. The introduction of over 1,000 speed restrictions in an attempt to remedy the accumulated maintenance deficit resulted in widespread paralysis and Chief Executive Gerald Corbett's departure.

Railtrack's project management

Railtrack's management of a flagship investment project – the west coast main line (WCML) upgrade – was also subject to damning criticism. This was intended to allow Virgin to run high-speed trains between London and Glasgow by May 2002, but fell behind schedule as costs escalated. By March 2000, enforcement action was threatened as the project was two years behind schedule, and costs had risen from £2.1 billion to £5.8 billion. The new Rail Regulator, Tom Winsor, claimed that Railtrack's approach was 'one of promises made and not kept' (Harper, 2000). The escalating bill demonstrated both poor project management skills and substantial interface costs. One analysis suggests the result of 'contractual interfaces' was that Railtrack had to spend around 2.5 times more money in real terms than BR to obtain the same result (Ford, 2001a). Nevertheless, *Transport 2010* proposed to compensate Railtrack for its overspending on the WCML through capital payments because of its 'exceptional nature' (DETR, 2000: 45).

As an alternative to dependence on Railtrack for major projects, a study for the (then) Shadow SRA floated the idea of using Special Purpose Vehicles (SPVs). These were envisaged as customised partnerships formed to tackle specific investment schemes (James & Nissan, 2000: 20). To date, no SPV is working. The first, including GoVia, Railtrack, Bechtel and the SRA, was integral to the new SouthCentral franchise, but 'hit a bureaucratic quagmire' and has been abandoned (Wolmar, 2001b: 24).

181

Railtrack in administration

The publication of *Transport 2010* was quickly followed by generous financial settlements for Railtrack. In October 2000, the Regulator allowed a 35 per cent increase in revenue from grants and access charges to £13.5 billion for the period 2001–2006 (ORR, 2000, Paragraphs 1.6–1.22). The costs of the Hatfield crash, initially estimated at £600 million, led to a revised settlement in April 2001 that allowed Railtrack to bring forward £1.5 billion of grant revenue from 2006. Despite the fact that the Regulator 'continually revised' his assumptions in Railtrack's favour (Stittle, 2002: 50), the company 'was haemorrhaging cash' (Ford, 2001b: 17). On 7 October 2001, it was put into administration by the Transport Secretary, Stephen Byers, who obtained a court order after refusing further financial support. This action was Byers' preferred alternative to re-nationalisation. However, the move created problems. In the short term, there were the costs of the 'administrators' fees', delays to 'enhancement projects', and the creation of 'confusion and uncertainty in the industry' (House of Commons, 2002: Paragraph 45). For the long term, the uncertainty about Byers' preferred replacement, a company limited by guarantee without shareholders, risks undermining the infrastructure improvements essential to *Transport 2010*. There is 'no evidence' that the generous funding settlement of 2000–2001 will provide 'greater incentives' for investment (Stittle, 2002: 54), and the government has not made it clear how the new company will raise debt finance or how a strong 'credit rating will be secured' (House of Commons, 2002: Paragraph 50).

In October 2002, after year in administration, Railtrack was succeeded by Network Rail (NR), a company financed by debt and limited by guarantee, which was officially described first as 'not for profit' and then as 'not for dividend'. Although its debts and borrowings were to be controversially excluded from the Public Sector Borrowing Requirement (PSBR), it was virtually a public-sector organisation, with a heavy direct and indirect financial dependence on the government. NR experienced continued difficulties in containing costs, and the 'managerial transformation' required by the SRA (2002: 15) remains elusive. Expenditure on the network in 2002–2003 was on course for a sum of nearly £6 billion, or two-thirds more than the Regulator had sanctioned. These figures gave rise to gloomy projections that maintenance alone might cost up to £30 billion over the period 2001–2006, and that no resources would be left for enhancement (Giles & Jowit, 2003: 17). Escalation in costs was accompanied by a decline in performance (with about 20 per cent of trains arriving late) and a fall in productivity of over 30 per cent after the Hatfield disaster (Giles & Jowit, 2003: 17). This expensive deterioration provoked comments even from friendly observers such as 'rail's costs have doubled in the last few years whilst efficiency is getting worse' and 'the industry is *awash* with money . . . the problem is that it is being spent rather badly' (Harris, 2003: 3). NR certainly intended to take engineering more seriously than its predecessor, but was initially reluctant to bring maintenance work back in-house. Some exceptions have now been announced, and the bulk of engineering work now seems unlikely to remain out-sourced.

Implications for investment by train operating companies

Rolling stock

Transport 2010 relies on the TOCs to increase investment in rolling stock through leasing from ROSCOs. Railway privatisation initially discouraged investment in rolling stock. In the lead up to privatisation, BR was forbidden to invest in rolling stock, and so no new stock was ordered in the 1,000 days before privatisation. The TOCs, which were awarded limited franchises (usually for seven years) on the basis of competitive bidding for subsidies, had every incentive to sweat their leased train assets by using 'cheap, limited-life equipment, with minimal space standards, fewer lavatories, and high noise levels' (Terry, 2001: 4). This was a consequence of the nature of the privatisation which, as Harman (1993: 21) forecast, 'could seriously reduce investment in new trains'. Thus, in 1998, the Rail Franchise Director reported that only £18 million worth of new rolling stock (i.e., 20 new coaches) was running on the railway two years after privatisation. The few longer-term franchises required the leasing of new rolling stock, but 'franchisees were not otherwise committed to provide any investment' (Wolmar, 2001a: 82). The Franchise Director criticised the 'generally disappointing performance' of many TOCs (Harper, 1998b).

By November 2001, there had been an improvement in the rolling stock position. Orders had been placed for over £3 billion worth of new passenger rolling stock, representing 3,229 vehicles – equivalent to roughly one-third of the existing fleet. Of these vehicles, however, only 573 were actually in service (SRA, 2002: 35). The trains took a long time to enter service because of Railtrack's 'extremely onerous safety case procedures' (Wolmar, 2001a: 212) and, in some cases, problems in manufacturing. Delays of up to two years were not uncommon.

Performance and regulatory problems

Delayed introduction of rolling stock was not the only problem. Most of the franchises went to bus companies that were used to managing through reducing costs. These companies therefore attempted to secure 'efficiency' savings through redundancies (Wolmar, 2001a: 83). Stagecoach implemented a voluntary redundancy programme involving 750 staff shortly after taking over at SouthWest Trains (SWT). The drawbacks of this approach were soon apparent to passengers. In 1997, Stagecoach was fined for the excessive number of train cancellations caused by driver shortage.

The temptation to economise on skilled labour persisted for some TOCs. In October 2001, the SRA announced a £2 million fine for Arriva because of an 'inordinate level' of train cancellations necessitated by insufficient drivers in its Northern franchise. The train drivers' union, ASLEF, estimated that the industry needed an additional 1,000 drivers – over 10 per cent of the numbers currently employed (Tighe, 2001). This shortage enhanced union bargaining power, and led to strike action in 2002 at SWT and Arriva as other grades sought parity.

The National Audit Office's report on passenger rail services (NAO, 2000b), *Shadow Strategic Rail Authority: Action to Improve Passenger Rail Services*, found problems with both the performance of the TOCs and the regulatory framework. Despite a complex and expensive monitoring system established by privatisation, the NAO (2000b: Paragraph 1) believed information for assessing train service quality was inadequate. There was too much reliance on self-certification, lateness was not penalised adequately, and the SRA tended to intervene only in cases of excessive cancellations or too few seats (NAO, 2000b: Paragraphs 6, 15).

The refranchising process

Transport 2010 recognised weaknesses with the TOCs, particularly inadequate investment and the inhibiting effect of 7-year franchises. Its solution is the refranchising process, which is 'central to the delivery of a better railway' (DETR, 2000: 43). Replacement franchises were intended to run for between 10 and 20 years, with review points every five to seven years when the agreements could be adjusted. However, ministers soon developed doubts about this strategy. The SRA recommended in December 2000 that GNER should be awarded a 20-year franchise for the East Coast. In July 2001, the Department for Transport announced its decision in favour of a two-year extension (Haigh, 2001a). It also issued a draft franchising statement charging the SRA 'with securing early improvements for passengers under existing franchises or by negotiating two-year extensions' (House of Commons, 2002: Paragraph 21). The renegotiation of franchises was well behind schedule, however, as only four had been awarded by Summer 2001, against a target of 18 by the end of 2001. Apart from GNER, one of the other three was also a short-term extension.

The plan also accepted the need to double the rates of performance payments and penalties applying to the TOCs, along with the importance of offering longer franchises in return for 'service improvements' (DETR, 2000: 44). These proposals reflect an ambivalent approach. The plan recognises the inadequacy of past investment by the TOCs. It also, however, expects newly enfranchised TOCs to make a substantial contribution to £7 billion of investment in rolling stock over ten years.

Financial problems of TOCs

There are several possible problems with this optimistic scenario. The subsidy to the TOCs has been fixed at £11 billion over the life of the plan, but this represents a fall in support in real terms since privatisation. Further, 16 of the 25 TOCs had declining profits or increasing losses in the financial year 1999–2000, prior to the Hatfield crash (Wolmar, 2001a: 201). This position was exacerbated by the crash and its aftermath, as the TOCs lost £63 million in revenue in the last quarter of 2000; they had expected revenue growth of £140 million (Wolmar, 2001a: 202). The £11 billion subsidy is likely to be used by TOCs as a contribution to track access charges, rather than as support for further leasing of rolling stock. The Regulator reduced the access charges for freight operators by 50 per cent in 2001, in an explicit attempt to 'facilitate growth' in line with the plan (ORR, 2001: 1). This was only possible, however, because the SRA agreed to compensate Railtrack for the resulting shortfall of £500 million from 2001–2006. A similar attempt to encourage passenger growth would require around £4.5 billion in additional subsidy over five years.

There are evidently major problems both in financing rolling stock and in the effective management of the introduction of new trains. The SRA (2002: 32) has described this as 'the greatest single challenge to the industry's operational performance over the next three years'. This challenge continues to present problems for the industry. In February 2003, it was revealed that hundreds of new commuter trains will have to be stored at SRA expense until at least 2005, as the power supplies currently available are inadequate to run them on the network (Clark, 2003: 25).

The franchise system

If the new franchises are to have strengthened performance targets on items like rolling stock, then more complex monitoring arrangements will be required. The current unsatisfactory arrangements, however, are hardly simple to operate. On the Railtrack–TOC interface alone, monitoring includes: 2,900 reporting points, 1,300 delay-attribution points, 500 contract monitoring points and 100,000 reports at those points (Kain, 1998: 260). A further difficulty with the TOC franchises is that they were chosen 'pragmatically' (Foster, 1994: 15), thus producing a far from optimal system. The original TOCs overlapped with each other, and the average franchise size was sub-optimal. The SRA intends to redraw the franchise map, but the number of franchises will, initially, only fall from 25 to 22. Ideally, the SRA would like a substantial reduction, and has long-term aims to simplify the structure 'by bringing services at key London termini under single control wherever possible' (SRA, 2002, p. 38). A study of economies of scale and density suggests that the optimal railway would have a network of around 4,000 kilometres, running about 120 million train kilometres per year. On this basis, four equally sized franchises would have been far more efficient than the original 25 (Preston, 1994).

Implications for safety

Transport 2010 aimed to ensure installation of the Train Protection and Warning System across the network, and full Automatic Train Protection on the high-speed passenger network. The case for giving a higher priority to safety and for investment in up-to-date measures is now more fully accepted. However, two key obstacles remain:

- The inherent difficulty in promoting a safety culture in what will remain a very fragmented structure with almost 100 separate enterprises.
- Achieving high safety standards 'may conflict with meeting other aims, such as increased frequencies or comfort of trains' (Harman, 1993: 22). The high cost of safety measures will consume a substantial proportion of the plan's public funding for infrastructure development. The SRA has pointed out that 'the Uff/Cullen programme may . . . compromise the economic viability of significant upgrade projects' (Haigh, 2001b).

These issues were tragically highlighted by the Paddington and Hatfield crashes. It was argued that: 'the oversight of safety on Britain's railways is almost as atomized as the running of trains and the track' (*Economist*, 1999b). Increasing use of subcontracting was leading to mistakes in signal repair and

---

Train protection systems

Train protection systems are designed to prevent a signal passed at danger from becoming a disaster. The most advanced system is Automatic Train Protection (ATP), which can bring a train to a halt independently of the driver and is effective at any speed. The most sophisticated version of ATP, in use in some European countries, is known as the European Train Control System (ETCS).

BR's trial ATP programme 'lost its way as a result of privatization', as it was considered too expensive at an estimated cost of between £2 and £3 billion (Wolmar, 2001a: 150, 187). Instead of ATP, the privatised rail industry opted for the Train Protection and Warning System (TPWS). A much cheaper system than ATP, the TPWS warns a driver if a signal is passed at red, and then applies the brakes if the driver does not take action. However, it is only effective at speeds up to 70 miles per hour (Wolmar, 2001a: 152).

The 10-year plan envisaged that the TPWS would be installed across the network by the end of 2003. This was overtaken by the Uff/Cullen Report on train protection systems, published in 2001, that recommended installing the ETCS across the network by 2010 (Wolmar, 2001a: 187). The cost of this is currently estimated to be between £3 and £5 billion (House of Commons, 2002: Paragraph 68).

---

maintenance. Corbett conceded that Hatfield resulted from structural weaknesses in the privatised system, acknowledging 'a conflict between performance and safety' (Wolmar, 2001a: 177). He had earlier conceded that the privatised system had not encouraged co-operation, accepting that 'a major culture change was required' (Travis & Wells, 1999).

The culture change, on which the plan insisted (DETR, 2000: 47), is likely to be hard to achieve given that privatisation 'has fragmented and weakened the culture in which safety was nurtured as a habit of thought' (Terry, 2001: 5). The profit motive remains, along with the complex contractual relationships between Railtrack's successor, its subcontractors, and the TOCS. These contractual relationships were highlighted again in May 2002 by the Potters Bar crash, which appeared to be caused by bolts coming loose from a set of faulty points.

Conclusions

Transport 2010 accurately identifies the lack of investment in the railway system as a fundamental problem. The Labour Government inherited a fragmented system, with TOCs running on short-term franchises, where reducing public subsidy had priority. The 10-year plan in *Transport 2010* relies on revenue support and large capital grants to 'lever in' private investment, with the optimistic prediction that £34 billion of private capital, representing half the planned increase in rail funding, will be forthcoming. There is, as yet, little evidence that the privatised system is capable of generating such investment. Furthermore, despite the recent increase in public support to £33.5 billion, funds are 'insufficient' given that investment is needed 'on a scale which dwarfs' the plan's figures (House of Commons, 2002: Paragraphs 67, 70). Within 12 months of the publication of the plan, the then SRA Chairman, Sir Alastair Morton, once an enthusiast, spoke publicly of 'a fair old hole' in the resources available, and of Railtrack as 'a very damaged and sick base for the industry' (House of Commons, 2001: Paragraph 62). Sir Alastair did not mention the SRA's own negative contribution. Instead, of the long-promised 'Strategic Plan', which established priorities for key infrastructure projects, it had succeeded by late 2001 in producing only a 'Strategic Agenda' which listed options (SRA, 2001). The new SRA Chairman, Richard Bowker, finally published the Strategic Plan in January 2002 (SRA, 2002). Although its modest proposals were welcomed by the industry, there was concern that 'the exact cost and the timescale' for implementation was lacking (House of Commons, 2002: Paragraph 11).

The SRA's second strategic plan, issued in January 2003, contained a shorter list of new projects and a greater volume of warnings about the need to reduce costs. It coincided with a cut of £312 million in the SRA's own budget and increased pessimism about the likely outcome of the government's public spending review in 2004. Suspicions arose that growth targets were being dropped, as a Department for Transport document in December 2002 made no reference to the original figure for freight and mentioned the passenger equivalent only on page 51 (DfT, 2002; Haigh, 2003). Extensive cuts in services in order to improve reliability were announced by the SRA in December 2002 and February 2003, with a capacity review to follow. 'The railway has got to get better before it gets bigger', according to one of its officials (Giles & Jowit, 2003; Jowit, 2003: 2). David Begg, an SRA Board member and government transport adviser, summarised rail's position bluntly: 'unless this industry drags down costs, it is in crisis' (Giles & Jowit, 2003).

Even after the collapse of Railtrack, the government continued to deny itself the advantages to be derived from re-nationalisation in implementing the 10-year plan. This would allow it to direct investment in the railways, reduce the cost of borrowing and enable the railways to regain the public sector ethos lost at privatisation (Wolmar, 2001a: 254). While Railtrack's record was 'appalling', SPVs are 'unproven' and, even though NR has been established as a virtually public-sector company, the government sill lacks an effective mechanism to overcome the fundamental 'problems of fragmentation' and make a reality of its plans (House of Commons, 2002: Paragraphs 45, 48, 71).

Acknowledgements

The authors are grateful to two anonymous referees for their helpful comments on an earlier draft.

Note

1 This article was originally published in *Public Money & Management* 22(3) (2003).

References

Clark, A. (2003). 'Public will pay up to £50M to ensure new trains stand idle', *The Guardian* (7 February), p. 25.

Department for Transport (DfT) (2002). *Delivering Better Transport: Progress Report*. London: DfT.

Department of the Environment, Transport and the Regions (DETR) (1998). *A New Deal for Transport: Better for Everyone* (Cmnd. 3950). London: HMSO.

Department of the Environment, Transport and the Regions (DETR) (2000). *Transport 2010: The 10-year Plan*. London: DETR.

Department of Transport (DoT) (1992). *New Opportunities for the Railways: The Privatization of BR* (Cmnd. 2012). London: HMSO.

Economist (1999a). 'Britain's railways' (3 July), pp. 85–90.

Economist (1999b). 'Inevitable' (16 October), p. 37.

Elliott, L. & Smithers, R. (1999). 'Paddington rail disaster: Privatization – Successful sell-off or cynical sell-out?' *Guardian* (7 October), p. 5.

Ford, R. (2001a). 'Railtrack "investment" – Money into a black hole?' *Modern Railways* (July), pp. 19–21.

Ford, R. (2001b). 'Byers blitzes Railtrack', *Modern Railways* (November), pp. 17–22.

Foster, C. (1994). *The Economics of Rail Privatization*. London/Bath: Centre for the Study of Regulated Industries.

Giles, C. & Jowit, J. (2003). 'Going nowhere: One in five trains is late, productivity has plunged and the network's costs may hit £6bn a year', *Financial Times* (30 January), p. 17.

Haigh, P. (2001a). 'Morton savages Minister's poor treatment of the SRA', *Rail* (31 October), p. 6.

Haigh, P. (2001b). 'Safety spending will delay upgrades, warns the SRA', *Rail* (31 October), p. 14.

Haigh, P. (2003). 'Role for rail targets is reduced in Darling's transport plan', *Rail* (8 January), p. 4.

Harman, R. (1993). 'Railway privatization: Does it bring new opportunities?' *Public Money & Management* 13(1): 19–25.

Harper, K. (1998a). 'Railtrack £17 billion "too little"', *The Guardian* (26 March), p. 21.

Harper, K. (1998b). 'New trains are running late', *The Guardian* (11 July), p. 24.

Harper, K. (2000). 'Railtrack blow to Virgin West Coast plans', *The Guardian* (28 March), p. 27.

Harris, N.G. (2003). 'It's not my problem', *Rail* (5 February), p. 3.

Harris, N.G. & Godward, E. (1997). *The Privatization of British Rail*. London: Railway Consultancy Press.

House of Commons (2001). *Select Committee on Environment, Transport and Regional Affairs: The Work of the Strategic Rail Authority, Oral Evidence (2000–01; HC434-I)*. London: HMSO.

House of Commons (2002). *Select Committee on Transport, Local Government and the Regions: Passenger Rail Franchising and the Future of Railway Infrastructure (2001–02; HC 239-I)*. London: HMSO.

James, T. & Nissan, D. (2000). *Rail Renaissance: Expanding the Rail Network in Britain*. London: Institute of Public Policy Research.

Jowit, J. (2003). 'More rail cuts raise fears of grand scheme', *Financial Times* (25 February), p. 2.

Kain, P. (1998). 'The reform of rail transport in Great Britain', *Journal of Transport Economics and Policy* 32(2): 247–266.

Nash, C.A. (2000). 'Privatization and deregulation in railways: An assessment of the British approach'. In: B. Bradshaw & H. Lawton Smith (eds), *Privatization and Deregulation of Transport*. London: Macmillan, pp. 159–176.

National Audit Office (NAO) (2000a). *Ensuring that Railtrack Maintain and Renew the Railway Network (1999–2000; HC 397)*. London: HMSO.

National Audit Office (NAO) (2000b). *Shadow Strategic Rail Authority: Action to Improve Passenger Rail Services (1999–2000; HC 842)*. London: HMSO.

Office of the Rail Regulator (ORR) (2000). *The Periodic Review of Railtrack's Access Charges: Final Conclusions, Vol. I*. London: ORR.

Office of the Rail Regulator (ORR) (2001). *Review of Freight Charging Policy: Final Conclusions*. London: ORR.

Preston, J. (1994). 'Does size matter? The case of Western European railways'. Paper presented to UTSG Conference, University of Leeds.

Railtrack (1995–1996 to 2000–2001). *Annual Report and Accounts*. London: Railtrack Group plc.

Stittle, J. (2002). 'Regulatory control of the track access charges of Railtrack plc', *Public Money & Management* 22(1): 49–54.

Strategic Rail Authority (SRA) (2001). *A Strategic Agenda*. London: SRA.

Strategic Rail Authority (SRA) (2002). *The Strategic Plan*. London: SRA.

Terry, F. (2001). 'The nemesis of privatization: Railway policy in retrospect', *Public Money & Management* 21(1): 4–6.

Tighe, C. (2001). 'Women get in driving seat to ease staff crisis', *Financial Times* (13 November), p. 7.

Travis, A. & Wells, M. (1999). 'Nationalize Railtrack, say public', *The Guardian* (26 October), p. 1.

Walters, J. (1998). 'Railtrack lines up a £17 billion future – Maybe', *Observer* (Business) (29 March), p. 8.

Walters, J. (2000). 'Rail boss in profit U-turn', *Observer* (Business) (2 April), p. 1.

Wolmar, C. (2001a). *Broken Rails: How Privatization Wrecked Britain's Railways*. London: Aurum Press.

Wolmar, C. (2001b). 'We must seize this chance to travel toward railway Nirvana', *Rail* (31 October), p. 24.

17. The Company Response to Government Policies on Transport[1]

JOHN ELLIOTT

The author presents a case study of how a large private-sector company has tried to respond constructively to current government policies on transport. The focus for implementation has been a Green Travel Plan (GTP), developed for company employees. A successful GTP needs to change the culture of the organisation, and provide both sticks and carrots to encourage sufficient numbers of people to change their travel habits. Delivering either or both of these requires a consistent and sustained approach by policy-makers, to match the efforts of private firms. Effective change depends on integrating the efforts of central government, local authorities, business, transport operators, police, the Highways Agency, individuals and the press.

Motor vehicles are recognised as one of the major sources of air pollution (RCEP, 1994), causing many premature deaths and serious medical problems as well as giving a much less pleasant environment in various other ways. The road accident toll alone accounts for more than 3,400 deaths per year in the United Kingdom, as well as over 34,000 serious injuries. Even if electric vehicles were to come into widespread use, we shall still be using non-renewable sources for many years into the future in order to provide the basic energy. By contrast, there are positive health advantages to 'greener' travel, not only from reduced pollution, but because walkers, cyclists and public transport users generally get more exercise than motorists.

The background to current policies

Recognising the seriousness of the threat from an ever-growing volume of traffic, both the Conservative and Labour Governments of the past seven years have moved cautiously towards policies that seek alternatives to unrestricted car use (DoT, 1996; Prescott, 1998). There is, in fact, nothing new in the need to reduce traffic. One of the most widely respected studies of modern transport planning, the Buchanan Report (1963: Paragraph 451) not only demonstrated this, but offered the elements of the solution:

JOHN ELLIOTT is Director, Parking Services with Legion Security plc (formerly Royal British Legion Attendants) and an independent consultant. He was previously Transport and Planning Manager for Pfizer until May 2002.

We think it will be necessary for transportation plans to be based on a conscious decision regarding the extent to which the demand for the optional use of cars can be met. The plans should contain measures to influence the demand so that it matches the provision that can be made. There is very little experience available at the present time of the best methods for influencing the demand, but in principle there appear to be four possibilities:

  (i) A system of permits or licenses could be used to control the entry of vehicles to certain defined zones.
 (ii) A system of pricing the use of road space.
(iii) Parking policy.
 (iv) Subsidising public transport so that it offers considerable financial advantages over the use of cars.

Interestingly, the Buchanan Report also says: 'We think people may have to be told fairly firmly where, and when, and how they can *use* their vehicles, but we feel sure they will demand the right of *ownership* . . . ' (emphasis in original).

The first step in achieving change is persuading people to understand why it is necessary. At the moment there is a gap in understanding, both among individuals and many commercial companies. Most people think that sustainability and air pollution are not problems that need to be tackled by individuals (Steg & Tertoolen, 1999). Most people think that *their* car is not the cause of congestion: rather, it is the other person's car that is the problem, or the 'authorities' who should provide more road space – but not too close to 'my' house!

To alter this perception means a big cultural change by society, which will take many years to feed through. Although there have been changes in attitudes towards drink-driving and smoking, for example, over the past 20 to 30 years, these campaigns have not touched all people. Speeding is now beginning to be accepted as a serious issue and the majority of people no longer boast about excessive speeds on motorways or in urban areas. Even so, only a very small minority behave in a fully responsible way over speed, and a great deal depends on trusting the motorist to drive sensibly and safely.

Government policy objectives

The acceptance of 'green' travel as a regular habit applies to an even smaller minority. Some people will positively choose to use greener modes, but the majority of us need incentives – the 'sticks and carrots' referred to in the Buchanan Report. Unfortunately, and despite the intentions of the White Paper, *A New Deal for Transport: Better for Everyone* (Prescott, 1998), many of the carrots have been undermined in recent years. The United Kingdom's public transport system is very poor compared to equivalent countries in Europe. The government's consultation paper on buses, *From Workhorse to Thoroughbred* (DETR, 1999), and the more recent legislation in the form of the Transport Act 2000, tackle only some relatively minor aspects of promoting alternatives to car use. Bus and rail fares continue to be much more expensive than the cost of motoring in many parts of the country. There are also a number of 'subsidies' presently in place to encourage car use: for instance, free parking places at work, free parking places in smaller towns, widespread provision of company cars, or generous travel allowances from employers for staff using their own car. Furthermore, societal values at present work against greener travel: for example, the status associated with cars and the lack of status in using a bus.

An *integrated holistic approach* is needed to the whole of the travel and planning package so that 'virtuous' behaviour is rewarded at every step. The government's *10-year Plan for Transport* (DETR, 2000), for all its good points, unfortunately gives only partial recognition to this principle. For example:

- Whenever new roads are planned, or measures used to relieve congestion, it would be reasonable for anybody using greener travel to be rewarded more than others (e.g., by being entitled to use bus and high-occupancy vehicle lanes).
- Similarly, pedestrians should not be delayed or have lengthened journeys in order that cars can suffer less congestion – traffic-light controlled pedestrian crossings should normally minimise pedestrian delay.
- Bus stations in shopping centres or industrial sites should be at the core of the mall, high street or industrial estate and certainly not further away than the car parks.
- Bus lanes (and high-occupancy lanes), if space permits, should be introduced on the approaches to, and within, all towns so as to improve reliability. Traffic queues should be relocated outside towns where appropriate and possible.

Such measures are, if we are honest, the logical implications of *A New Deal for Transport*. Although the White Paper did suggest some of the sticks and carrots (e.g., road pricing and workplace parking charges), these are not in place yet nor are they adequately supported in a positive manner by the government. Instead, a very blunt instrument is now being used, by asking companies to produce green travel plans (GTPs) and by rationing workplace parking spaces. (Again, there is nothing new in the idea of reducing parking space to limit traffic – see box below.)

The remainder of this chapter looks at the effect of this policy instrument on a major pharmaceutical company, Pfizer Ltd, which has tried to make a positive response to the government's approach.

The implications for private-sector companies

There is a coincidence between government policy aims and companies' own self-interest, although many firms have yet to realise this. If we want to minimise company costs, and especially if other measures such as road pricing and parking place charges are introduced, it is strongly in a company's

---

The Buchanan Report (1963)

The question of how much parking space should be provided in *new buildings* needs to be considered from two points of view, namely, liability and convenience of access and circulation . . . (Paragraph 454)

. . . the application of arbitrary parking standards to new buildings may produce an accumulation of parking space which the network cannot deal with.' (Paragraph 455)

To summarise, we think present parking policies need re-examination to ensure that traffic difficulties are not being 'built in' by the provision of too much parking space in the wrong position, and that owners and developers are not being burdened with liabilities which are not really for them to carry . . . (Paragraph 456)

---

interests to reduce car dependency. It also makes sound commercial sense, as excessive traffic delays commercial operations and, for workers, it causes frayed tempers and less productivity. It can even waste time at work when, after a bad journey, people talk about traffic problems (the 'Reggie Perrin factor'). Excessive use of space for cars, whether moving or parked, is a waste of land that could be developed for other purposes.

The cost of provision of parking can be significant. At the Pfizer sites at Sandwich in east Kent and at Walton Oaks near Reigate in Surrey, the company has calculated that each new space costs typically £2,000–£3,000 for its construction, along with access roads, lighting and so on (but excluding land costs). The annual running costs of a parking space, including amortisation, are typically £400–£500. The company also realises that the traffic impact of its Sandwich site is greater than the local road network can satisfactorily bear. Currently, up to 5,800 people, including consultants and visitors, come to Sandwich each day, and approximately 500 are employed at the United Kingdom head office at Walton Oaks. At Sandwich, there are at the moment a further 500 building workers active on site, and it has been estimated that, for every Pfizer worker, there are another five people employed as a direct result in the region.

While the highway authorities are planning some increase in road capacity in the vicinity of the Sandwich site, particularly for buses and high-occupancy vehicles, there is a real need to change travel habits. This is quite a difficult task for a rural area. Working in Pfizer's favour, the Sandwich site is a concentrated travel destination, while the major local settlements are similarly concentrated and the land is relatively flat. This makes cycling relatively easy, at least in the summer when the weather is favourable; it also allows reasonably good bus services to be provided from the major settlements. Because of Pfizer's very large employment size in relation to the local communities, car sharing can make a significant contribution to reducing car use. With sea boundaries a few hundred yards to the east, 12 miles to the south and eight miles to the north, longer distance trips come only from the west and this further aids the radical approach to transport arrangements for Sandwich. As a condition of any new developments, the local planning authority, Dover District Council, required Pfizer to produce a GTP. It also introduced some controls on parking spaces, and required a second entrance to the site (which was much needed in any case). For the latest development on the Sandwich site, Pfizer is committed to a reduction of 15 per cent in its car:people ratio. The company may, however, want to go further, in order to offset the impact of future traffic congestion.

The Walton Oaks site was developed recently, owing (among other reasons) to pressure on Sandwich. There, the situation is very different: the site is immediately adjacent to the M25 motorway and the potential places where staff can live are spread out over the whole of south London, Surrey, Sussex and parts of Kent. There can be no significant corridors of travel to such a site, which is in any case very much smaller: about 10 per cent of the employment size of Sandwich. Furthermore, the site is some five or six miles from the nearest towns with good railway services – namely Redhill and Epsom. There is an escarpment immediately to the south, which makes cycling from that direction very difficult.

In order to secure planning permission for the Walton Oaks site (a 'brownfield' site within the green belt), an exceptionally strict Section 106 planning agreement from Reigate and Banstead District Council and Surrey County Council was accepted. This agreement includes an incentive of £1,000 per annum to each member of staff who foregoes use of a parking space, provision of £100,000 over five years for improved public bus services and very limited parking provision. Parking spaces, including those for visitors, were rationed to 300 for 500 staff (plus visitors) in the first phase, and to 475 spaces for 900 staff (plus visitors) for the second phase.

The Pfizer plans and strategies

In seeking to respond to the government's policy aims, Pfizer's strategy is designed to encourage all staff to use the highest level that they can practically reach in a transport hierarchy the company has adopted. Employees can either: walk, use public transport, bicycle, car share, motorcycle or use a single-occupancy vehicle. As part of the culture change process, the first of these three modes are labelled 'green', the next two are 'amber' and the final one 'red' (in parallel with the colours of traffic lights). Unlike some other travel hierarchies, public transport is placed above the bicycle, as it is available to all and is far less dependent on the weather or time of year.

John Whitelegg Associates had a major role in launching Pfizer's GTPs, both for the existing site at Sandwich and for the new development at Walton Oaks. At Sandwich, an extensive survey of staff was carried out in 1998,

Table 1. 1998 Whitelegg survey results*

Transport mode	Percentage using
Walk	1.5
Public transport	6.7
Bicycle	5.7
Car share	17.7
Motorcycle	1.6
Single-occupancy vehicle	66.7

* Pfizer needed a 10–20 per cent change in car:people ratio.

resulting in 2,350 questionnaires being returned from the staffing complement of 3,800. Focus group discussions were held with 250 staff, and discussions organised with internal and external people critical to progressing the travel plan. At Walton Oaks, the task was very different: creating a GTP for a new site close to London and in the green belt, which had to be acceptable to the district council, county council and central government (both the Government Office for the South East and the Minister in Whitehall). The package that has evolved from the Whitelegg study probably has more teeth than any other GTP, but the plans will only work if the various arms of government continue to play an active and supportive role.

At Sandwich, the proportion found to be travelling by each mode were as shown in Table 1.

The Pfizer travel strategy is based on seven elements:

- Cash incentives to those not using a parking space on site ('Parking Cash-Out').
- Staged improvements to public transport, including trains and shuttle buses.
- Cycle/motorcycle facilities.
- Car sharing system.
- Infrastructure improvements.
- Better site access and on-site networks.
- General enablers and publicity.

The parking cash-out scheme (PCO)

This scheme is the combined stick and carrot, which cements the whole travel plan together. The company was, like most organisations, in effect providing a hidden subsidy to those that drive to the site, of approximately £400–500 per annum. This annual subsidy is not available to those who use public transport or walk, and is obviously perverse in sustainable transport terms.

There is very little elasticity information on parking demand with cost, or on any cross-elasticities. A £2 per day charge or benefit between parking and not parking was felt sufficient to encourage a number of staff at Sandwich to seriously consider alternative travel arrangements. However, it should not cause people to search too hard for spaces outside the site and should not be enough to encourage other operators with spare land to engage in competition. At Walton Oaks, the sum is £5 per day; this may generate other problems of off-site parking, but a traffic trust fund has been set up to tackle traffic or parking problems when, and if, they occur in the immediate vicinity. Interestingly, as part of the decriminalisation of parking in Kent, controlled parking was introduced for the town of Sandwich about six months before PCO went live. This substantially reduced the temptation to park off-site and try to collect the cash incentive.

Pfizer has a sophisticated security system with proximity cards issued to all people working on-site. These recognise individuals as they pass through turnstiles or enter certain buildings. On the first occasion the card is recognised in a day, 20 parking points are awarded to the member of staff. The same cards are used to exit the car parks, at which time 20 points are deducted from the person's credit. Unused points are turned into money and paid automatically through the payroll system (20 points = £2). At Walton Oaks, the 'credit' is 50 points and £5.

Points are used rather than parking charges, since (office) parking is a tax-free good in the United Kingdom. Tax is paid on the cash value when it appears in the pay packet. The finer grading of each point being worth 10 pence will allow differential charging for different car parks or different reward levels for different types of worker in the future, if ever required. It was also initially intended that unused points could be turned into fares on Pfizer contract buses. Since bus fares on contract or scheduled services can now (from April 2002) be subsidised by the employer without tax problems, unused points can be transferred to any bus fares, also tax free.

The system is also designed to automatically give greater rewards to the greenest travel, and intermediate benefits to car sharers, because only one person's security card is used for exiting a car park. In the development of the system, a wide variety of working patterns as well as obvious potential abuses were considered. The system provides good data on cars and people, from which to monitor the key performance statistic (the car:people ratio). This simple statistic is probably the most important figure we should all be targeting for GTPs.

For towns and counties, a slight refinement on this performance indicator is probably needed in order to reflect distance travelled. The road traffic reduction target (partially) enshrined in the Traffic Reduction Act 1996 is a similar key figure that is easily measured and means something tangible. Traffic congestion and pollution effects are much harder to measure and target. Pollution levels for individual vehicles are a more appropriate target to give the motor industry than to transport planners.

197

Staged improvements to public transport

Promotion of good public transport is a key factor and all Pfizer's initial energies went into providing as good a service as possible within the budget available. Good public transport is the fundamental carrot of the plan. It was important, therefore, that bus fares should be attractive and substantially less than using cars. The philosophy behind fares is that they should match, as closely as possible, the petrol costs of motoring. Thus when the incentive scheme is included, the cost of the bus should be less than car sharing (the marginal cost of motoring is typically double the petrol cost) – thus supporting the transport hierarchy explained above.

Pfizer provides contract bus services to the Thanet towns of Canterbury, Deal and Dover and intermediate destinations within east Kent, using the Stagecoach Group. The terms of the contract have built-in incentives on quality and on attracting passengers to all bus services by both Pfizer and the operator. Revenue is shared on the contract service (but no longer on the remaining scheduled service). These shares vary if a bus is late, misses a passenger, is dirty, or if the driver is discourteous.

Free fares were considered but, at the time, they would have attracted tax. The company was also aware that wider objectives for local authorities, and the country as a whole, were to reduce overall traffic volumes and so there needed to be some incentive not to travel too far. It is hoped that a virtuous circle of improved service, more passenger demand and further improvements to the service will be maintained.

Previously, regular north–south local bus services serving Thanet, Deal and Dover used to stop at Pfizer's site. The operational hours, frequency and destinations of these services had all been increased over what was provided originally. The bus services enabled people to travel at half-hourly intervals throughout the working day, thereby helping part-time workers or people having to go home for mild emergencies, appointments and so on. The time-tables were designed to meet the needs of shift workers 364 days of the year (most live either in Thanet or Deal). Evening frequencies were increased so that research experiments in the Pfizer laboratories could be finished.

In planning bus services, it is important to have an extra safety net of a bus to get people home if they are delayed by anything at work. Where possible, both contract and scheduled services were adjusted to connect with trains at all the surrounding railway stations, so that from whatever direction people arrived they could make an onward connection. Unfortunately, Stagecoach withdrew their service in 2001, and Pfizer have been forced to introduce some further shuttle bus services to cover part of the shortfall.

Trains: The Sandwich and other shuttle services

From the Whitelegg study, the main concentrations of staff were found to be in the towns served by the buses, plus Sandwich, Minster, Herne Bay and

Whitstable. It was also found that two-thirds of Pfizer staff lived within one mile of the 1998 contract bus service, and 45 per cent within one mile of the local railway stations.

With the low number of people using trains, and the nature of rail services in the area ('end of the line' services to London), and a station over one mile from the site, improvements to trains were a low priority. Nevertheless, the company did operate a local on-demand minibus service to an outpost office 100 yards from the local railway station in Sandwich. By acquiring an additional minibus and extending the hours of operation, a reliable 10-minute interval service could be provided to that office, a link to the station and to the town's hotels (for conferences and courses) and to the shops, restaurants and pubs, and provide a good home-to-work service for all those living in Sandwich. This bus service is now carrying 500 people a day (up from 60 in 1998), bringing in and taking home between 150 and 200 people, 62 per cent of whom said they would have used their car otherwise, and about 20 rail passengers (up from two in the Whitelegg report). Some of the regular users have sold their second car.

Ideas have been put forward to divert the railway line and create a Pfizer halt, but these are very expensive without substantial patronage. The next interim step has been to negotiate fares with the train company, Connex, for extra marginal passengers. These are at a cost slightly above the equivalent bus fares and provide a greater range of destinations/origins for Pfizer staff. These fares are to and from all the surrounding stations (Ramsgate, Sandwich, Minster and Birchington), to suit as many public transport users as possible, and link with the contract and other bus services described above.

At the Walton Oaks site, there are good frequent rail services to a wide range of destinations at Redhill and Epsom (about five miles away), and infrequent services to Tadworth and Betchworth (about two miles away). A number of free minibus services are run to these stations and the surrounding housing, although they are inclined to be badly affected (when most needed) by local peak period traffic congestion. The company also runs a high-quality coach service from east Kent to Walton Oaks, with park-and-ride points for anybody living in between the two main establishments. However, this service can be seriously affected by congestion on the M25 motorway.

Cycle/motorcycle provision

Pfizer is providing the necessary facilities (e.g., changing rooms, lockers and showers) to further encourage the use of bicycles and motorcycles. These are being incorporated in new building contracts and, where appropriate and economical, added to some existing buildings. On-site routes are being provided as part of the site development plan. Pfizer also provides pool cycles for general 'intra-site' movement and cycle sheds are being built or upgraded.

The company is working with local authorities and others to provide safe cycle routes to work (the site is fortunately adjacent to national cycle routes to all the larger settlements in the area: Ramsgate, Sandwich, Deal, Canterbury and Dover). The most critical of these routes is to Ramsgate and the other Thanet towns. The main road is quite terrifying to all but the most experienced cyclists. An off-road route to Ramsgate has been completed and was formally opened on National Cycle-to-Work Day 2000.

At Walton Oaks, the geography does not lend itself to cycling, but motor-cycling will be attractive to many. Pfizer has provided advice on relocation and is assisting with motorcycle training.

Car sharing

The proportion of staff who were car sharing at the Sandwich site before the plan was introduced was high (18 per cent). The PCO scheme now provides benefit to those who car share, but this benefit is not as great as for those using the bus service, cycling or walking.

A map-based computer car-share system has been developed and commissioned. This allows anybody to enter their home and office details, hours of work and so on, together with certain preferences, like smoking/no smoking, sex of other ride-share partner, radio choice, together with an outline route. The system automatically throws up the best 'matches' and gives internal e-mail names and telephone numbers. It is then up to the individuals to arrange their travel. A facility also allows for last-minute searches for people who are stuck, or where travel arrangements change. At Walton Oaks, the company is working with the local authorities and other local employers on a district-wide car-share scheme.

Infrastructure improvements

Serious and varied traffic congestion occurs in east Kent and this will grow as Pfizer increases its workforce and as the local area is regenerated. The growth rate is likely to be well in excess of efforts by Pfizer and others to encourage greener travel. The Pfizer site is also bisected by a main road, and access along this same road to some industrial sites – and, indeed, Sandwich town itself – is far from ideal. A package of schemes involving road and public transport improvements has been developed by the two district authorities and the county as the East Kent Access Scheme (EKAS). This is part of Kent County Council's Local Transport Plan (LTP). The main *raison d'être* of this scheme is industrial regeneration and ensuring existing jobs are retained and new jobs can be provided in the area.

The government's new approach to transport appraisal (NATA) is based on five over-arching objectives:

- To improve safety for all travellers.
- To contribute to an efficient economy and support sustainable economic growth in appropriate locations.

- To promote accessibility to everyday facilities for all, especially for those without a car.
- To promote integration of all forms of transport and land-use planning.
- To protect and enhance a built and natural environment.

The East Kent Access Scheme, and specifically the roads element, meets all these criteria well. However, for many years, a somewhat flawed cost-benefit analysis has been used for assessment of road schemes. Unfortunately, and surprisingly, the 'measured' elements of this analysis still appear under the heading of 'efficient economy' and in 'accessibility' under NATA. The inclusion of this cost-benefit analysis will continue to show roads as giving reduced peak car hour congestion, and therefore desirable.

The East Kent Access Scheme is intended to provide positive economic regeneration effects, and also reinforces greener travel as part of Pfizer's overall transport plan. The scheme, which will take some years to develop, gives positive advantage to buses and high-occupancy cars. Reserved lanes are provided in each direction for these vehicles and if congestion occurs, other vehicles have to queue. A similar long-term benefit should accrue around the Walton Oaks site when bus and high-occupancy vehicle lanes are introduced.

Better site access and on-site networks

As an integral part of its site development, Pfizer is providing better and more convenient access for pedestrians, buses and cycles. The principle is that the network of paths and routes should always be more convenient than the road routes in and out of the car parks. An investment of over £1 billion has been made in buildings and other facilities on site in the past eight years, and route improvements are blended with these works.

General enablers and publicity

Winning hearts and minds is fundamental to delivery of the Pfizer plan, along with the need for company policies to work in the same direction. Essential elements include:

- A progressive company car and car use policy.
- Senior management leading by example.
- Good information on alternatives (a company intranet scheme).
- Briefing sessions and explanation of why change is necessary.
- Monitoring targets to chase progress.

Results

Measuring small changes in travel patterns is always difficult, and staff changes that typically occur make it even more complex. Now that the PCO system has been implemented, it is possible to monitor changes, reasonably

Table 2. Results of the 2001 Whitelegg survey (percentages)

	1998	2001
Bus	6.7	11.8
Bicycle	5.7	5.2
Single-occupancy vehicle	66.7	58.8
Car share	17.7	20.4
Walk	1.5	1.4
Motorcycle	1.6	2.0
Train	0.0	0.3

accurately, in the number of people exiting car parks and the number coming in each day, but only since June 2001. Ticket sales by Stagecoach, or regular counts on minibus services, also give some indication (this information points to a significant increase in bus use). Changes in car and bicycle numbers were much harder to estimate, owing to a number of temporary arrangements during building programmes. In April 2001, Whitelegg repeated the 1998 survey, at the same time of year. The results are shown in Table 2.

The gratifying result shown in Table 2 is attributable to a more reliable public transport service and better coverage. It represents a 75 per cent increase in relative market share of public transport, or approximately two-and-a-half fold increase in passenger numbers. This compares very favourably with the 10 per cent proposed increase in bus usage over the period covered in the government's *10-year Transport Plan*. Car sharing, already high among Pfizer employees, increased further. The result for cycle use is slightly disappointing, but this could be explained by the very wet weather in April 2002 (the survey question referred to 'normal travel mode').

The key statistic – namely, car:people ratio – changed from 75:100 to 68:100 despite a number of factors working in the opposite direction. This 9 per cent reduction in the proportion using cars from an already reasonably 'green' site was a very positive effect of the changes. When PCO went live in June 2001, the typical ratio was 62:100; however, this was in the summer months and the summer/winter variation is known to be considerable. The results from the analysis so far are shown in Table 3. The figure for April 2001, established by the Whitelegg survey, is included in the table for reference. It is unfortunate that the company does not have an accurate measure of the car:people ratio on a comparable basis just before PCO went live.

Table 4 shows a typical weekly variation of staff and car numbers. Despite Friday having a higher car proportion, the critical planning days for traffic and parking are Tuesday, Wednesday and Thursday (and during winter months).

At Walton Oaks, which opened on 10 December 2001, the car:people ratio is typically 66:100. This figure needs to be improved, although it is very

Table 3. Car:people ratio per month for Sandwich

Month	People in cars
April 2001*	0.68
June 2001	0.62
July 2001	0.62
August 2001	0.63
September 2001	0.65
October 2001	0.65
November 2001	0.65
December 2001	0.64
January 2002	0.65

* The figure for April 2001, established in the Whitelegg survey, is included for reference.

Table 4. Staff attendance and car park exits for the week commencing 11 February 2002

Date	Staff on site	Car park exits
Monday, 11 February 2002	4,782	2,994
Tuesday, 12 February 2002	4,818	2,854
Wednesday, 13 February 2001	4,968	3,163
Thursday, 14 February 2001	4,805	3,041
Friday, 15 February 2001	4,307	2,746

creditable for this particular site. The planning obligations were imposed at the time when the 1998 transport White Paper was published, although neither local nor central government has made much progress in delivering the policy. Utilisation of the bus service to the site at Walton Oaks is much better than expected, as more staff have made real efforts to locate close to the site.

Conclusions

On the basis of experience at Pfizer's Sandwich and Walton Oaks sites, an effective GTP should aim to both change the culture of the organisation and the public at large, and provide both sticks and carrots to encourage a sufficient number of people to change their travel habits. To deliver either or both of these requires the efforts of public and private sector bodies to be closely integrated, including central government, local government, businesses, individuals, the press, public transport operators and the police.

The results from the past three years' work look promising, both in terms of culture change and travel behaviour. A very stretching target of a 20 per cent reduction in the car:person ratio on-site was set deliberately. Moving towards this target does require leadership from all levels of government, including tax changes and highway policy. My experience at Pfizer suggests that the government needs to be more positive about a concerted programme of reduction in traffic, and the press and opposition parties should not undermine these efforts. The whole agenda is far too important for political point-scoring and courting short-term popularity.

A small thing that would improve everybody's motivation is understanding that a modest reduction in traffic results in a big reduction in congestion and, hence, big initial benefits from changing travel habits. Pfizer has certainly made some impact, especially considering that staff levels in the recent period have been rising. The key conclusion I draw is that those who give up their cars need to benefit most, not those who are left on the road. To achieve this will require ex-motorists to save money, and ideally to save time as well; this requires a net transfer away from car use towards the greener modes of travel at national, local and company level.

Note

1 This article was originally published in *Public Money & Management* 22(4) (2002).

References

Buchanan Report (1963). *Traffic in Towns*. London: HMSO.

Department of the Environment, Transport and the Regions (DETR) (1999). *From Workhorse to Thoroughbred: A Better Role for Bus Travel*. London: HMSO.

Department of the Environment, Transport and the Regions (DETR) (2000). *Transport 2010: The 10-year Plan*. London: HMSO.

Department of Transport (DoT) (1996). *Transport: The Way Forward – The Government's Response to the Transport Debate* (Cmnd. 3234). London: HMSO.

Prescott, J. (1998). *A New Deal for Transport: Better for Everyone* (Cmnd. 3950). London: HMSO.

Royal Commission on Environmental Pollution (RCEP) (1994). *Eighteenth Report: Transport and the Environment* (Cmnd. 2674). London: HMSO.

Steg, L. & Tertoolen, G. (1999). 'Sustainable transport policy: The contribution from behavioural scientists', *Public Money & Management* 19(1).

Index